THE NEW WORLD OF

The Wall Street Journal

EDITED BY
CHARLES PRESTON

———◆———

Simon and Schuster · New York
1963

First Printing

Library of Congress Catalog Card Number: 63–19278
Manufactured in the United States of America
By American Book-Stratford Press, Inc., New York

CONTENTS

THE NEW BEHEMOTHS—BIG GOVERNMENT . . . BIG UNIONS

WINDOW ON THE WORLD

WINDOW . . . OUT OF THIS WORLD 185

THE BUSINESS OF WORDS 201

POLITICAL LABELS—READ WELL BEFORE USING 245

THE NEW WORLD OF

The Wall Street Journal

FOREWORD

Durability is not one of the qualities ordinarily found in newspaper writing. But *The Wall Street Journal* is not an ordinary newspaper.

Newspaper stories are generally ground out under the pressures of men, machines and the always impending next edition. The day after a story appears, it is dead—and the paper on which it was printed is consigned to the proverbial fish stand.

After a respectable period has passed, yesterday's news story may generate its own importance as a measurement for today's events: What was the total of corrugated boxes produced last year at this time? Where were the Mets in the league standings a year ago this week?

On occasion, what appears to be yesterday's stale news finds its place in the history books: an assassination, a shipwreck or a violent market drop.

No matter how hot or lukewarm the news event, *The Wall Street Journal* has revealed the essential vitality of business news.

For business is exciting. There can be drama in railroad carloading, tension in TV set production—particularly if your own livelihood is connected with these fields. To share *The Wall Street Journal*'s discovery is to learn that the excitement and significance of business news affects everyone in this country—indeed, in the world.

The background of the American canvas is business.

Steelmaking is business, baseball is business, baking is business and bookmaking is business; as the fine detail of the American panorama emerges, we find everyone involved in some activity that must mean business. The simple biologic and economic truth is that to survive man is required to produce a valued goods or service.

If you are not a regular reader and may have fancied *The Wall Street Journal* strictly a financial newspaper, you are in for a pleasant surprise. A sampling of the contents of this volume quickly reveals the wide range of the *Journal*'s diversity of interests.

For as a national business newspaper, it is inevitable that *The Wall Street Journal* covers and uncovers so many of man's activities and pursuits. The impact of politics on business and business on political affairs earns its proper attention in the *Journal*. As the stories in this collection indicate, there is no limit to the topics which interest *Journal* readers—as businessmen concerned with dollars and cents—and as citizens curious about the world around them.

For all its steady, calm appearance, *The Wall Street Journal* is, in fact, a most energetic and exciting newspaper. Its foresight and ability to wed journalism and electronics makes it the newspaper phenomenon of the 20th century.

In 1929, when it inaugurated its San Francisco edition, *The Wall Street Journal* became the first newspaper to publish simultaneously on the East and West coasts. By 1963 the *Journal* was being printed at six different points throughout the nation, and indeed, has become the first truly national newspaper.

Journal subscribers across the nation—from Spokane, Washington, to Tampa, Florida, read the same paper on the same day.

If efficiency and speed of communications reduces distance and the sense of space, certainly *The Wall Street Journal* has contracted our borders to the dimensions of a small town.

Though newspaper stories supposedly perish with the next edition, the following pieces covering the period from 1959 to 1963 continued to entertain and inform this reader after three and four readings. I hope you find them similarly durable and profitable reading.

CHARLES PRESTON

EVERYBODY'S BUSINESS—
THE VARIED WORKDAY

Recruiting Firms—

Head-Hunters and Hatchet Men

NEW YORK—A big corporation here was all set to hire a man for a $60,000-a-year marketing job.

The president and three vice presidents had interviewed the candidate twice, but as a final check they asked Handy Associates, Incorporated, an executive recruiting firm in New York to look the man over.

"We blew him right out of the water," recalls John Handy, president of Handy Associates. "They were hiring the man as he had been 10 years before. In the meantime, he had run out of gas. It would have been a terrible mistake to hire him."

Executive recruiting firms are being called on increasingly for advice and aid in filling upper-level corporate jobs; the demand is drawing more firms into the field.

"When we came into the industry in 1953, there were perhaps a half dozen companies in the business," recalls Frank Canny of New York's Hoff, Canny and Bowen. "Today there are 50 to 75 executive search firms." Mr. Canny's own firm now fills about 75 executive positions a year, about five times as many as it did in 1953. Mr. Canny's definition of an executive position is one paying $15,000 or more, a yardstick agreed upon by most executive recruiters who as a rule don't try to fill jobs paying less.

Among corporations turning to executive recruiters to fill positions in the $15,000-and-above category are such companies as General Electric Company, Chrysler Corporation, General Mills, Incorporated, General Dynamics Corporation, Radio Corporation of America, Republic Steel Corporation and Lever Brothers Company.

The American Management Association reported recently that 99 per cent of the companies it surveyed said there was at least a 50-50 chance they would have to bring in outside executives within two years —and 64 per cent said they definitely would have to bring in new executive blood.

Why must so many companies go outside when executive develop-

ment programs are flourishing in industry and when most companies
try to promote from within?

The rapid postwar expansion of American industry has created a
shortage of executives, according to Edward A. Raisbeck, Jr., a senior
partner at Thorndike Deland Associates of New York, an industry
pioneer which has been filling executive jobs since 1923. "This business
is built on the fact there aren't enough good people in the world," he
says. "There's a mad scramble for them."

There has been a sharp rise in the demand for new executives since
the current economic slowdown began, the recruiting firms say. "We've
had a decided increase in business in recent months," says Hardy Jones,
vice president of New York's Ward Howell Associates, Incorporated.
"We find more businesses replacing vice presidents in charge of operations—men whose job it is to watch over costs."

The recruiters also report that many companies are bringing in new
men to stimulate their sales and marketing efforts. "Our business has
increased a great deal since October 1—primarily in filling marketing
jobs," says Mr. Canny of Hoff, Canny and Bowen. "That's exactly
what you'd expect in a business downturn."

The demand for executives still varies widely among industries and
companies. Human weaknesses sometimes may put a company on the
spot, suggests Thorndike Deland's Mr. Raisbeck. "Many executives
object to having a real strong No. 2 man," he says. "So, when something happens to No. 1, the corporation has egg on its face."

Mr. Canny says: "In data processing, electronics or containeriza-
tion—where we're looking for a man right now—the fields are so new
there hasn't been time to develop a lot of executive talent."

At New York's Boyden Associates, Incorporated, Paul Wilson says
his firm is sometimes called in after a merger "where the acquired company isn't ably staffed." Another common case is the company in
which all the major executives are in the same age group and "they all
grow old together," Mr. Wilson says.

Once a company decides it must "go outside" for an executive, it
doesn't necessarily rush to the phone and call in the "head-hunters,"
as executive recruiters are sometimes called by their clients. The company may advertise in a newspaper, let business associates know it is
looking for an executive, and spread the word among members of a
trade association or a professional society.

The stiff fees charged by executive search firms may keep some customers away. An executive in one major corporation says: "I think
their fees are pretty obviously too high, and that's one reason we
haven't used them more."

Most recruiting firms have a minimum fee for finding an executive: It's $3,000 at Hoff, Canny and Bowen and about $5,000 at

Handy Associates. In general, the search firms charge about 20 per cent of the executive's first year's compensation. Thus, the fee for filling a $60,000-a-year post comes to $12,000.

Some recruiters exhibit considerable sensitivity over the fee question. "I don't think it would contribute anything to discuss our fees," says Mr. Wilson briskly. Others defend the fee system. They point to the thoroughness of their search (90 to 120 days for the average executive, says one) and to the many valuable hours high-paid company executives would otherwise have to spend in the search for good candidates to fill a vacant position in their corporation. Although high fees discourage some companies from hiring recruiters, the search firms have captured a great deal of business. An executive with top personnel responsibilities for one of the country's biggest corporations suggests why: "They can make a thorough search and analysis of your competitors which you can't do yourself. And they can keep our company name out of it—in the initial stages, anyway."

Some of America's top executives have been introduced to their companies through executive search firms.

Mr. Handy relates that he presented Boone Gross to Gillette Company as a candidate for sales manager. Mr. Gross was hired, and now he is president of Gillette.

Ward Howell Associates has among its "successes" the following: Dause Bibby, president at Remington Rand, and Samuel Auchincloss, president of Tracerlab Incorporated.

"We guarantee a candidate for two years," says Mr. Handy, as he settles back in a Queen Anne chair in his 15th-floor Park Avenue headquarters. With no desk in sight, Mr. Handy's private office has the look of an 18th-century parlor. As he has his shoes shined and signs a sheaf of papers, the recruiter says that only once in seven years has he had to replace a man under the two-year guarantee.

Some "head-hunters" appear reluctant to admit the possibility they may make a mistake. Ask Mr. Wilson of Boyden Associates, Incorporated, if his firm ever has recommended the wrong man for an executive job and he retorts sharply: "We don't dare to make a mistake." Pressed for an isolated case or two where perhaps a Boyden-blessed executive went sour, he replies firmly: "I can't think of a single instance where we've had to replace a man."

Others in the industry, however, will own up to an occasional goof, though they are careful to insist on anonymity. One veteran recruiter cites this case: "We placed a man with a company as a sales manager; he had been very highly recommended by one of our most trusted reference-givers. Six weeks after he got the job, the company president called us. The man had been on a binge for two weeks and they couldn't even find him. We supplied another man without charge." He adds ruefully: "Even the best of your contacts can slip you a turkey."

But by and large, executive recruiters do come up with able executives, according to their top corporate clients. How do they do it?

First, they study very carefully the job and the company itself. "The toughest kind of a search is one for a man to fill a poorly defined job," says Bob Huttemeyer, an affable six-footer who has chalked up 14 years' experience in hunting for executives for Thorndike Deland.

He warns that job titles don't tell you much. "A director of communications may be on the president's staff in one company—with over-all staff responsibility for all types of corporate communications from TV to the annual report. In another company he may be not much more than the mail boy."

Besides trying to get the company to describe the job accurately, the recruiter, before he begins to hunt for candidates, tries to understand thoroughly the "nebulous and unspoken conditions surrounding the job itself," or the "climate" of the job.

Mr. Huttemeyer describes some of these conditions: What kind of men will the new executive be working with? Is it a shirt-sleeve group in which some executives would feel uncomfortable? The recruiter also tries to check on possible nepotism; he wants to know whether the president's son is going to be president some day.

"Joining a company," says Mr. Huttemeyer, "is something like getting married, where you love the girl, but inherit the whole darned family. Now, although the boss's wife may not hold a position in the company, it's well to evaluate her influence and to lay it on the line for a job candidate."

Ethical conduct is another consideration. "I've seen a terrific executive leave a fine company because he couldn't agree with the way the president acted on business trips. I've seen another good man quit in disgust when he found out that his new company was engaged in practices that, although 'common in the industry,' were really unethical."

Once the search firm has nailed down the kind of job that is open and the kind of man it thinks can best fill it, the hunt begins. The recruiters turn to their filing systems which contain the records of all the business contacts they have built up over the years.

Mr. Handy describes his "$250,000 IBM setup" which he says enables him to get the most out of his files on 100,000 executives: "Let's say an electronics company needs a president. We can run the cards through our sorting machine and come up with 250 men in the electronics field making over $20,000 a year."

Pointing to a long row of green filing cases, Rawle Deland of Thorndike Deland says: "Those files are invaluable. In there are the names of 150,000 executives."

He explains that if he gets an assignment to find a chief fiscal officer for a manufacturer, he'll pull out the files of all the treasurers or assistant treasurers the recruiting firm has talked to in the past five years. "These are from our 'preferred list,' people we feel are capable," he says, holding up six green jacketed folders containing data on 150 to 200 fiscal officers.

Mr. Deland scours this list looking not only for prospects but also for "resources" or "reference givers," as they're called. These are people who have suggested good candidates in the past. "In some ways," says Mr. Deland, "we place more emphasis on our resources than on prospects. We want to get to know key people in an industry who can steer us to the good prospects. This is much more practical than to try to know all the good prospects yourself."

Executive recruiters agree on the importance of developing "resources" whose judgments can be trusted. They admit it isn't easy.

"You could probably find people who'd say nice things about Al Capone," comments Hoff, Canny and Bowen's Mr. Canny. He notes that many people are inclined to say "nice things" about an acquaintance but are reluctant to state honestly his weaknesses.

One search man classifies some other undesirable reference-givers as follows: The hatchet man—enjoys knocking everyone. The unforgiving one—once you've left his company you're dead. The cave-of-the-winds—says nothing but words.

At times a search man finds his files of little help. Bob Huttemeyer cites a job he is trying to fill now: a director of fluid flow research. "Now, who has a file on a bunch of fluid flow specialists?" he asks. "I didn't even know what they were when I started out." After several weeks, however, he has developed a file some two inches thick.

He explains how he did it: "I went to the Chemists' Club Library in New York and went through all their publications getting the names of the authors of articles on fluid flow. I even discovered the field has a trade magazine—*Hydraulics & Pneumatics.*"

Once in touch with a prospect, executive recruiters lean heavily on personal interviews with the man. Frank Canny describes how he conducts "an interview in depth": "I let the man do as much talking as possible. I ask him to go back to before his college days and tell me about his background. It's amazing how much you can learn by letting a man talk—both from what he tells you and what he glosses over."

Mr. Handy says some of his interviews may last nine hours and "amount to a psychological test."

Recruiters say that in interviewing candidates it is important to know one's own prejudices so as to discount them. Rawle Deland lists a clutch of prejudices an interviewer may have: "Bow ties, pimples, fast talkers, slow talkers, mustaches, rimless glasses, patterned stockings, Continental suits, 'insincere' ties, English haircuts."

Although recruiters usually shy away from executives who have been fired from their most recent positions or who appear to be chronic job-hoppers, they sometimes are sympathetic toward men who have left certain jobs. "There's certainly no disgrace involved in anyone leaving a certain drug company in New York," says one recruiter. "The only question we'd have about the man is why he ever went to work for them in the first place."

In a rare instance, a search firm will duck an assignment entirely. The head of one firm recalls such a case: "Several years ago a family-owned company wanted an executive vice president. The idea was that he was to run the place while he brought along the president's nephew to the point where he could take over. I looked over the nephew and decided it was an impossible assignment—the nephew just didn't have the talent or the ambition."

ED CONY

November 29, 1960

"I hope you realize that you are speaking to the Chairman of the Board of Directors of one of the world's largest corporations."

Here Come the Debs

NEW YORK—At midnight, the lights will dim in the crowded Grand Ballroom of the Plaza Hotel here. As an orchestra plays softly, a spotlight will follow a succession of 46 white-gowned young women as they parade up the middle of the ballroom on the arms of escorts in white tie and tails.

The names of each girl and her parents will be announced, and each girl will curtsy low. Onlookers will respond with polite clapping.

The occasion will be the New York Junior League's annual Thanksgiving eve debutante ball—"one of the really top parties," as a former participant describes it. The affair will signal that another winter coming-out season is in full swing.

It will be a busier one than ever. In New York City, 29 debutante balls are scheduled for the winter season, nine more than two years ago. Thousands of debutantes, mostly college freshmen 17 to 19 years old, will take part in other balls around the nation, such as Chicago's Passavant Cotillion, the Veiled Prophet Ball in St. Louis and the Ak-Sar-Ben Coronation and Ball in Omaha. Dozens of suburban communities will hold their own deb dances. And on top of all the group affairs, doting parents will give an endless succession of private parties to honor debutante daughters.

The practice of making formal debuts is flourishing even though it has lost much of its original purpose, which was to introduce to "society," including prospective husbands, demure young ladies until then largely restricted to the family circle. "Now," observes one Greenwich, Connecticut, matron, "most girls go out with boys and run off for college weekends long before they become debutantes."

The custom endures because "coming out is a status symbol—it's part of the American aspiration for social status," says Marianne Strong, who heads a New York "social public relations" firm. Miss Strong's services include advising would-be social lions on such matters as whom to invite to a cocktail party and what charity balls to attend.

The spreading popularity of the coming-out ritual is increasing the business of a wide variety of people. Among the chief beneficiaries are "social secretaries," women who, for a fee, counsel debs and their families, arrange parties and draft invitation lists. Essential to the job, notes Katherine Palmer, a New York social secretary, is a close reading of the daily newspapers to keep track of the comings and goings and marital status of potential guests.

High-priced dress shops, dance orchestras, caterers, hotels, florists and other firms also are profiting from the trend. Meyer Davis, who provides orchestras for debutante functions, says he's booked heavily three or four years ahead; his deb business will bring in $729,000 this year, up $9,000 from last year. Comments the Society of American Florists: "Our members have definitely felt the increase of debutante parties in their business." A New York tent firm reports the renting of canopies for outdoor deb parties during the summer debutante season has grown from almost nothing to 20 per cent of its total volume over the past 15 years.

Debutante affairs were once largely confined to old cities like Boston, Newport, Rhode Island, New York and Philadelphia, but they now are a nationwide phenomenon. The *Debutante Register,* a partial listing of the nation's debs published annually at $45 a copy, carries 3,300 names in its 1962 edition, compared with 2,200 the previous year. A sizable part of the increase, according to the publisher, Society Associates, Limited, of New York, was in Southern California.

In theory, any girl can come out, and nowadays debutantes are drawn from a broader social and economic spectrum than a few years ago. But, realistically, it still takes a prominent family or reasonable wealth for a girl really to join the debutante whirl, with her own coming-out graced by social notables and her mailbox crammed with invitations to other debuts and parties. Even within the upper reaches of the debutante world, there is quibbling over the prestige attaching to various debuts. A girl coming out in Boston this winter is convinced that in New York it's possible to buy your way into society with a splashy debut. "But it won't work in Boston," she insists.

Many private coming-out parties are lavish. Henry Ford II was reported to have spent $250,000 to honor his daughter Charlotte during the 1959 Christmas season in Grosse Pointe, Michigan. Some 1,200 guests attended, and the decorations alone were said to have cost $60,000.

This year's summer debutante season saw several elaborate parties. The debut of Leslie Clement, daughter of Mr. and Mrs. James Higbee Clement, Kingsville, Texas, was marked by a whole weekend of celebrating at that state's giant King Ranch; guests flew in from such faraway places as Portland, Oregon, New York City and Miami to nibble frijoles and tamales and dance to Mexican music. Here in New York some 600 guests had leis flung around their necks by Tahitian dancers as they boarded a chartered commercial passenger vessel which was the setting for a coming-out party for Anne Terry Pierce, daughter of Rebekah Harkness Kean, a Standard Oil heiress. Amid South Seas decorations, the guests danced, drank champagne and sampled Tahitian delicacies as the boat cruised up the Hudson.

Increasingly, however, the trend is to "mass debuts"—balls at which a number of girls are presented. "Girls come out en masse because they might not be able to afford by themselves a party on the scale they would like," says society band leader Lester Lanin. Adds Emil Coleman, another band leader popular with the deb set: "It's not good form any more for people to show how much money they can spend."

Frequently, joint debuts are arranged by groups of parents, who split costs. Thus, the families of 15 girls who will come out at a cotillion in Englewood, New Jersey, this week are each paying $250. Other balls are held under the auspices of organizations, such as the Junior League in New York, though the parents of the debutantes still help foot the bills. New York Junior League debs, who have been thoroughly drilled in how to walk and curtsy in the presentation ceremony, are "provisional" members of the League.

Debutante balls often benefit charitable causes. Some critics complain the affairs are frequently so costly that little is left for charity; they suggest the ties to charity serve mainly to salve the consciences of participants who might otherwise feel ill at ease over lavishing large sums on debutantes. All the same, debutante parties sometimes do produce substantial amounts for charity. Over the past seven years, the deMarrillac Cotillion has raised $50,000 for charity in the Catholic diocese of Brooklyn. The New York Junior League ball, while not primarily a fund-raising event, in 1961 earned a surplus of almost $7,000 for social service in New York City.

Not all debutante ball profits go to charity. A few balls are "owned" by social secretaries such as Mrs. Henry Duncan Wood of New York, who pockets the surplus from her annual Greensleeves Ball. For the ball Mrs. Duncan chooses 10 debutantes, each of whose families pays $800 for the privilege, and sells tickets to a select group at $25 per person.

What do parents and girls caught up in debutante affairs think of all the fuss? Though most fathers profess to be disinterested, it's obvious many like the idea of having a debutante daughter. Mothers usually insist girls benefit. "It's important for a girl to learn how to meet people," a New York mother says. "She gets finesse and experience out of being a deb."

After protesting it was all mother's doing, the debs themselves generally concede that they enjoy the glitter and excitement of debutante balls and that it's flattering to be the cynosure of society for a while. But here and there a debutante expresses doubts about the whole business.

"You meet people, but it's awfully superficial," says a Boston deb. "All you ever say is 'What school do you go to?' and 'Oh, do you know so and so?'" The motive behind many debutante parties, ac-

cording to this girl: "A lot of people who aren't in the top, top society
want to get in, so they give a party."

NEIL ULMAN

November 21, 1962

———◆———

THE HYBRID FIG LEAF

We can't pretend it's to please the male
That women are slaves to fashion.
For the sons of Adam in vain bewail
The raiment we spend their cash on.

But nevertheless, as the seasons wheel,
We let the designers costume us
In clothes that most of us privately feel
We'd hate to be caught in posthumous.

And whether in sacks or in whalebone stays,
And whether we freeze or smother,
Eve's daughters now, as in fig leaf days,
All dress to distress each other.

—GEORGIE STARBUCK GALBRAITH

———◆———

Spanish Shepherds

Ease Labor Shortage

KERMAN, CALIFORNIA—José Luis Echamendi uses a chunk of
bread to wipe the last of his noontime stew from a tin plate. Holding a
worn wineskin at arm's length, he washes down the stew with California burgundy.

His meal over, Mr. Echamendi and a co-worker leave their ram-
shackle trailer home and resume moving a flock of 400 sheep slowly
across the spacious San Joaquin Valley.

These two sheep herders are part of an unusual work force—

Basques imported from northern Spain by Western sheep men to tend woolly flocks that range through the rugged Sierras and Rockies. Wool growers, plagued by falling meat and wool prices, say they would go out of business without this labor supply.

This year, a sheep grower's association in nearby Fresno is importing some 230 Basques—a mountain-dwelling people from Europe's Pyrenees—to nursemaid members' flocks. Next year, estimates the association, the number will be even larger. All told, nearly 800 Basques, brought in temporarily under special U.S. legislation, are now working as herders through 10 Western states.

The reason: American youths, apparently preferring higher-paying and less-lonely occupations, haven't the slightest interest in meandering around the mountains with a thousand or so bleating animals.

Though no bonanza by U.S. standards, employment here pays Basques many times what they could earn back home in the Pyrenees. As sheep herders here, they earn about $200 per month plus "room and board." The latter usually means a tent or a trailer, plus a burro or two with a load of provisions. One important food item provided in California: wine for the wineskins.

Unlike the typical range hand of television Westerns, who seemingly works only for Saturday nights in town, the Basques for the most part shun cities during their entire U.S. stay. Explains dark-haired, 18-year-old Luis Villenueva as he stands by his trailer home: "I want to save my dollars."

This, of course, is why these Spanish citizens volunteer for the lonely U.S. jobs in the first place. As present immigration laws make it difficult for them ever to enter America on permanent visas, they come here vowing to save as much as possible and take it back. At the end of their three-year stays, sheep men say, most herders return home with $5,000 or $6,000. This cash reserve gives returning herders a sense of financial independence that would be hard to achieve by other means.

"Basques are proud and independent people," says Philip Erro, a second-generation Basque himself and a leading sheep man here. "They don't like to work for other people, so this program gives some chance of getting started on their own."

Independence has always been a characteristic of the reserved Basques, a people of unknown ethnic origins who inhabit the mountainous area shared by Spain and France. Raising sheep has historically been one of their major occupations; many Western U.S. sheep men are descendants of Basque immigrants. In the postwar years, these wool growers found their own sons and other youths—now Americanized—no longer were interested in tending flocks, and they also found U.S. immigration laws kept them from bringing over enough men from "the old country" to fill vacancies on a permanent basis.

The growers asked for special legislation, and following Congressional hearings in 1956, Basques have been allowed to come to America under the same Federal laws which bring other foreign nationals here for jobs that can't be filled by the American labor force. The same laws, for instance, allow importation of Mexican and British West Indies laborers for toil on American farms during harvest seasons. But the latter are seasonal workers, and for the most part only supplement the domestic work force. Basques are guaranteed three full years of steady employment by sponsoring sheep men, and take jobs that simply can't be filled by reasonably qualified Americans, says a sheep men's representative.

In Fresno, the Western Range Association, a group representing most large range operators in the West, acts as a clearing house for this labor program. Sheep growers send in the names of individuals they want to sponsor—usually a friend or relative of someone already on the payroll—and the association makes proper arrangements with U.S. and Spanish governments.

ROBERT KEATLEY

November 21, 1960

THROUGH A GLASS, LIGHTLY

My wife's no connoisseur of wines,
And she'll admit it to you gladly;
We serve you white with meat because
It doesn't stain the cloth as badly.

—LOYD ROSENFIELD

Food Salesman's Success

CHICAGO—A few days ago a salesman, displaying expensive, exotic food in the home of one of Chicago's wealthiest women, was asked the price of a case of imported Danish shrimp.

"Madam," said the salesman airily, "if prices concern you, may I suggest the A & P?" The woman's $600 food order climbed shortly to $770.

This story is related by the salesman, Rex D. Kane, president of Sey-Co Products Company, Van Nuys, California, and confirmed by the woman customer. Mr. Kane cites such strategy as the major reason annual volume of his carriage trade food business has climbed 50 per cent in three years to about $500,000.

Sey-Co, whose catalog bills its products as "the world's rarest delicacies," sells 200 imported food items to some of the nation's wealthiest families, mostly by personal appointment.

The company sends its catalog to an international mailing list of 100,000 families. It counts 11,000 U.S. families as active customers. "The average income of our customers is $50,000 a year and 100 of them are millionaires," Mr. Kane reports proudly. Orders are taken by Mr. Kane and 10 other traveling salesmen, and average around $300 at a crack.

One order from the widow of an industrial executive last year amounted to $4,084 and included such items as three cases of Japanese crab meat, 100 tins of black bean soup with sherry, and four dozen containers each of Brazilian hearts of palm, Belgian carrots, Nova Scotia lobster, beluga caviar and pheasant *pâté*. Mr. Kane's list of customers, besides an imposing roster of American industrialists, includes such individuals as Margaret, Countess of Suffolk and John Ma, one of the heads of the Asia Trust Company, Bangkok, Thailand.

Mr. Kane's methods help him compete with the many other firms trying in various ways for a share of the fast-growing gourmet food market. This year, sales of these imported and specialty foods are expected to hit $130,000,000. Reese Finer Foods, Incorporated, of Chicago, draws attention with fried Mexican worms and chocolate-covered ants. Mail order steaks are a mainstay of Pfaelzer Brothers, part of Armour and Company in the Windy City. New York's Cresca Company lures customers for its delicacies by packing them in a $150 home bar on wheels, and Liberty Import Corporation, also of New York, and S. S. Pierce Company of Boston distribute through retail stores a broad line of exotic foods.

Mr. Kane emphasizes quality and variety; he recently returned from a two-month world shopping tour. But he maintains his business could not succeed without a special brand of salesmanship. While the company has been in business since 1934, volume soared to its present level only after perfection of the "carriage trade approach," which is now drilled into each salesman. "These people are a different ilk than the average," he contends. "They were weaned on champagne and feted on caviar, educated in special schools and staffed with servants who know how to serve. If you kowtow to them you're the same as the gardener and you can't sell them a can of hash."

Top rule in what Mr. Kane calls his "million-dollar formula" is "maintaining control of the situation by talking to customers on even terms." He adds: "These women admire men who talk directly to them. I do it by continually telling myself that the only difference between this rich woman and old Rex is her money."

A California heiress reports that he "talks very directly, almost sharply," but she adds quickly that she regards him as "a perfect gentleman." She generally manages to get him to disclose the price before she buys, but observes: "Mr. Kane usually has to score a point first— he has to point out that price is secondary to quality or that it's a minor factor in my case."

Some customers indicate that they buy from him despite his approach, rather than because of it. "Mr. Kane is an extremely self-confident man," says the private secretary of a wealthy Chicago customer. "Frankly, his approach doesn't always go over too well and he's really trading pretty heavily on the quality of his product."

Mr. Kane's sales pitch includes the conjuring of scenes of "tiny Danish shrimp dabbled with spicy Russian dressing and served with crisp Japanese cocktail crackers." Says Mr. Kane, "You have to be a pitch-man to sell high society. You can romance a can of artichoke bottoms into a $96 sale (four dozen) if you paint a good picture." A favorite line: "Madam, I'm doing you a favor by sending you a case."

Problems of the business include movie people and women who offer him cocktails, Mr. Kane says. Movie stars are notoriously bad payers, he contends, and liquor "distracts from the food products and slows down the sale."

Potential customers? Most of their names are obtained from present clients. In a typical case Mr. Kane will suggest that "Mrs. Jones doesn't know me and I know it's not an imposition for you to call her and say I'll be by in the next 30 minutes."

Sey-Co products cover a wide range of items, all of them produced to specification and packed under the company label, Mr. Kane says. Top seller is Japanese crab meat, bought from floating canneries and billed as 86 per cent leg meat; it sells at $1.75 for a 6½-ounce tin. Peeled miniature Danish shrimp for cocktails and salads costs $1.40 for a three-ounce tin, and four ounces of beluga caviar is $8. French *pâté de foie gras* is $7.75 for four ounces.

The Sey-Co president, 51, dark-haired and dynamic, dropped out of Milwaukee's West Side High School at 14 to work at odd jobs. He doesn't mix socially with the wealthy people to whom he sells. Comments Mr. Kane, "I don't feel inferior but when the day is over I want to relax."

KENNETH G. SLOCUM

July 25, 1960

"After being a housewife so long, I suppose it's hard for you to adjust to the office routine."

She's the Boss

A clipped French poodle pads about the office of the president of Bonwit Teller stores in Philadelphia.

The vice president-treasurer of Whitaker Cable Corporation, a Kansas City, Missouri, maker of automotive electrical equipment, starts the working day by preparing breakfast for the chairman of the board in the company cafeteria.

Always on display at the office of the president of Beech Aircraft Corporation in Wichita, Kansas, is a flag signaling the boss's mood of the moment; a smiling sun on a royal blue field, for example, proclaims business is going swimmingly, while a predominantly black flag bearing the word "woe" may mean a big order got away or a production schedule wasn't met.

It should come as no surprise that, except for the breakfasting board chairman, the executives in these examples are women—Mildred Custin, Adalain Lee Taylor and Olive Ann Beech, respectively. They all demonstrate that women can hold down demanding executive posts. But they also show that life around the office is likely to have a distinctive flavor when the boss is a lady.

Besides bringing feminine touches to business management, women frequently bring special problems. They may have trouble inducing co-workers to respect their leadership and customers to accept them as top representatives of their firms. The male president of a company may wonder whether he should hold the chair for the female vice president when she sits down at the conference table. The woman executive may wonder how she should go about firing a male subordinate. And women in low-ranking clerical and secretarial jobs may be resentful when one of their sex joins management.

Many women executives have made impressive records despite such problems. Miss Custin of Bonwit Teller and Company of Philadelphia, which has three women's clothing stores in that area, has lifted sales 20 per cent since taking over as president four years ago. When Mrs. Beech assumed the presidency of Beech Aircraft in 1950 after the death of her husband, the company's volume was running at an annual rate of $16.5 million; in the firm's most recent fiscal year sales were $67.7 million.

A competitor says of Mrs. Beech, who owns a big block of Beech Aircraft shares: "If she sold her stock tomorrow, she would still be there. She's a damn good businesswoman."

Women executives often insist their sex doesn't make any difference in the business world. "It has never been my experience that being a woman has hindered or helped my ability to progress," says Miss Taylor of Whitaker Cable.

All the same, Miss Taylor uses only her initials when signing letters, a common practice among women executives. While Miss Taylor's motive may not be to avoid calling attention to her sex, that's undoubtedly why many women stick to initials—which suggests that they sometimes feel a bit ill at ease in their executive roles.

"This is a man's job," concedes Elsa Blum, hard-driving, chain-smoking vice president and production manager of Fritzi of California Manufacturing Corporation, a San Francisco women's apparel producer. "You have a capacity of 25,000 blouses a month and orders for 30,000. The question is what pattern to cut first, what to push ahead and what to let fall behind. I have to decide."

A number of women executives note there's no place in business for the emotional thinking and emotional displays normally considered female prerogatives. A woman executive must "pay the price" that goes along with business success, observes Mrs. Beech. "She can't throw a fit of hysteria just because she can't face up to something."

Some women executives have shown they can be just as tough-minded in business dealings as their male counterparts. Reflecting on the success of Margaret Brand Smith, a woman lawyer who is president of Union Bankers Insurance Company of Dallas, a male associate says: "Margaret can make an off-the-cuff decision and never flinch if it turns out wrong. That's why she makes a good executive. A lot of women are afraid to make decisions, and they're always worrying about defending and justifying themselves."

Margaret Laughlin Mitchell, now vice president and general manager of Stouffer Foods Corporation's restaurant division, is quick to admit that she didn't climb to the executive level through gentle feminine tactics alone. "I had to get rough, and I did," she says. Mrs. Mitchell believes in "firm" management and has no qualms about firing subordinates, "especially if they try to outwit me or lie." Only last December she discharged a male restaurant manager. "I told him he used his time poorly and filed inaccurate reports," she says.

Nevertheless, some women executives rely heavily on persuasion and suggestion. "I don't manage my men—I cooperate with them," comments Kathryn Margaret Schien, chairman and executive vice president of Products Research Corporation. Products Research is a Burbank, California, chemical company which Mrs. Schien and her late husband helped organize in 1945; its volume last year topped $8.5 million.

Discussing Harriet Wilinsky, sales promotion manager of Filene's store in Boston, a male subordinate says: "She realizes she is a woman in a man's world. She's sharp as a tack and when dealing with men gives the impression of deferring to their better judgment. Later you realize that she has planted the seed of an idea that you come up with."

Most women executives maintain their sex causes no special problems with subordinates or with fellow executives. "It's a matter of respect," observes 35-year-old Elsa Blum, the clothing manufacturing executive. "They know I've done every job in the plant—and always a little faster."

Inevitably, however, some men find female bosses a severe blow to their egos. "I'll never again have a woman executive telling me what to do," vows a former associate of Mrs. Smith, the insurance company president. Louise Hess, merchandising vice president of Chicago Printed String Company, a maker of gift wrap products, says that in her former post of sales manager she often called on department stores with her salesmen. "Older salesmen never could bring themselves to introduce me as the sales manager—it was always Miss Hess from Chicago," she recalls.

Miss Hess's presence also "confused" the company's men executives at first. "They didn't know whether or not to hold the chair for me, and they couldn't comprehend that I found it more fascinating to talk business with men than housekeeping with women," she says. Because the men hesitated to ask her to join them for lunch, she lunched alone "for a solid year." Miss Hess began to feel accepted when she noticed male executives no longer made any move to help her seat herself.

Jealous women subordinates have caused problems for more than one woman executive. "I may be a traitor to my sex, but I think I have more trouble with women than with men—although I don't have much difficulty with either," says Miss Custin of Bonwit's. In a chapter written for a book to be published this spring, psychologist Dr. Harry Levinson, director of the Menninger Foundation's division of industrial mental health, maintains that "male subordinates respond better to women superiors than do female subordinates." Usually, says Dr. Levinson, "women would rather have men as supervisors."

Even when completely accepted within their own companies, women executives may encounter problems with outsiders. "I just resent dealing with women executives," says a Dallas businessman. "I don't think women belong in business."

Barbara G. Quigley, vice president of the international division of Gabriel Company, a manufacturer of auto shock absorbers, says a male Filipino customer once exploded when he received a letter from her concerning a problem. The letter forcefully suggested the course of action the man should take, but the Filipino felt it was not a woman's place to address him in such fashion. Miss Quigley wrote another letter to soothe him. "Had I not backed down a little, we might have lost our shock business in the Philippines," she says.

Women executives can't avoid falling into embarrassing or annoying situations occasionally. Some say they feel uncomfortable when business conventions turn roisterous. Ethleen Lasseter, a First National Bank of Atlanta trust officer, complains about attempts to put her "in with all the wives" at conventions.

Other women executives—particularly those who go by their initials —tell of inadvertently being invited to executive stag dinners or to affairs at men-only clubs. J. M. (Julia) Montgomery, a widow who is a highly successful general partner of a Washington, D.C., securities firm, recalls an Investment Bankers Association gathering in Philadelphia at which room assignments had to be reshuffled when she was assigned a male roommate in advance.

Mrs. Smith of Union Bankers Insurance fumes because American Airlines refuses to admit her to its Admirals Club. The club maintains private lounges in airports for top executive passengers. "It's just a little thing, but it burns me up," says Mrs. Smith.

Some women in management assert that traditional bias also affects their pay scales. "Even doing a man's job, women have difficulty getting the same salary," says one woman executive. "I've found that right along." Even so, many women are deep into the five-figure category, and in general they can afford to indulge their whims and live comfortably.

Miss Taylor of Whitaker Cable hums along in a 1962 "black cherry" Lincoln. Edith Martin, a vice president of Pittsburgh's Pennsylvania National Bank, travels abroad most summers, and Filene's Miss Wilinsky—who in private life is Mrs. Sylvan A. Goodman—says she and her husband "frequently hop a plane for Hong Kong or some place."

Mrs. Schien of Products Research, at $90,000 a year one of the highest-paid women, dwells in a handsome French Provincial-style house complete with air-conditioning and a swimming pool. One day recently, Jane Ford, executive vice president and part owner of a Beverly Hills, California, investment banking firm, rented a four-place airplane and piloted it the 400 miles to San Francisco—solely because she craved a lunch of crab legs and abalone steak at a celebrated restaurant there.

Many women who have attained high-ranking jobs in business have not been able to fit marriage into their busy lives. "Holding a job like this and being married wouldn't work," says Miss Blum. The German-born apparel firm vice president is separated from her husband.

Some women executives are happily married, however. Occasionally the wife earns more money than her husband. This is true of Stouffer restaurants' Mrs. Mitchell, whose husband runs his own food brokerage business. Though such a situation might easily strain domestic relations, Mrs. Mitchell says all is harmonious in her home.

Louise Hess of Chicago Printed String, who is Mrs. Wallace Landau after business hours, suggests that in one way her career contributes to domestic peace. "Many of my women friends complain that they want to go out evenings, but their husbands are too tired from work," she says. "That's no problem at our home." Both she and her husband, owner of a small manufacturing company, are reluctant to budge from home after a day at the office.

February 25, 1963

WRITTEN PERMISSION

Sign in window of paint store: "Husbands Choosing Colors
Must Have Note From Wives."

Doctor's Prescription

Helps Sterling Drug

NEW YORK—In the executive dining room at the Times Square headquarters of Sterling Drug, Incorporated, is a scale. At least once a week, every Sterling executive steps on it and records his weight on a near-by chart. If he has gained from the previous week, his colleagues are sure to needle him. And if the gain is five pounds or more, the expanding executive faces the prospect of banishment from the private dining room until his bulge disappears.

The weight-watching program is being carried out under the orders of a 58-year-old doctor named John Mark Hiebert—who also happens to be chairman and president of the big pharmaceutical firm. In its systematic, precise methods, the attack on executive waistlines is typical of the whole approach of the combination physician, researcher and manager to the job of running Sterling.

"Mark Hiebert is a man who has been trained in the scientific method," observes one of his vice presidents. "As a result, he approaches everything from an objective, scientific view."

Dr. Hiebert, who joined Sterling as a research employee in 1934, became chief executive early in 1960. He succeeded the late James Hill, Jr., the top official of the company for almost two decades. The contrast between the two men could not have been more marked. Mr. Hill was an ebullient, hard-selling businessman with an accounting background; he tended to run the company as a one-man show. The methodical, reserved Dr. Hiebert prefers to assign carefully defined areas of responsibility to subordinates, whose performances he then analyzes by means of an elaborate system of reports.

"It's quite a change from an accountant to a medical man," says Dr. Theodore Klumpp, a physician himself and president of Sterling's Winthrop Laboratories division. "Jim Hill was a dynamic man. Mark Hiebert is equally dynamic but in a more quiet way."

Under both these diverse personalities, Sterling Drug has made considerable progress. Between 1951 and 1959, the last full year of Mr. Hill's reign, world-wide sales climbed from $153.2 million to $228.9 million; earnings increased from $1.46 a share to $2.65 a share. Last year, with Dr. Hiebert in command, sales totaled a record $258.9 million and profits a record $2.95 a share.

As he strives for further gains, Dr. Hiebert faces some formidable challenges. In the drug industry, a steady stream of new products is imperative if a company is to remain successful, and one of Dr. Hiebert's major responsibilities is to insure that Sterling does not fall behind in the search for new and improved drugs. Last year the firm introduced more than 100 new products or variations of existing products.

Another problem confronting Dr. Hiebert and other drug industry officials is the widely publicized charge by Senator Kefauver's investigating committee that some drug prices are exorbitant. Pharmaceutical makers insist the allegation is unjustified; they say critics do not take into account the large sums the companies must spend to develop new drugs. Nevertheless, the industry still faces the possibility of legislation, proposed by Senator Kefauver, that would limit exclusive patent rights on a new drug to three years instead of the present 17. Such a law would undoubtedly drive down many drug prices, but industry spokesmen assert it would also wreck research programs by weakening the incentive to come up with new drugs.

Sterling is one of the nation's largest drug companies. It has 44 manufacturing operations in the United States and 24 foreign countries. The company is best known to the general public through its scores of non-prescription medications, such as Bayer Aspirin, Phillips' Milk of Magnesia, Fletcher's Castoria and Ironized Yeast. Between a third and a quarter of its sales, however, come from a wide range of prescription drugs, particularly analgesics and anesthetics; Novocain is one of the more familiar products in this category. During World War II, millions of GIs became acquainted with Sterling's yellow-colored antimalaria pills, Atabrine, the first substitute for quinine.

Sterling has also moved into some non-drug fields, including the manufacture of printing inks and vanillin flavoring. More recently the company began promoting a new sewage burning process devised by one of its executives.

Difficulties encountered in trying to establish a medical practice in the depression year of 1934 led the young Dr. Hiebert to join the Sterling organization originally. The son of a Hillsboro, Kansas, Mennonite Brethren minister and educator, he had worked his way through the University of Kansas and then Boston University School of Medicine; his jobs had included laboring on a harvesting crew and teaching all nine grades at a 47-pupil country school in Kansas. At the completion of his medical training, he had traveled between Boston and Kansas looking for a spot to earn a living as a doctor.

"I covered a lot of territory by jalopy," recalls Dr. Hiebert, a tall, trim man with receding gray hair. "I would stop in many towns and talk with the head of the local medical society about setting up a practice. They all told me I had fine credentials and that they would like to have me. But then they added that they were getting paid in potatoes themselves, and a new doctor wouldn't be able to make a go of it."

Dr. Hiebert's first job with Sterling was as a $3,800-a-year "research attaché" with the Winthrop division in Chicago. His chief duty was to arrange with medical institutions to do clinical studies of new Winthrop drugs. One of the projects he worked on was the introduction in the United States of sulfa drugs, whose germ-fighting abilities were considered close to miraculous in those pre-antibiotic days.

After three years in Chicago, Dr. Hiebert was transferred to Sterling's headquarters in New York. Shortly thereafter, he moved into the management side of the business and began to catch Mr. Hill's eye. His initial management assignment was to help establish a new subsidiary called Alba Pharmaceutical Company. In charge of research and product development, he quickly built a line of successful products. One of the most successful was Demerol, a pain-killer of German origin which is still one of the most widely used pain relievers in obstetrics.

Dr. Hiebert progressed steadily up the executive ladder. When Alba was consolidated with the Winthrop division just before World War II, he became executive vice president of the Winthrop operation. In 1944 Sterling acquired Frederick Stearns and Company, a Detroit drug firm, and Mr. Hill picked Dr. Hiebert to run it. Three years later Dr. Hiebert recommended that Stearns' operations be absorbed into other divisions, thereby causing the abolition of his own job. Recalled to New York, he worked as a vice president and assistant to Mr. Hill. Then in 1955 Mr. Hill, who had been both chairman and president, relinquished the latter title, and Dr. Hiebert was made president. In this post, he was the obvious choice to succeed Mr. Hill as chief executive five years later.

Dr. Hiebert's accession to the top executive post at Sterling, a job which pays him $145,600 a year, has resulted in no sharp changes of direction for the company. But his personality is clearly leaving its imprint on the mood, manner and emphasis of management.

The gregarious Mr. Hill was well known outside Sterling. He enjoyed convivial lunches with Wall Street drug industry analysts and traveled constantly; at the time of his death, he was in Paris personally carrying on negotiations on behalf of Sterling. By way of contrast, Dr. Hiebert, who is slow to unbend with casual acquaintances, is more inclined to operate within the company. He often arrives at his unpretentious 31st-floor office by 7:30 A.M. and works there till late in the evening. Sterling's executive dining room was his idea; he wanted to avoid drawn-out business lunches at midtown Manhattan restaurants.

Dr. Hiebert's colleagues agree that one of his most deep-seated traits is the tendency to carry habits of thinking instilled in research into the rest of the drug business. He shies away from snap decisions and refuses to jump to conclusions. "In research you learn to disbelieve everything until it's proven," says Dr. Hiebert.

One of his associates explains what this means in practice. If a new advertising approach is tried for a particular product and sales subsequently spurt, the normal reaction would be to credit the gain to the new advertising and immediately use the new approach on a wide scale. But Dr. Hiebert would reserve his decision until a thorough investigation had been made of every factor that could affect the drug's sales, including the weather, the incidence of disease and any setbacks to competitors' products. Dr. Hiebert's caution also means extra-careful testing and evaluation of new drugs; as a result of this policy, Sterling, unlike some of its competitors, has encountered no difficulty in clearing new drugs with the increasingly strict Food and Drug Administration.

Dr. Hiebert's penchant for system and order has brought changes in Sterling's management organization. Under Mr. Hill, the company was completely dominated by the chief executive. "Jim Hill," recalls one long-time Sterling executive, "was his own controller, president, chairman, advertising manager and production foreman."

While Mr. Hill was undoubtedly responsible for Sterling's rapid growth in the 1940s and 1950s, most of the company's executives now agree that the firm has become too large for the "tycoon-type" of management. They say that Dr. Hiebert's broader distribution of authority and responsibility, though it might be the wrong prescription for the many companies in which management decentralization has already been carried to great lengths in recent years, is working well at Sterling.

Dr. Hiebert has steadily pushed more and more authority and responsibility on to vice presidents, general managers and other officials down the line. Executives who formerly had to clear every move with Mr. Hill now are much freer to operate on their own. To insure that their efforts will benefit the company as a whole, vice presidents are being trained to look at actions and decisions from an over-all company viewpoint rather than from the narrow view of their own divisions.

Says Dr. Hiebert of his subordinates: "They are being given as much responsibility as they will take with only two reservations—that I be kept abreast of the important things and that I have the opportunity for guidance."

Comments a Sterling vice president: "Mark still keeps his hands on the pulse of the company, and the major decisions are still his. More and more, though, he's letting others be the experts in their own fields rather than trying to handle everything himself."

In part, Dr. Hiebert stays abreast of Sterling's operations by daily informal contact with key officials and by formal weekly meetings with executives. The weekly sessions are usually held on Tuesday mornings and are designed for the gathering and exchanging of information rather than for decision-making. A typical meeting may cover such varied topics as the plans for a new salicylic acid plant abroad, a joint venture with an Indian firm and revisions in the company's pension plan.

But Dr. Hiebert's principal tool for keeping on top of the business is a device he terms a "budget." This is a master plan drawn up annually for each division. Besides outlining a division's finances, a budget—in his use of the term—details plans for advertising, new products, new plants and market expansions. The division officials have wide latitude in drafting their budgets and carrying them out, but Dr. Hiebert must approve each budget and must approve major changes made during the course of the year. These stipulations assure him ultimate control over all phases of Sterling's operations.

Dr. Hiebert receives periodic reports from division heads which enable him to see if budget goals are being met. Reaching into a cabinet behind his desk, he pulls out a thick sheaf of these reports. Laid out on legal-sized paper, they consist of three columns headed "Subject," "Action This Month" and "What Will Be Done Next Month."

"Most people fail because they don't stop once in a while to take inventory of themselves, consider what they've done and where they're going," says Dr. Hiebert. The reports force subordinates to take such inventories. Also, he observes, "going on record that something is to be done is the greatest motivator around."

Not surprisingly, in view of his background, Dr. Hiebert takes a closer interest in the company's research program than did Mr. Hill, who felt more at home in the financial side of the business. Reflecting the boss's research background, the company's big Sterling-Winthrop Research Institute at Rensselaer, New York, last year opened an addition containing 112 new laboratories. Its budget has risen 40 per cent in the past two years.

Among the new products which emerged from Sterling's laboratories last year were a new drug for treating asthma, a new dental anesthetic and a new hormone drug that helps build up bone, muscle and red blood cells in undernourished or underweight children and in elderly persons. Sterling researchers are now working on everything from a new arthritis drug to a long-range basic research program in contraceptives.

Dr. Hiebert frequently prods researchers into pursuing new lines of investigation. At his behest, Sterling scientists currently are exploring anew the uses of aspirin, Sterling's biggest selling product and the most commonly used medicine around the globe. The scientists are studying aspirin's possible value in such diseases as diabetes and heart ailments.

Dr. Hiebert often reads the full scientific reports on new drugs and he follows medical journals closely. At least once a month, he spends an evening going over research projects with the head of the Sterling-Winthrop Institute.

Because such night work is common, Dr. Hiebert and his wife Dorothy, who was also trained as a physician, live during the week in a one-bedroom apartment on East 34th Street in Manhattan. On weekends the Hieberts retreat to a Port Washington, Long Island, house purchased a dozen years ago for $35,000. There, in an elaborate kitchen outfitted with gas, infrared and charcoal cooking units, the drug executive indulges in his chief hobby—the creation of "tasty but low-calorie" dishes.

JERRY E. BISHOP

March 26, 1962

MONSTER'S MATE

Electric brain, your fame is mounting!
You've greatly simplified accounting,
Yet in my modest operations
I find new rules and complications:

"Detach this stub." Just as you say!
"Leave this space blank." And I obey.
I put my number down and then
I print my name. ("Use ball-point pen.")
I shun all bending, perforation
Or other forms of profanation.

Electric brain, I'm not denying
Accountants' work you're simplifying,
But I'm the simple fellow who
Is simplifying work for you!

—MIKE MITCHELL

Freud in the Market

NEW YORK—When you buy or sell a stock, are you really trying to lose money? And, when you get mad at your broker, are you unconsciously venting your anger on a father-image?

The answers may be yes, says a Detroit psychoanalyst. His patients have shown an affinity for irrational stock market behavior. The psychoanalyst, Dr. Henry Krystal, told the American Psychoanalytic Association here that many unconscious drives may help shape the ups and downs of the stock market.

There have been few previous attempts by psychoanalysts to study economic behavior, asserts Dr. Krystal, a balding, bespectacled assistant professor of psychiatry at Wayne State University College of Medicine. Of course, psychologists and pollsters have been picking consumer brains for some time to fathom deep-seated prejudices and emotions that influence buying. But psychoanalysis is a different thing, dealing as it does with those memories and conflicts that are beyond conscious recall.

"Psychoanalysis," said Dr. Krystal in an interview, "is the tool with which we can understand the unconscious component of stock market and economic behavior."

What can psychoanalysis tell us? For one thing, it suggests that stockbrokers are sometimes father-images in the unconscious mind of the customer. To the child, the father is expected to be an eternal source of infallible good advice. One patient recently came to Dr. Krystal after a broker advised him to buy Walter E. Heller and Company stock. The broker said it was a good buy because the company's chairman was also chairman of the President's Council of Economic Advisers. The patient later discovered that Walter Heller, chairman of the finance company, was not the Walter Heller who advises the New Frontier. The man, his confidence in his broker shattered, sold all his stocks and called for psychiatric help.

Parents, of course, are far more than generous providers of good advice and comfort, according to Freudian theory. "There's a place in the history of every child when his boundless greed must be stopped short by his parents," says Dr. Krystal. "This results in anger, but the child still loves his parents. A conflict arises and the child feels guilty about it." These feelings of guilt and conflict are buried in the unconscious and in adulthood may appear in seemingly unrelated acts, such as a stock purchase, says Dr. Krystal.

To support this point, he cites a successful professional man in his early forties who had accumulated a large bank account, earmarked for a real estate purchase. When the market fell earlier this year, the man plunked all his cash into stocks, telling himself he would make a fast profit on a later upturn in prices.

But then he became full of self-doubts and turned to Dr. Krystal for help. He was encouraged to describe his dreams. In one dream, the patient was walking on a street and a man approached, saying, "Hand over your money." To the psychoanalyst, the dream took on special significance as other details of family life unfolded. The patient recalled severe lectures from his parents when, as a child, he had eaten a basket of fruit and the skin off a goose that was to be the family dinner. On top of the reprimands, he had his tonsils removed shortly thereafter. By the queer associations of the mind, the pain of tonsillectomy became punishment for his greed.

It became clear, says Dr. Krystal, that the man associated any gain or reward with a later punishment. Unconsciously, he wanted to lose the money he had invested in the market. The market obliged shortly afterward by slipping further downward. The man, who needed funds immediately for his real estate, sold out at a loss.

Another man was luckier in the market, but also had his problems. He sold all his stocks as soon as the market downturn began last March. When he presented himself to Dr. Krystal, he told of a simple dream in which he was spraying a pesticide on a rose bush in his back yard. He also told how his father had made a fortune in the stock market of the 1920s and then lost it in 1929. Unconsciously, says Dr. Krystal, the patient was competing with his father by his stock sale this year. "It was a form of one-upmanship, in which he showed that he, unlike his father, was prepared," he says. "The rose bush spraying was a symbol of his preparedness."

Besides the more serious psychic conflicts that Dr. Krystal describes in his patients, he sees other signs that amateur investors are playing the market with childish abandon. Stock trading is often done "with the idea that you must play the market to prove you're a man," he says. "No one brags about losing a job or a business deal, but many people will freely joke about their losses in the market."

HERBERT G. LAWSON, JR.

December 27, 1962

Bounced Bosses

In San Francisco an unemployed former $20,000-a-year treasurer anxiously scans job listings at a state employment service office. In a Chicago suburb an ex-vice president works worriedly on the third hundred of a series of letters to firms he hopes can use his services. In New York a former general sales manager, now a magazine advertising salesman, ruefully contemplates his cut in annual income from $25,000 to $12,000.

All these ex-executives, widely scattered as they are, share a common lot: they can't find jobs as bosses. Their sudden ousters from long-held executive posts stem from corporate reorganizations, not incompetence. But their age, their own bewilderment at their plight and the complexity of executive hiring systems have thus far posed a three-decked barrier to efforts to regain their former lofty status.

Although no one keeps tabs on the number of unemployed executives, talks with more than a score of executive recruiters and management consultants turn up a nearly unanimous opinion that the number of unemployed executives is growing.

A New York executive recruiter reports inquiries from unemployed bosses have tripled in the past two years. A Chicago executive job counselor, who advises job-seeking executives, says about 25 per cent of his clients are unemployed, compared with a "normal" average of 15 per cent. The rest are employed but are hunting better or more agreeable posts. A Los Angeles employment official reports "hundreds" of executives out of work due to cutbacks in aircraft manufacturing. "Heads have really rolled around here," he says.

Reasons: Mergers eliminate many top jobs. Rapid technological advances drastically curtail demand for traditional products of many industries, causing retrenchments. Even when outright dismissals don't result directly in these cases, changes often spawn office intrigue, policy rifts and personality clashes which lead to executive ousters, management consultants say.

But aren't such bounced bosses quickly snapped up by companies proclaiming a dearth of management talent? Many are, but by no means all of them. "A top executive is fortunate if he finds what he wants in six months," says William Clark, a New York executive recruiter.

The plight of ex-executives, unpleasant as it may be, should be of more than passing interest to active bosses. New owners are not always respecters of seniority and past performance. "A man should always have an anchor to windward," counsels a management consultant. "When he sees these things happening to others he should be thinking: What would I do if this happened to me?"

For mergers continue at a record clip and some of the biggest consolidations are yet in the offing. The Federal Trade Commission, which tries to keep track of significant mergers, counted 525 instances in which merger talks were either started or completed during the first six months of 1960. That was equal to the pace of 1959, when the agency counted 1,050 cases in which merger negotiations were begun or were completed. Several more are under consideration among railroads. And in the airline business, plans for mergers have been announced, between United Air Lines and Capital Airlines and between Trans World Airlines and Northeast Airlines, which might touch off marriages by other carriers. Says a veteran vice president of a smaller airline about to be merged: "Almost all of our executives are going to go."

The shock of a dismissal leaves many a bounced boss bewildered as well as embittered. Notes a jobless executive: "The thing a man has to battle more than anything else is a sense of not belonging. You've been a key part of an organization for years, and it's a real blow to your morale to be let out."

And although most ousters have a gracious appearance—they're usually termed resignations—appearances can be deceiving. For example, not long ago the entire management of one electronics company was fired by telegram by new owners. "Most executive dismissals are abrupt, although precautions are taken to make them look like a carefully considered move on the part of management and the individual," says one employment specialist.

Moreover, for the average medium-salary unemployed person, finding another job is a clear-cut matter of making the rounds of company personnel departments. Employment agencies abound that are anxious to lend a hand, but few agencies cater to the executive trade. Ex-executives face an artful chore which most of them are sadly equipped to handle.

"Most of these men are babes in the woods when it comes to getting jobs," declares Bernard Haldane, president of Executive Job Counselors, Incorporated, New York. "There isn't anything as stupid as the average business executive trying to sell himself," says Sidney Edlund, another New York counselor.

Many ex-bosses have little idea how to write a résumé which will entice an employer, say job experts. Some specialists advise ex-executives to write "reports" analyzing their past experience, forgetting the standard résumé format. But this can be carried to extremes, as in the case of the ex-sales executive who explained at length how he had successfully licked his alcohol problem 15 years ago.

A short, but successful, letter employed by a former purchasing agent: "I have been signing checks on a single-signature basis for $1.5 million per year. I would be interested in exchanging references." This succinct statement netted him interviews from all seven of the companies to which he wrote and, in short order, a job.

Many ex-executives, who pride themselves on past success, have a hard time accepting rebuffs. "You get a few rejections and it's darn hard to hold your head up," admits an unemployed boss lately relieved of his $25,000-a-year post in a retrenchment. "It's the wrong attitude to go in and talk to someone exuding failure. No one wants to hire someone like that, but one of the hardest things to realize is that nothing is wrong with you."

It's plain that job-hunting at executive levels is no job for an amateur and many ex-bosses are just that. Employment specialists note that experienced job switchers usually recognize the earmarks of a potentially untenable position and, if possible, move on before being let out. On the other hand, long-time executives are more likely to hope they can hold on to their jobs. "Almost without exception, they are rudely disappointed," says John Powers of Cadillac Associates, Incorporated, one of the few executive employment agencies.

Such men often have worked their way up in one company and have never looked for a job. With little idea of job-hunting techniques, unemployed bosses also find themselves outside most executive hiring systems. According to Executive Manpower Corporation, a New York consulting firm, companies fill more than half their posts by promotion and rely greatly on executive recruiters when they do go outside for talent. And recruiters hardly ever choose ex-executives for their clients. "About 99 per cent of the people we get for positions are already employed," remarks Hallam B. Cooley, vice president of Handy Associates, an executive recruiting firm.

To remain on equal footing with employed job rivals, ex-executives can't appear too eager for a job, even though unemployed. It's all right to be "available," say employment specialists, but anything so gross as asking for a job is out. "It's a nerve-racking job," concedes a job expert, "but an executive has to keep his dignity or he is through."

What this boils down to is a sort of subtle sell. But before ex-executives can make their muted pitch they have to get to the right people. "You've got to hitch a top man, the president if possible," says a sacked personnel manager who discloses that personnel officials seldom have authority to hire executives above the $15,000 level. "They have to get to someone in top management," agrees Clark Ryder, a

Los Angeles employment official. "Often no one else in the company will know of plans to hire an executive."

Getting to top officials can be a tough chore. Most ex-executives rely on passing word of their "availability" among friends and business acquaintances, but this doesn't always work. "That's the only way I know how to do it," says one ex-executive, but after two months of waiting for an introduction he glumly reports little success. And an employment expert observes: "Friends don't really know their qualifications and can get them into embarrassing positions."

When ex-executives do maneuver themselves into job interviews, they have to know when to stop playing cagey. "The executive has to sell his mind," says Richard D. Gleason, a Chicago executive counselor. "Companies aren't interested in what a man has done, but in what he can do for them," remarks a management consultant.

One ex-personnel manager is convinced a blunt approach will eventually get him back on the other side of the desk. He opens each interview by saying: "If you want a detail man or a yes man for this job, I'm not your man. If you want a man who is friendly, but aggressive and at times a little impatient, I'm your man." He's nobody's man yet, but he is confident his frankness will be rewarded.

In an interview, most unemployed executives falter in treading the fine line between underplaying and overplaying their hand. "They talk too much and try to overly impress the employer," claims one employment agency official. But a company executive counters: "They sit in that chair, don't tell me anything, and dare me to find a reason to hire them."

An ex-executive's age is often a painful handicap. Most former bosses are middle-aged, and companies with extensive training programs are often reluctant to hire men past 35. "Age is everything," contends a 54-year-old former boss who has been job hunting unsuccessfully for 21 months.

Employment officials disagree on this factor's importance. "Age is generally only an excuse for not hiring a man," says Mr. Gleason. "The reason is that he fails to sell himself." Many job experts, however, advise older ex-executives to concentrate on small firms. "We are practically never asked to secure a man who is over 50," says Mr. Cooley.

The few job counselors advising ex-executives are mostly headquartered in New York and Chicago. Unlike employment agencies, they usually don't seek out jobs for their clients but drill them on the techniques of job-finding and résumé-writing. One such service was started by Mr. Gleason, a former General Electric Company personnel official, in Chicago six years ago. He takes only 200 or 250 clients a year, turning down some whose "marketability" is questionable, and charges

$500 for his service. His firm also offers counseling to groups of eight or ten men at $250 per person. Most of his clients are still employed, though angling for a change.

Employment agencies find executive placement unprofitable because it takes so long to line up a middle-aged former boss with a job. Robert Schwarz, president of the National Association of Employment Agencies, says none of the group's members specializes in placing high-salaried men. "I tried the employment agencies and found that nobody wanted to talk to a 48-year-old man," recalls a controller ousted in a merger.

Most trade and professional groups shy away from close involvement with job-hunters, but a few private organizations, such as the Sales Executives Club of New York, sponsor job-hunting services. The club has expanded its service to non-member sales bosses and now has 1,300 résumés on file, all but about 10 per cent of them from men who were forced out of their jobs, according to Henry Astwood, director of the job service. Oddly, ex-sales executives don't seem any more adept at job hunting than other former bosses. "Of those 1,300 résumés, 90 per cent don't have five cents' worth of sell," says Mr. Astwood.

In at least one instance, bounced bosses have banded together to try to solve their problems. In Berkeley, California, Ralph Moore of the state employment department became concerned about a year ago about the number of former top officials who were registering for unemployment compensation. Most of them seemed completely demoralized, he recalls, so he invited them to get together to talk over their difficulties.

Out of such informal gatherings has developed a weekly meeting group (with transient membership, of course) which dubs itself Experience Unlimited. Every Friday the 20 or so current members meet to swap job-hunting tips.

About 120 men have joined Experience Unlimited for varying periods in the last year. Only about 30 got jobs through the group but members are enthusiastic. "It's a wonderful morale booster," says a current member. "It lets you know that other capable men are in the same boat through no fault of their own."

Fortunately, most ex-executives are financially able to ride out a lengthy period of unemployment. Employment officials say most ousted executives receive about three months' severance pay, and presidents get up to a year's salary. Some bosses with contracts get even bigger settlements.

Nonetheless, ousted bosses have financial worries. For one thing, they often lose substantial pension benefits when sacked, and they usually can't recoup these losses even when they find another job. A long period of unemployment can also cut heavily into their savings.

In such circumstances the temptation to accept a low-level job offer is strong. Many ex-executives frankly admit they're ready to take the first job that comes along after a few months of fruitless searching. A job counselor notes: "When a man has been out of work for six months he begins wondering about himself and can get pretty upset over it. It takes guts; he has to keep calm and not jump at the first Grade B job he is offered just to shut up his friends." Warns another employment official: "If he drops back too far in the corporate hierarchy he may hurt himself and never be able to regain stature."

NORMAN C. MILLER, JR.

August 16, 1960

"I finally found a man smart enough for the job. But he was too smart to take it."

Judo Enjoys a Boom

Like most housewives, Mrs. Sue Folmer of Dallas devotes most of her time to tending her home and caring for her two young children. But twice a week, this 125-pound blonde spends 30 minutes slamming 180-pound men to the ground.

Mrs. Folmer's vigorous hobby, shared by a growing number of other Americans, is judo. It's the sport version of jujitsu, the self-defense art practiced by Japanese warriors for more than a thousand years. Users of judo, which ironically means "the gentle way" in Japanese, rely on a variety of kicks, blows, throws, pulls and holds to subdue an opponent.

More than 20,000 judoists now belong to the Judo Black Belt Federation of the United States, compared with only 11,000 last April and about 3,000 five years ago. The federation, which helps promote the sport, takes its name from the black belt worn by judo experts. Many of its new members learned judo fundamentals at YMCAs. Instruction also is given by about 700 schools and clubs accredited by the federation, compared with only 125 five years ago.

"Most people come here with the intention of learning self-defense," says Vincent Tamura, owner of the Tamura Judo Institute in Dallas, where Mrs. Folmer takes her lessons. "But then they gradually become interested in the competitive sport aspect. For children, judo develops coordination and self-confidence, and businessmen and professional people look to it for exercise and emotional release."

Mrs. Folmer began taking lessons "because my six-year-old son was a student and I had to learn how to fall so he could practice his throws. Already my three-year-old daughter is interested and practices with her brother and me every night."

Says Leon Goldberg, a 60-year-old Los Angeles household goods salesman who took up judo three years ago: "I felt that if I could do something to handle trouble I could relax. I've come to love the activity of the sport and I feel better now than I felt when I was 25. It gives me a light, sure feeling to know I don't have to be a yes-man."

Judo training paid off for John H. Mandell, 40, a Torrance, California, optometrist, when he was attacked by a holdup man three years ago. "I heard a rustle behind me and when I turned around I was hit on the head with a lead pipe," Mr. Mandell recalls. "As I was falling I automatically used a circle throw (a foot in the pit of the stomach) which sent the man flying over my head and knocked him out. If it wasn't for my judo reaction he definitely would have finished me."

Mr. Mandell has been taking judo lessons for four and a half years. At first he was mainly interested in self-defense. "But once I got into it," he says, "the sportsmanship and the physical conditioning became more important. My only regret is that I didn't start learning judo as a child."

Taking up judo requires an initial investment of about $25, according to Donald Pohl, secretary of the Judo Black Belt Federation. Of this sum, $15 goes for a white cotton judo suit and the rest for instruction books. Students pay an average of $5 for a half-hour lesson at commercial schools. Dues to non-profit clubs, which give members a chance to develop their skills by competing against each other, average about $5 a month.

The Detroit Judo Club, one of the largest in the country, last year took in about $48,000 in dues from its 500 members and proceeds from the sale of judo suits and instruction manuals. A good part of this money went to pay staff members and maintain the clubhouse—a one-story building with a large, matted "dojo," or workout area, and dressing rooms.

Last June the club sponsored a tournament at the University of Detroit gymnasium which drew about 4,000 persons who paid $1 or $2 for tickets. About 500 judo tournaments are held in the country each year, including club competition, collegiate matches and a national tournament staged by the Amateur Athletic Union.

Mr. Pohl of the Black Belt Federation claims that judo slowly is developing into a good spectator sport as people learn more about it. "Judo has a lot of suspense and drama in it once you learn what it's all about," he says. "It's intriguing to know that if you blink, you might miss seeing a guy tossed on his head."

Another Oriental combat technique, called karate, is also attracting increasing interest from Americans concerned with defending themselves. It combines elements of jujitsu and Western-style boxing. Although a karate expert can kill or maim an opponent with slashing blows of the hands and feet, U.S. schools generally teach less lethal versions of the technique. Karate isn't as popular as judo in the United States, according to Alice McGrath, a Los Angeles judo and karate instructor, because "it's so much newer than judo that there just aren't enough trained teachers."

DAVID H. KELSEY

November 20, 1962

The Moonlighters

For three weeks, Gordon Neumann, a deputy sheriff in Portland, Oregon, will grab a cat nap after his graveyard-shift tour of duty and then report to a local department store. There he will don a red suit and white beard and take up his part-time job for the Christmas season—playing Santa Claus.

Deputy Neumann is one of this nation's army of "moonlighters," people who boost their incomes by working at two jobs. Also numbered among moonlighters are teachers who drive cabs after school, factory hands who vend cold drinks at evening sports events and firemen who paint houses on their days off.

The prevalence of moonlighting is the source of considerable concern around the country, a *Wall Street Journal* survey of scores of personnel executives, union officials and two-job workers themselves indicates. Some industry personnel managers, while not flatly opposing the practice, worry that second jobs may sometimes fatigue employees and result in poor quality work. Union spokesmen generally denounce moonlighting, arguing it isn't fair for one man to have two jobs when some workers are without a job of any kind; they also say it thwarts unionism's drive for a shorter work week and increased leisure. As for the workers who feel compelled to hold two jobs, their chief complaint is that the long hours of labor leave them with little free time.

According to Government figures, an estimated 4.3 per cent of the U.S. work force held two jobs last year. This was up from 2.9 per cent in 1950, though a shade under the 4.4 per cent level of 1958. The increase since 1950 is generally attributed to the trend in many industries to shorter work weeks, which leave workers more time to devote to second jobs. Many Government and private economists predict even shorter work weeks are in prospect for the future, so opportunities for moonlighting may well multiply. Says an executive in the steel industry, where the Steelworkers Union now talks of a 32-hour week: "I'm sure the shorter work week would lead to more moonlighting."

Despite the possibility of an increase in moonlighting over the next few years, the proportion of workers with two jobs appears to have remained fairly stable in recent months. On the one hand, the current slowdown in business has cut the hours of work in numerous industries and led more workers than usual to seek supplemental income from part-time jobs. But the slowdown also means many firms need fewer part-time employees than normally.

"More and more people are trying to find second jobs," says Marian Miller, assistant manager of a Los Angeles employment agency. The agency finds it's able to place about four of every ten part-time-job seekers, most of whom are blue-collar workers. An employment agency in Galesburg, Illinois, reports many workers are eager for part-time jobs in filling stations and elsewhere. But, says a spokesman, "there's not much open—even the filling stations are laying off here."

While most companies haven't noticed a jump in moonlighting recently, increases have occurred in a few instances. At the Sacramento, California, plant of Aero-Jet-General Corporation, maker of solid propellants for missiles, roughly 1,200 of the company's 7,000 hourly wage earners are moonlighters, up from 700 a year ago, according to a spokesman for the International Association of Machinists. And the director of industrial relations for a Chicago steel mill says more of his firm's employees may be taking odd jobs as house painters and filling station attendants because of the steel industry's reduced operations.

Moonlighting is by no means confined to workers in temporarily depressed industries. Some workers who could get by with the earnings from their primary job take another job after hours because of a powerful drive to raise their living standards; these industrious folk would rather have extra money for a new car or a dishwasher than a few more hours of leisure.

Others turn to moonlighting because they find that even by putting in a full week at their principal job they can't pay the bills they pile up and make ends meet. "People tell us their main job just isn't enough to cover the cost of living," says an official of an employment agency.

A vivacious, 27-year-old secretary in Los Angeles recently spent four months working from 8:30 A.M. to 4:30 P.M. in one insurance office and then hurrying to another to work as a typist till 9:00 P.M. "I ran up bills at practically every department store in town, and I couldn't see how I could pay them off any other way," she explains.

A squabble involving the cost of living and moonlighting is now roiling the New York City police department. Claiming their salary gains have failed to keep pace with the rise in living costs, many New York policemen have taken off-duty jobs to supplement their incomes. This violates a department policy forbidding moonlighting and has roused the wrath of Police Commissioner Stephen Kennedy. Fines have been levied against a number of policemen for working at outside jobs.

In Portland, Mr. Neumann, the Santa Claus-playing deputy sheriff, and a number of his fellow law officers are also having moonlighting problems. The Oregon Supreme Court last week ruled that the deputies could not hold outside jobs. The prohibition won't take effect until after the Christmas season, but Mr. Neumann may well not be able to play Santa Claus next year.

Most employers are more tolerant of moonlighting than are these law enforcement agencies. Many place no restrictions on outside employment as long as efficiency doesn't suffer. "We don't care if a man works 24 hours a day as long as he doesn't fall into a machine in our plant," says a spokesman for a major Midwest manufacturer of household appliances.

"We have no company policy against an employee holding two jobs and leave the question of a worker's efficiency up to his supervisor," says W. Dudley Coursey, assistant vice president in charge of personnel for Texas Instruments, Incorporated, Dallas.

Occasionally companies have rules prohibiting moonlighting by employees but are lax about enforcing them. "As far as outside employment goes, in our book of rules they're not supposed to do it," comments an official of the New York, New Haven and Hartford Railroad. "But what they do on their own time is their business."

Several New Haven conductors pick up a few extra dollars by working during idle hours between the morning and evening commuter rush. One conductor, for example, hops off the 6:17 A.M. out of Danbury, Connecticut, doffs his uniform at Manhattan's Grand Central Terminal and dashes off to work as a mail-order clerk at a discount house a few blocks away. In midafternoon, he dons his blue uniform again in time to punch tickets on the 4:47 P.M. back to Danbury.

Inland Steel Company takes a generally lenient attitude. "If we can not provide full-time employment for workers, we can't discourage them from taking on part-time work," declares Robert A. Graney, director of industrial relations. But the Chicago steel maker has one reservation. "We have strong feelings against workers trying to hold another full-time job as they did during World War II," says Mr. Graney. When employees try to handle two full-time positions, he explains, they can't have "the stamina to work efficiently or safely."

A big paper producer indicates its attitude toward moonlighting varies for different categories of workers. The company doesn't mind if production workers lead double lives because so far this has never raised any problems. But the paper maker has let it be known that management frowns on accountants, lawyers and other white-collar specialists working at two jobs. The company believes an employee in one of these positions "can't really give his best if his time is split two or three different ways," says the personnel director. "It's like the Army—we have the right to demand 24 hours a day if we need to."

More firmly opposed to moonlighting than most firms is Food Machinery and Chemical Corporation of San Jose, California. "We intentionally try to discourage moonlighting because it starts reducing efficiency in the plant," says Phillip Olson, director of industrial personnel. "If a fellow is holding two jobs, it has been proven he doesn't do his best in either job." In a similar vein, William Nicholas, assistant to the personnel manager of Tidewater Oil Company's western division, says of workers who hold two jobs: "We would prefer they didn't do this. You just can't serve two masters well. People who do this can't get the rest they need." Tidewater is not troubled by moonlighting to any extent currently, however, according to Mr. Nicholas.

A food chain operator suggests that the employer for whom a moonlighter works part time may occasionally have problems, too. This retailer has found it wise to place moonlighters in jobs where they won't deal with the public, since fatigue often makes them irritable and inclined to snap at customers.

Arnold Moss, secretary-treasurer of San Francisco's Garage and Service Station Employees Union, expresses a typical union viewpoint on moonlighting. "Guys holding one and a half jobs or two jobs deprive another man of work," he complains.

Moonlighting frequently arouses bitterness between workers in different fields. Mr. Moss, for example, lashes out at "the guys who make good money during the week, like carpenters and other people in the building trade," for taking service station jobs in the evening and on weekends. San Francisco carpenters, in turn, are mad because crews of firemen sometimes take on carpentering jobs in their free time.

December 1, 1960

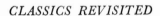

CLASSICS REVISITED

Apollo: Game played on horseback.
Aphrodite: Athenian baby pants.
River Styx: Driftwood.

—EDMUND A. BRAUN

And Moonlighting Bosses

LOS ANGELES—What do hard-driving corporate executives do to relax after a day of wrestling with management problems? Some find other businesses to manage as a sideline.

An airline president, for example, operates a mortuary and two cemeteries, and an oil firm executive raises orchids commercially. Another oil executive serves after hours as the president of a company which invests in small businesses. A construction company official helps run the New York Yankees baseball team.

Moonlighting, as the practice of holding down more than one job is known, usually is thought of as a practice of low-paid workers who don't earn enough at one job to make ends meet. But moonlighting executives are, for the most part, highly paid men with a zest for business that can't be satisfied by their regular jobs. Making money sometimes isn't a primary motive, but most of the moonlighting bosses obviously hope the side activities profit.

Some companies bar executive moonlighting. "We don't like it because we feel our executives should devote their time to our company," says the president of one big corporation. But at some other firms the top man himself moonlights and thus isn't likely to clamp down on subordinates' outside ventures.

One moonlighting chief executive is Samuel Mosher, chairman of Signal Oil and Gas Company, headquartered here. His after-hours business, orchid-raising, started as a hobby, which is the case with many such enterprises. Now he is believed to be the largest orchid marketer in the world. His Dos Pueblos Orchid Company ships more than two million orchids annually, as well as three million carnations. Mr. Mosher devotes most of his weekends to the orchid company's activities.

A few years ago, two dozen moonlighting executives joined forces to buy the Strasburg Rail Road, a four-and-a-half-mile line winding through Pennsylvania's Amish country from Strasburg to Paradise. The road was about to be junked, and the executives paid $22,000— the scrap value—for the line. One of their number became president, and the rest became vice presidents.

The executives originally conceived of their railroad as a big toy. But with the addition of vintage steam engines and the restoration of old-fashioned passenger and freight cars, the Strasburg developed into a profitable excursion line, charging adults $1 a ride. The railroad even hauls a little freight now. "We've got some debt to pay off, and then we'll be able to slice a melon," says the president, Henry K. Long. Mr. Long is also president of Champion Blower and Forge Company, Lancaster, Pennsylvania.

The moonlighting activities of Del Webb, the construction man whose sideline is baseball, are an outgrowth of his early years as a bush league ball player. Mr. Webb is chairman of Del E. Webb Corporation, a Phoenix-based construction and real estate development company. He is half owner of the Yankees.

"I guess I spend an average of four to five hours a week on the Yankees," says Mr. Webb. His partner, Dan Topping, supervises the club day-to-day, explains Mr. Webb, but "I get daily reports, and we confer on major decisions, such as trades."

Some executives engage in more than one business activity after hours. Hung Wo Ching's principal job is the presidency of Aloha Airlines, a Hawaiian line that flies passengers throughout the islands. On the side he is president of three corporations which own two cemeteries and a mortuary in Hawaii and he heads a real estate firm with big holdings in the Waikiki Beach area. He also is involved in California real estate development, and he currently is setting up a vending machine business in Boston.

Some corporate executives find outside jobs extremely burdensome. Meyer Luskin, president of Southern California Petroleum Corporation, serves as the president of a small business investment firm as a sideline. "I spend about six hours a week on it, and the time comes out of my hide," says Mr. Luskin.

Moonlighting ventures can sometimes produce headaches rather than profits. Consider the Hungry Tiger, a Sherman Oaks, California, restaurant owned by five executives of the Flying Tiger Line, including President Robert Prescott.

"We bought the restaurant a little over a year ago, and we've got $85,000 in it, including about $50,000 of our own cash and some bank financing," says Leonard Kimball, a vice president of the cargo-carrying airline. "Our break-even gross is about $15,000 a month, but we've never done better than $10,000. We just don't know anything about the restaurant business, and we haven't had any luck finding a manager who does."

February 18, 1963

———◆———

WEATHER VAIN

Week of weather far from pleasing,
Snowing, blowing, raining, freezing,
Hangs icicles on roof and tree,
On bathroom fixtures—lingeries!

—HAROLD WILLARD GLEASON

Archaeologists Seek Ideas

to Aid Modern Man

TIKAL, GUATEMALA—An archaeological autopsy is under way here in the heart of the dank and dense Peten rain forest in northeastern Guatemala to determine why a civilization died 10 centuries ago.

More is at stake than the dusting off of musty pages of ancient history. Archaeologists, anthropologists and botanists digging in the shadows of the Temple of the Giant Jaguar are turning up some information that may prove useful to modern man.

The trowel and shovel target is the ancient city of Tikal. Located near the British Honduras border in deep jungles, it was the focal point of the Mayan empire—a society that was speeding toward lofty pinnacles in architecture, astronomy, the arts and mathematics before the birth of Christ.

Tikal's structures today are mostly covered by mounds of dirt and debris. Stand in the center of Tikal's great plaza, where patches of jungle have been cleared. On one side has emerged the "Northern Acropolis"—a huge terraced substructure supporting a compact group of 16 temples of varying sizes and heights. An even larger temple facing the plaza, the Temple of the Giant Jaguar, slowly regains its original form as workmen clean debris from its limestone blocks. The Temple of the Masks and rambling stucco buildings called "palaces," also ringing the plaza, still are overgrown with trees, although entrances have been cleared.

Inhabited for the past 1,000 years by monkeys, snakes, peccaries, jaguars and other jungle creatures, Tikal is the oldest and biggest of 125 or so ceremonial and urban centers the Maya spread across 125,000 square miles of Central America's Yucatan Peninsula. Scientists aim to find out why Tikal and the other centers were abandoned.

"We are not digging solely because we enjoy it; there are broad objectives," insists Edwin Shook, 48-year-old archaeologist-engineer from Philadelphia who directs Project Tikal, a joint excavating venture of the Guatemalan government and the University of Pennsylvania Museum.

Among the objectives: added knowledge in the fields of history, art, architecture, astronomy and mathematics. The Maya, for example, were adept at city planning; they came up with the concept of the zero; and they concocted a calendar that some experts consider more accurate than the modern Gregorian.

Mr. Shook believes Tikal may provide clues to help solve some modern-day dilemmas. Take the problems of fast-expanding world population, for example. "The Maya developed in a tropical environment," he notes. "How they did it is important today, because we are going to have to spread out into the tropics if population trends continue."

Adds another long-time student of this Indian race: "If we can determine why the Mayan society reached such high peaks only to deteriorate abruptly, perhaps we can erect barriers against similar happenings in our own civilization."

On a more prosaic level, scientists cite anticipated benefits for American agriculture from resurrection of the ancient city and from the study of its environs. Most of the principal food crops grown today in the United States originated with the Maya; scientists note that they may be able to develop hardier domestic plants, such as corn, if they can trace the wild kin.

Tikal is not the first Mayan center to be assaulted by teams of archaeologists, architects, engineers and anthropologists. Archaeologists now are poking into scattered Mayan ruins up and down the valleys of the Usumacinta, the main waterway of the Maya which now forms the western boundary of Guatemala's department state of Peten. The river flows into the Gulf of Mexico.

In Mexico, near Mérida, Yucatan, a series of mounds on a site known as Dzibilchaltun are being unearthed. At Kaminaljuyu, a Mayan site in Guatemala's scenic and volcano-ringed highlands where today one million descendants of the Maya still live, archaeologists are bent on exploration, excavation and restoration. Indeed, exploration and reconstruction already have been completed at dozens of Mayan centers scattered from Chichen Itza in northern Yucatan to Copan in Honduras.

Most studies of the Maya are comparatively recent, having been made only since the 1920s. Dozens of unexplored Mayan ruins dot the Peten hinterlands. Archaeologists continually spot ruins from the air, but are unable to reach them on the ground.

Much about the Maya remains a mystery. Their hieroglyphics, for instance, can be only partially deciphered. No one knows from where the Maya came, or how they originated their civilization. Nor does anyone know yet why their scientific and cultural attainments came to an end some five centuries before the Spanish invaded Central America in the mid-16th century. Scientists are pinning their hopes on Tikal, located roughly in the geographical center of the Maya country.

"We look on Tikal as the biggest city; it may have been the origin of the Mayan civilization. At least there is more opportunity to learn about the Maya here," says red-bearded John Rick, a Canadian anthropologist.

Although the origin of the Maya is not clear, archaeologists are convinced they existed in the Guatemalan highlands thousands of years before the birth of Christ. A theory drawing increasing support is that the Mayan spurt of building got under way near this region where the oldest remains have been uncovered. One monument found here is dated, in the Mayan numerical equivalent, 292 A.D. The Maya probably were building their cities long before they got around to dating their monuments, scientists say.

Evidence to date indicates the Maya were the most advanced civilization to evolve in pre-Columbus America, and that their civilization endured from 2,000 to 3,000 years. The Maya learned to control fire, they developed an agriculture, and they were able to build resplendent cities of stone with roof vaultings that still are sturdy today. But scientists say the Maya knew nothing of three other civilization tools: beasts of burden, the wheel, and metal tools. With stone instruments, however, they quarried giant limestone blocks from the jungle floor and they chiseled, in even harder stone, images of their deities and intricate writing.

The Maya were dominated by powerful priests under a rigid theocracy. One scientist estimates that Tikal had a population in its heyday of around 200,000, of whom 60,000 were laborers working full time on building bigger and better temples and palaces for the omnipotent priesthood. The priests were the scholars and astronomers. They plotted the exact length of the solar year—365.24 days—by studying the sun.

Then, for unknown reasons, the Maya in the 10th century abandoned their cities to the jungles. The ruins remained hidden for centuries.

JAMES C. TANNER

June 22, 1960

———◆◆———

CASH, CLARIFIED

$1,000,000,000: An economic concept.
$1,000,000: A fortune.
$100,000: A tidy sum.
$10,000: Capital.
$1,000: A nest egg.
$2.00: Real money.

—BILL IRELAND

Jobs and Emotions

After a number of employees of Hanes Hosiery Mills, Winston-Salem, North Carolina, had separately visited Dr. Richard Proctor, the company's psychiatric consultant, about difficulties they were having with the same foreman, Dr. Proctor concluded the foreman probably was the source of the trouble, not the employees.

Investigating, Dr. Proctor found the foreman was having personal problems at home "which naturally he couldn't leave at the gate outside when he came to work in the mornings." A few talks with Dr. Proctor made the foreman aware that his personal difficulties were causing friction at work. Soon complaints about the foreman stopped.

Cases such as this are by no means rare. Companies are becoming increasingly aware of the importance of their employees' emotional health and are doing something about it. Like Hanes, many corporations have set up psychiatric programs, either directly employing psychiatrists or establishing referral systems in which workers suspected of being emotionally disturbed are sent to outside psychiatrists, with the companies often picking up the tab for the first few "diagnostic" visits.

"There are very few large companies now that aren't aware of the importance of the mental health problem," declares Dr. Alan A. McLean, chairman of the American Psychiatric Association's committee of psychiatry in industry. The APA estimates more than 400 psychiatrists now are devoting part or all of their time as consultants to companies sponsoring mental health programs. Four years ago an association survey turned up only 144.

Besides concern for their workers' welfare, companies have both legal and economic reasons for their growing interest in mental health.

Now pending in Kansas is a case that represents the second time in three years that a state workmen's compensation board has been asked to decide a company's legal obligation regarding the emotional stability of an employee. In the first such case, involving a General Motors assembly line worker in Michigan, the employee was upheld by the Michigan Workmen's Compensation Commission in his contention that GM was responsible for a mental disorder he had incurred.

The Kansas case was brought by a 32-year-old printer who seeks compensation from a Wichita printing shop on the ground that he is suffering from a serious mental disorder caused by an "intolerable job situation" at the printing concern. He claims friction between owners of the shop kept him in such confusion that it eventually led him into a state of paranoia, a mental disorder in which the victim suffers from delusions of persecution.

If the printer is upheld, the case may have a significant impact on the hiring practices and medical programs of thousands of companies already alerted by the Michigan ruling.

It's difficult to pin down precisely the extent of the mental health problem in offices and factories. But some idea of its scope can be gleaned from an estimate by the National Association of Mental Health that one of every ten Americans suffers from emotional disturbances.

Corporate psychiatrists are convinced that emotional problems figure prominently in the estimated 12-billion-dollar loss which U.S. industry suffers each year in absenteeism, employee turnover, alcoholism, industrial accidents and lowered productivity caused by friction between workers.

Many times, a worker's problem can be talked out in a few visits with the company psychiatrist; about all the employee needs in such cases is a sympathetic ear. Industrial psychiatrists rarely undertake any long-range treatment of employees, preferring to limit themselves to diagnosis. If psychotherapy is needed, they usually let psychiatrists in private practice handle it.

Several firms have conducted studies of the effects of such psychiatric help for workers and have concluded it has economic justification. Consider Hanes Hosiery's experience.

Some years ago, Hanes became concerned with the high turnover and widely varying production rates of some groups of employees. Causing the biggest problems were 1,400 "loopers," highly skilled women workers who operate sewing machines which close the toe of a stocking. The work is extremely exacting since the loopers must place 40 stitches an inch by hand over points on a dial that is constantly rotating. The worker is under considerable pressure because the slightest error makes the stocking defective.

Despite the fact that the loopers were thoroughly tested and sent through a 14-week training period, Hanes found that absenteeism in that department ran a high 6 per cent. Also, two-thirds of the women visited the mill dispensary at least once a month, and about 500 were giving up the job each year. "We felt that establishing a psychiatric section to help round out our medical program would perhaps be the answer to our problem," declares Gordon Hanes, president of the firm.

The company brought in Dr. Proctor, a faculty member at nearby Wake Forest College, as a part-time psychiatric consultant. Dr. Proctor immediately set out to encourage troubled loopers to visit his office. At first the response was slow, but later the number of patients picked up and he now deals with about half a dozen a week. "They learned that whatever they tell me stops at my office," Dr. Proctor says. "I don't mention a thing a patient tells me to management without permission of the patient."

In a recent study of 40 loopers who came to him, Dr. Proctor found that within six weeks the average production of the employees rose 6.2 per cent, errors dropped 20 per cent and visits to the dispensary fell markedly. Turnover and absenteeism rates also dropped. "Through common-sense psychiatry we have been able to reduce significantly the problems we have with emotional disturbances among our workers," Dr. Proctor says. "Analogous programs carried out by other companies have obtained similar results."

Among companies with full-time psychiatrists: International Business Machines Corporation, Du Pont, U.S. Steel Corporation, and Continental Insurance Companys (American Fore Loyalty Group).

Corporate psychiatrists say that usually their greatest difficulty is spotting employees who need their treatment. "The nervous or mentally ill individual cannot be identified by size, shape or personality," explains Dr. Gerald Gordon, chief of the psychiatric section of Du Pont. "He can't be spotted in a crowd and often his illness is not apparent to his associates."

To help overcome this difficulty, many companies have begun briefing supervisory personnel on symptoms of emotional disturbance. Industrial psychiatrists also pick up clues from continuing studies of company medical and personnel records. Excessive unexplained absenteeism is one fairly certain sign of trouble, for instance.

Executives frequently are brought into corporate mental health programs, mainly to instruct them in how to recognize emotional disturbances but also to teach them how to manage the mental health problem. At Topeka, Kansas, the Menninger Foundation, a center for psychiatric training and research, regularly holds seminars for decision-making executives on mental health. The week-long sessions, conducted three times a year, usually are filled to capacity and Menninger is expanding the program. Among the subjects considered: psychological motivation, psychological factors in supervision, and executives' emotional problems.

Menninger also has established a separate department which specializes in industrial mental health. Launched a few years ago with the aid of a $105,000 grant from the Rockefeller Brothers Fund, the department now is supported by contributions from more than a score of corporations and business-supported foundations.

As corporate interest in mental health grows, research emphasis is gradually shifting toward prevention of emotional disturbances. Psychiatrists from the University of Cincinnati are conducting a five-year study of emotional problems in industry under a $150,000 grant from the U.S. Department of Health, Education and Welfare. The aim is to find ways to prevent or cut down on mental illness in plants and offices.

GEORGE G. GRAVLEY

March 5, 1963

"Besides benefits such as profit sharing, medical services, bonuses, life insurance, loan funds, pension plans and educational courses, I'm looking for a job that offers a challenge."

Footnotes on a Revolution

Just about 30 years ago there took place in kitchens all over America one of those minor revolutions which, once they have been won, leave so few monuments behind them that they are practically forgotten.

This particular revolution was plotted during the early 1920s by a middle-aged Midwestern specialty salesman of an inventive turn of mind, named Otto Frederick Rohwedder.

What Rohwedder set out to do was to abolish the bread knife. He announced to his family and friends and everybody else who would listen that he would make the bread knife an obsolete piece of equipment in the average American household. He succeeded in doing just that.

Rohwedder invented sliced bread. More precisely, he invented the idea of pre-sliced bread. He arranged to build, and persuaded a commercial bakery to install, the first machine specially designed to slice bread on a wholesale scale as part of the manufacturing process. This made it possible, once and for all, to answer the question as to whether sliced bread would sell.

Had there been good consumer opinion surveys in the summer of 1928 when this machine was first put to work, these surveys unquestionably would have shown public opinion almost solidly against sliced bread. The objection was very simple and very emphatically recorded in many individual instances: "Sliced bread will dry out." Everybody knew sliced bread would dry out because, as a matter of domestic experience, bread unwrapped and sliced in the kitchen did dry out.

This opinion was generally shared by bakers, too, until their convictions were shaken by Rohwedder's salesmanship or demonstrations. What really pushed them into sliced bread was the thought, in a period of extremely tough competition, that something new in a product so basic to them as bread might possibly catch on—though they didn't really think it would.

Even the inventor at first thought elaborate measures would be needed to hold bakery-sliced bread together. The first experimental machine, soon abandoned, had arrangements built into it to pin a loaf of sliced bread back together with oversized, sterilized hairpins. The pins would not hold. So shallow boxes were tried out. The first sliced bread was sold in those shallow boxes, wrapped in the usual waxed paper.

The boxes led into a patent suit, but by the time this was settled nobody was using boxes. It developed that the whole process was simpler than had been supposed—the bread could be sliced on its way to the wrapping machines and did not have to be held together at all, except by the waxed paper.

In a few short years, every big bakery and most of the small shops were selling sliced bread.

When sliced bread swept across the country the demand for slicing machines far outran the ability of Rohwedder and his associates to perfect and manufacture the machines. So most of the equipment came to be made and sold by somebody else.

Few consumers today—or at any earlier day for that matter—know or care who makes bread-mixing machinery and bread-slicing machinery and bread-wrapping machinery. Nor do they hear of inventors in this specialized field.

Otto Rohwedder, aged 80, died on election day. There was a notice in his local newspaper, but there was a lot of other news that day and it could be said that his passing attracted little attention outside a rather small circle. He did not become rich or powerful from his invention; in fact, he probably would have made more money if his career as a salesman and sales manager had not been interrupted by a venture into manufacturing and finance.

But he did abolish the bread knife.

BERNARD KILGORE

November 22, 1960

Busy Professors

Edward H. Litchfield, chancellor of the University of Pittsburgh, leads a double life.

In a typical week he may spend Monday through Wednesday attending to academic duties in Pittsburgh. Thursday morning may find him boarding his personal Beechcraft—equipped with telephone and dictating equipment—for a flight to New York City.

There, in his role of board chairman, he presides over management meetings at SCM, Incorporated (formerly Smith-Corona Merchant,

Incorporated). An Avco Corporation directors meeting may also claim a couple of hours of his time. Some weeks Chancellor Litchfield flies west to South Bend, Indiana, for sessions of Studebaker Corporation's board of directors or executive committee, on both of which he serves.

Mr. Litchfield dramatically points up how far from the campus educators are wandering these days. Few are as deeply involved in business as he is, but increasing numbers of college faculty members, particularly in scientific, technical and business administration fields, are doing part-time work outside the academic world. Some are managing businesses. Many more are serving as consultants to industry and government at daily fees ranging from $100 to as much as $500 for a few top men, plus expenses.

Says George Baker, dean of Harvard Business School: "Industrial demand for consultants is so great that if it were to get any bigger we would have to close the school."

The growth of educators' extracurricular activities is not without its critics. Though praised for sparking a big expansion of the University of Pittsburgh, Chancellor Litchfield has been charged with delegating too much authority to his numerous assistants. Some colleges are worried that teaching and research may suffer because professors are devoting too much time to outside work.

"I doubt if there is a university president in the country who is not concerned about the problem," comments Herbert E. Longenecker, president of Tulane University in New Orleans.

Many schools believe that a reasonable amount of faculty involvement in the workaday world is healthy. It aids the flow of information between the campus and business and government to the benefit of all parties, they contend.

"It's very important for teachers to maintain contact with business and industry to derive realism from the outside world," says Myles Mace, assistant dean of Harvard Business School. Massachusetts Institute of Technology, whose professors are in especially strong demand by industry and government, views faculty consulting as another way to fulfill a university's function of disseminating knowledge.

Nathaniel H. Frank, a physics professor at MIT and chairman of a committee which has been reviewing MIT's policy on outside work by faculty members, suggests that as a practical matter such activity is unavoidable. "The need for top talent exceeds the supply, and we must recognize that as long as this condition exists the nation must use talented people in multiple capacities," he says.

All the same, some educators fear professors may be spreading themselves too thin as off-campus employment opportunities multiply. American Telephone and Telegraph Company used 729 college consultants in 1960, up from 450 five years earlier. Du Pont Company says its use of college consultants has jumped about 25 per cent since 1958. Raytheon Company, a Boston-area electronics firm, hired 15 per cent more faculty members as consultants in 1962 than the previous year. The National Science Foundation, one of the many Federal agencies which uses consultants extensively, has 445 of them now; a year and a half ago it had 358.

The increasingly complex technology of modern industry is a major reason for the strong demand for expert consultants. "Industry, moving from production of heavy, rather uncomplicated goods into the high technology fields of today, found it needs brain power—and colleges have a supply," says a Harvard administrator.

Companies say the hiring of a consultant is often the most economical, efficient way to tackle a problem. "We turn to consultants when we need specialized knowledge for a specific project for a limited time and when it is impractical to hire a full-time man," explains a Raytheon spokesman.

Besides serving as consultants, many professors are plunging into business management and ownership as a sideline. Robert Liberman, a Boston University law professor, is the founder and president of Technical Fund, Incorporated, a small mutual fund; Professor Liberman says he devotes an average of 10 hours a day to the fund, in addition to carrying a full teaching load.

Across the country, Stanford University Professor Rolf Eliassen, a specialist in sanitary engineering and water resources, runs the West Coast operations of Metcalf and Eddy, a Boston-based consulting engineering firm. Another Stanford faculty member, business policy teacher Robert Katz, a director of one small business investment company, is currently helping to form another and is part-owner of an optics firm.

From the school's point of view, the major drawback of outside work is that it may take too much of a professor's time. "Sometimes it gets to be a case of the tail wagging the dog when professors use the school as a launching pad for their own activities," says the provost of an Ivy League university.

"It is almost inevitable that a professor doing consulting will get overcommitted on an outside project from time to time," concedes P. W. Cherington, a transportation professor at Harvard Business School who is highly sought as a consultant. One solution, says Mr. Cherington, is "working 80 hours a week to get out of the overcommitment." Another remedy is to follow the example of Mr. Cherington and several of his associates; they set up United Research, Incorporated, a consulting company with its own staff, to handle some of the requests for help that come their way.

Many colleges, either through informal understandings or formal regulations, try to limit faculty members' outside work to one day a week. A school which recently adopted the one-day-a-week rule is Northeastern University in Boston. "We formulated a new policy limiting outside work because of the great increase in requests by professors for time to do consulting," says K. G. Ryder, dean of administration. Dean Ryder estimates the demand for consultants is growing "about 10 per cent a year."

Opportunities for outside work vary markedly from field to field, a situation which often creates faculty friction. Specialists in some technical and scientific fields frequently have more consulting offers than they can handle, and experts in solving management problems are also much in demand. In 1960 U.S. engineering teachers averaged $2,479 in outside income on top of an average teaching salary of $8,534.

Professors and instructors in the social sciences and the humanities, on the other hand, rarely have an opportunity to pick up consulting fees. The resulting income disparities inevitably produce discontent, college officials say.

MIT and other large institutions carrying on multi-million-dollar research programs have found that faculty members' off-campus jobs can sometimes raise questions of conflicts of interest. One of the chief tasks of Professor Frank's committee at MIT has been to devise rules to avert such conflicts.

Mr. Frank cites two examples of the kinds of conflict of interest that can arise at schools like MIT:

MIT and a company are competing for a multi-million-dollar Government contract for basic research. A young MIT physics professor working in the field in which the Government is interested is hired by the company as a consultant. In seeking the contract, the company lists the MIT faculty member as one of its experts—which means, in effect, that the professor may be helping to steer research funds away from his own institution.

Another delicate situation might arise when the college decides to buy a large quantity of scientific apparatus for a research project, and it turns out that some of the suppliers employ MIT men as consultants. "If we buy from one of those which employs one of our men, some questions could be raised," says Professor Frank.

CAL BRUMLEY

January 14, 1963

Self-Service Market Employees

Siphon Off Millions a Year

The enterprising manager of the meat department in a big Boston supermarket developed a profitable sideline. He would sign for meat that was never unloaded from the delivery truck, permitting the driver to sell it to various small markets. He and the driver would then split the proceeds, a tidy $10,000 a year.

Such employee dishonesty is a growing problem of supermarket operators. Losses from these internal thefts currently amount to more than $100 million a year, according to some management consultants who make it their business to uncover such thefts and protect markets from them. The consultants hold management itself largely to blame for the losses.

"Customer pilferage is penny ante compared to what is taken by trusted employees," says Norman Jaspan, president of a New York management engineering firm which bears his name. He adds that "99 per cent of all dishonest practices are committed by employees who were honest when first employed" by the supermarket.

Saul D. Astor, head of Management Safeguards, Incorporated, and Lincoln M. Zonn, a polygraph (lie-detector) expert who heads his own firm, maintain that employee dishonesty is nourished by: unenforceable rules, unenforced rules, excessive pressure for profits, and poor morale.

Explaining how unenforceable rules encourage stealing, Mr. Astor asserts: "If a man doesn't have the time and the crew to check everything being delivered for his department, then he'll have to sign for it blindly. And when he finds he can do that, he's tempted to enter into collusion with the driver." To cover his thefts, a department manager may juggle his books, overstate spoilage or use other devices.

The meat department manager of an Indiana supermarket got kickbacks from a meat truck driver by accepting inferior quality meat and signing vouchers for first quality.

Just as harmful as unenforceable rules are practical ones that are not enforced, says Mr. Astor.

At a Long Island supermarket, which required all rear doors to be locked, employees complained of poor ventilation, so the manager permitted a back door to be left open. One clerk, apparently needing more fresh air, made frequent trips outside—and each time carried a case of merchandise with him. He deposited the cases in his car, which always was parked near the door, another infraction of the rules. During nine months he hauled out $14,000 worth of goods. He was the chief supplier of his grandfather's corner grocery store.

Dishonesty sometimes infects a supermarket's entire staff. A big chain was about to close a large supermarket it had acquired earlier in a Midwestern city because the store was not holding its own against competition. An investigation, however, disclosed that all the 18 full-time employees and five of the nine part-time helpers were taking home more than their paychecks. The assistant manager, for instance, admitted taking stamps, coupons, premiums and merchandise. Over two and a half years the employees' larceny added up to more than $400,000.

Employees of a Boston supermarket made a practice of helping themselves to candy, fruit, cigarettes and other merchandise as they went about their jobs. The manager couldn't very well object because everyone knew that he and his assistant had a cozy corner in the basement where they prepared on a stove each day lavish lunches of steaks and lobster taken from the store's supplies. All these siphonings were costing the store about $10,000 a year.

When a store is lax about enforcing its rules, checkout counter attendants frequently are tempted to cut prices unofficially or give goods away to friends and relatives. At a New York supermarket, the checkers were in league with the managers of the dairy and meat departments. Each manager was stealing about $10 worth of goods from his department each week and giving an equal amount to others in the cabal. The loot was being passed through the checkout counters by children of the thieves and the loss was between $7,000 and $8,000 a year.

More than 62 per cent of the thefts which Mr. Jaspan's firm has uncovered in supermarkets were "traced to employees on the supervisory and executive levels."

The manager of a West Coast supermarket set up his own checkout cash register in addition to those supplied by the chain's stockholders; he took in $70,000 before he was caught. The big-hearted manager of a Massachusetts warehouse owned by a food chain, which allowed dented can goods and other damaged merchandise to be given to charities, donated $85,000 worth of unscarred merchandise over a three-year period to his church's needy. The grateful church members gave this Robin Hood a testimonial dinner.

Max Edmond, an assistant manager of a Food Farm supermarket on Staten Island, New York, was charged by police with arranging a holdup last month of the market where he was employed. Police said

Mr. Edmond admitted he had a part in the $3,200 robbery of the store by two men who appeared at closing time.

Some managers resort to larceny, Mr. Astor notes, when too much pressure for profits is put on them. Says Mr. Jaspan: "When we impose upon people impossible tasks, impractical budgets, or unrealistic quotas, something usually snaps."

Managers have used several devices to cover their thefts. One which Mr. Jaspan cites is "to prematurely post price increases within two minutes after receiving notice that such a change is being planned— and then stall, in some cases for two days, before taking a required price reduction."

Other methods include manipulating inventories, trading stamps and coupons; overstating damage and spoilage; padding overtime; selling items at full price while listing them as cut-rate tie-in sales; submitting register receipts discarded by customers with notations that refunds have been issued on them.

Mr. Astor explains that when his firm examines a store suspected of harboring larceny his investigators include engineers, accountants and systems analysts. When they have determined that merchandise is disappearing, sleuths are planted on the premises as regular employees to spot the culprits in action.

Mr. Zonn's job is to extract signed confessions from the guilty employees. His chief instrument is the polygraph.

In the New England operation of one chain Mr. Zonn tested 115 employees and came up with 91 signed confessions of thefts totaling $160,000. He explains that when he starts probing into a nest of this sort, the investigation proceeds "like the bursting of a star shell—one employee tattles on the next one."

He also screens employees before they are hired and runs checks on those who have been found guilty of minor thefts in the past and given another chance. At present he is serving about 450 stores with polygraphs. Such tests, he says, "not only find the guilty but also clear the innocent."

Mr. Jaspan recommends that "periodic unannounced checks of employee behavior should be made on all levels of an organization. Employees should know that these checks are a normal part of management control."

One chain which makes such checks is Red Owl Stores, Incorporated, operating in the upper Midwest. It inventories its meat supplies in each store once a month and its groceries every six weeks. Employees of the store do not take the inventories. It's done by representatives of the company's internal audit staff who arrive unannounced on the scene.

Some findings which Mr. Zonn's and Mr. Astor's investigations have turned up include: more merchandise than cash is stolen and with fewer guilt feelings; the most serious thefts usually are the work of long-time employees; improper handling of trading stamps (thefts, overpayment, tearing) is minor compared with merchandise losses.

VICTOR J. HILLERY

March 16, 1960

———◆●◆———

SEARCH PARTY

"It isn't lost, it's in the files,"
She says, and very sweetly smiles
And keeps on looking, drawer by drawer,
Both left and right and higher, lower.
"It's in the files, it isn't lost,"
She says, with papers madly tossed,
And shrewdly plays her little game,
For "lost" and "filed" are much the same.

—RICHARD ARMOUR

Billie Sol and the Sugar

The late W. C. Fields, that astute student of the larcenous heart, discovered that you can't cheat an honest man. So don't give all the credit to Billie Sol Estes.

To be sure, he lifted the old shell game of the Texas county fairs—now you see it, now you don't—to magnificent heights. A man who can play sleight-of-hand with huge liquid fertilizer tanks by the simple device of switching serial numbers faster than the eye can see, well, he deserves a place alongside such super performers as the great Ponzi or Ivar Kreuger, the European master whose matches burned the most sophisticated fingers of Wall Street.

But Billie Sol had a lot working for him.

For one thing, none of it could have happened if the quick buck hadn't exercised a certain charm for a number of earnest farmers, hard-headed moneylenders and devoted public servants on the Government payroll. Possibly none of them intended anything really dishonest (who would sell his soul for a suit from Neiman-Marcus?) and it isn't proved that anybody did anything illegal. It's merely that sleight-of-hand requires the sucker to look the other way, and what will divert the gaze quicker than the promise of an "easy thing"?

Another part of the Fields theory is that where the sugar is there will the flies gather. So there is the rather elementary fact that the Agriculture Department takes billions of dollars every year from all the people and pays it out to some of the people. The Department also disposes of other things of large monetary value, such as crop allotments which are in effect licenses to farm. Transfer an allotment from one man to another and you have done someone a real favor.

In fact, there was quite a bit of scandal some years back over the grain storage program. Billie Sol just showed more imagination in putting two and two together, the attraction of sweets scattered about and the little touch of larceny that always lurks in the mortal heart.

The combination is a sure-fire mixture for scandal, and though at the moment it centers on the Agriculture Department you can find the mixture almost anywhere in the Federal Government today. The Government not only handles more than $90 billion every year; it has all manner of other goodies to give away. Profitable television licenses. Urban renewal programs. Copper stockpiling contracts. Favorable income tax rulings. There is today hardly any area of the national life, or any part of the economy, where the decisions of public officials —and sometimes the actions of Government clerks—do not mean money in the pocket for somebody.

In the days of Teapot Dome a scandal in the Government could stun the nation precisely because it was rare. And it was rare because the opportunities for anything more than a little fudging on a channel-dredging contract were rare. Today Government scandals roll around with the inevitability of the equinoxes. And while they create some excitement, you can hardly say the populace is outraged.

And for us that's the saddest part of the whole affair. We agree with President Kennedy that some people will always succumb to the temptation for a little bit of larceny. What's sad is that Washington's reaction was more embarrassment than shame, the country's response more a chuckle than a roar. What's saddest is that everybody is so interested in the Government's sugar that hardly anybody minds the flies.

For to be fair about it all, in a day when workers get paid for not working and farmers for not farming, it almost seems natural to get paid for a fertilizer tank that isn't there.

VERMONT ROYSTER

May 24, 1962

———◆●◆———

CHECK, MATE?

The writers in the darkest plight
Are those who simply hate to write:
The bug by which they have been bitten
Is not to write, but to have written.

—MARGARET FISHBACK

A Lesson in Vigilance

It's been some 22 years now since the Richard Whitney case, which ended with his expulsion from the New York Stock Exchange and later imprisonment for mishandling other people's money. That case was a national scandal.

Just recently another stock exchange member was expelled and one of the firm's partners has been charged with "fraudulent acts." But this time there has been no public outcry against the whole of Wall Street.

That alone, we think, suggests how much the intervening years have changed not only the complexion of the financial community and the stock exchange itself, but also the attitude of the public toward Wall Street.

But there is more to this particular story, and we think it is worth telling how it all came about and what the reaction to it has been among those most immediately concerned.

The story began last spring when the New York Stock Exchange, as it has been doing for many years now, called for a routine surprise audit of member firms' accounts. One purpose of this audit is to make sure that every member firm maintains at all times a fixed, and safe, ratio between its liabilities and its capital. In measuring a firm's capital the rules are exceedingly strict; the value of its stock exchange membership, for example, cannot be included and even the bluest of blue chip stocks are valued at only a part of their current market value.

As a result of this routine audit, it was found that Du Pont, Homsey and Company of Boston, a relatively small firm, was in technical violation of this capital ratio rule. By itself this is not unprecedented; perhaps five or six times a year some firm may, very briefly, fall short on its capital requirements; in every case it is immediately required to bring its capital up to the mark.

In this instance, however, there was a prior violation on record and the exchange officials decided to bring charges against the firm before the Board of Governors and to discipline it. Thereupon a special auditor from the exchange was sent to go over the books more thoroughly.

This auditor did not like what he saw. He was promptly reinforced by the exchange's chief auditor and for several weeks the accounts of this firm were thoroughly scrutinized. The result was that the Securities and Exchange Commission and the district attorney's office were notified.

It seems to us that the significant thing here is not that a bad apple has cropped up among the stock exchange members, but rather that the bad apple was found in the process of a routine check to make sure of compliance with definite and strict requirements. Furthermore, both the requirements and the check on them were instituted by the stock exchange itself. Neither the SEC nor the district attorney had anything to do with uncovering the situation.

And there is more. In an unprecedented statement, president Keith Funston said that the exchange "feels that its moral responsibilities (in protecting the firm's customers) are not ended with the act of expulsion" against the Boston firm. If, after the firm's accounts are straightened out, there are losses to some customers, then the exchange itself hopes to make restitution.

Here, then, is a clear lesson in the rewards of self-vigilance. Sound rules and a system for spotting transgressors quickly; prompt and forceful action at the first faint signs that all is not as it should be—these are the essential ingredients for avoiding more Federal intervention and, more importantly, for protecting the financial community's good name and the money of those who come to it. If this case suggests anything, it is the need for even more vigilance and a full appreciation by all exchange members that sound exchange rules are the best safeguards.

For it is in this way that the New York Stock Exchange, as an institution, fulfils its true function. It is not the function of the stock exchange to sell stocks or drum up business for its members. In addition to providing a market place, its job, which it has performed so well in this case, is to be sure that all who do take their business there can do so in confidence that their affairs are honestly conducted under the watchful eye of a vigilant guardian.

VERMONT ROYSTER

October 10, 1960

White Collar Crime

Amazing. Such was the reaction of most people to news that a brokerage's accounting vice president—a fast man with a computer— had clipped his firm for a quarter-million dollars.

But it wasn't too amazing to Norman Jaspan, management consultant, head of Investigations, Incorporated, and professional criminologist on gray-flanneled wrongdoing. In his thoroughly provocative *Thief in the White Collar,* co-written with Hillel Black, a book on embezzling and what preventive management can do about it, Mr. Jaspan makes the point that very little white collar crime sees the light of public print.

Yet the magnitude of white collar crime is appalling. What catches most of public and perhaps police attention is ordinary theft—burglary, safe-cracking, pickpockets, auto thefts, hijacking, armed robbery, et cetera—which will amount to about a half-billion in stolen goods and money in 1960. But embezzlement, the violation of an employer's trust, will account for a cool billion-dollar series of thefts in 1960. Mr. Jaspan estimates another five billion dollars will change hands this year in kickbacks, payoffs and bribes. And the Internal Revenue Service will collect some $1.7 billion in penalties, interest and back taxes because of understated returns and tax evasions, if 1957 is any guide.

Comments the author: "The tragedy of white collar crime is not just the cost in dollars and cents, but the corruption of our most respected citizens, the professional worker, the executive, the top government and union official."

What's behind the corruption? Personal factors—like the shipping manager who enjoys playing the horses with company funds, the secretary who acquires an irresistible fascination for mink and forges her boss's signature, or the incorrigible super-operator. Contributing factors include war and postwar upheaval, international tension, malfeasance in public office, general moral laxity, and a lack of preventive management.

Preventive management probably can never eliminate the embezzling and shakedown rackets 100 per cent, given human nature as it is. And many of our laws are also conducive to corruption, as can be seen in Mr. Jaspan's discussion of the findings of the McClellan Committee on Improper Activities in the Labor or Management Field. But—and this is the big point of the book—solid preventive management can greatly cut down the size of the annual bite of white collar crime.

For example, the author, whose clients include banks, manufacturers, hotels, airlines, mining companies, retailers and government agencies, advises a system of dual responsibility in sensitive work functions. Take payroll. Preparation of payroll and payment of employees should be handled by two different groups of workers. Again, persons who maintain inventory records should not be allowed to participate in the physical counting of inventory.

Mrs. Jaspan also believes in occasional testing of the company's security program through "created errors." A created or controlled error is one that is deliberately inserted into an employee's or department's operation. The idea is to evaluate the accuracy and care with which personnel carry out their assigned tasks. A company, for instance, may arrange with a vendor to ship short or overship on a specific shipment to determine whether receiving personnel detect discrepancies in quality or quantity shipped.

Norman Jaspan concedes white collar crime is a moral problem. But he insists that the businessman and executives in charge must bear some responsibility. For their vigilance can remove much of the temptation.

WILLIAM H. PETERSON

March 30, 1960

ECONOMICS AND ECONOMY—
THE THEORY AND PRACTICE
OF MONEY

"You're suffering from high-income pressure."

How to Pick a Pocket or Two

To a small-town fellow come to the big city it was bound to happen sooner or later, and finally it did. On the way to Wall Street, that den of iniquity, our pocket was picked in the subway, that haunt of the huddled masses.

Along with a couple of credit cards, an unfilled prescription for the drugstore and a shopping list from the lady of the house, this skillful disciple of Fagin made off with $100, which for years we've kept secreted in the back of our wallet against such grave emergencies as running out of expense-account money in San Antonio or St. Paul.

Now being imbued with a Puritan ethic, we do not approve of pickpockets, especially those who pick our own. But in all honesty we must confess that purely from the standpoint of the nation's economic balance sheet there was no net loss to the country. Indeed, if some of the economic theories bruited about today are correct, it could be argued that the nation's economy had been helped thereby.

For our loss of $100 was somebody else's gain of $100, the one canceling out the other insofar as economic statistics are concerned. Furthermore, since there was a transfer of funds from one party to another there was a gain in the Gross National Product as well as the National Income. The fact that we paid an exorbitant price for the service received—namely, a lesson in personal finance management—is no concern in abstract economics.

Finally, we suspect the unknown artist of the subway is less well-endowed with worldly goods than we are, less likely to keep the money out of circulation as idle savings for a rainy day. So this transfer of our funds to his pocket probably resulted in an increase in the nation's consumer spending.

Whatever our personal feelings, then, the result represents a consummation devoutly to be wished by the influential thinkers of the day. The whole object of current economic policy is to increase the transfer of funds, raising the statistics of national income and the GNP, and especially such transfers of funds as may increase consumer spending. The sociological objective is called the "redistribution of income."

Hence the great emphasis on Government spending, which has gotten to be a large part of the GNP. There's no surer and more efficient way to transfer huge sums than to take taxes from citizens of, say, New York and spend them in New Mexico or Mississippi. According to this thinking, it's a further help if the dollars can be transferred from corporations and rich folk, who might have a proclivity toward savings, to the hands of those who will inject it more quickly into the spending stream.

We are told that the good effects of all this are enhanced if the Government, unlike our friend on the subway, can spend more than it takes or at least seem to. Big deficits, especially those arising from tax cuts, allow more dollars to be put in some people's pockets without appearing to take quite so much out of other people's pockets.

True, this is illusory; what the Government spends it must take away from somebody in some form. Nonetheless there's no denying it's less painful to steal a bit from everybody's dollars by inflation than to take the money away from them in immediate taxes.

On the subway we had a blissful ignorance of being plucked until, much later in the day, we found ourselves less well off than we thought. And even now we think there must be many a helpful pickpocket who wishes that policemen understood the ethics of the new economics.

VERMONT ROYSTER

March 13, 1963

The above editorial was reprinted by many newspapers and magazines. The press departments of both *Time* and *Newsweek* also commented on the editorial, *Time* sending a photographer to *The Wall Street Journal* and printing Editor Royster's photograph with its article.

It was this magazine commentary which apparently reached the Russian magazine *Soviet Press,* house organ of the USSR Union of Journalists. Following is the comment of Mr. I. Davidow, appearing in the *Soviet Press*:

It is possible that the above figures (in the preceding item, concerning the cost of the New York newspaper strike to those involved and to the Government) acquired special interest in the reasoning of Mister Royster, the editor of the newspaper *Journal* (town of Vermont, state of Connecticut).

"Whose Pocket Is Being Picked?"—Such was the disturbing theme of the leading article by Royster in a recent number of the aforementioned newspaper. The event which suggested this theme to Royster was an adventure in the New York subway.

However, as the author himself writes, when one commutes from a small town to a big one, sooner or later such an adventure is bound to happen, and indeed it did.

"On the way to Wall Street, this nest of vices (As we see, Royster is not lacking in powers of observation.—I.D.), my pocket was ravished in the noisy and bustling throngs of the subway," the editor of the *Journal* stated.

Royster, from whose pocket the thief extracted documents, druggists' prescriptions and $100, properly admitted that he used what had happened to him as the theme for his statement. True, it was in rather unexpected form: He came to the conclusion that "according to economic theory, if somehow an adroit pocket-picking operation could immediately be put to use, it could be of great aid to the economy of the U.S.A."

In what manner?

"We do not excuse the habit of picking someone else's pocket, particularly if this pocket belongs to us," writes Royster, "but in line with contemporary thought it is necessary to halt before these facts and do some thinking."

And Royster pursues these reflections further. At that moment, as $100 moved from our pocket to another, we read in his article, the Gross National Product, as well as the national income of the United States, showed a definite gain, in that money migrated "from a corporation of rich people, with a tendency toward accumulation, to the hands of those who quickly will put it in circulation."

In a word, pickpockets perform a socially useful function.

Later on, this economist from Vermont draws the courageous and, it would seem, justifiable conclusion that the American ruling circles, as a matter of fact, practice this very same "economic policy" of the pickpocket in the New York subway, whether by means of inflation or by taxes, etc.

We will not intrude with an analysis of the scientific value of the *Journal* editor's reasoning. We only pay just due to his journalistic skill in interpreting certain phenomena in American life as it really is.

Inflation and Business

For almost a generation now, the thinking of the country has been pretty much dominated by the idea that inflation is a sure warranty of prosperity.

True, inflation has been complained of on many grounds, such as its unfairness to widows and pensioners and its propensity for turning ecomic life into a rat-race. But while these ill effects have been deplored, it has still been accepted as gospel that inflation will nonetheless keep business swirling and provide a bulwark against depression.

As preached in Washington, this gospel says that while inflation cuts the purchasing power of each dollar, this effect is more than offset by the increased number of dollars which increase purchasing power and raise the gross national product. It's even been argued that by this simple device a multi-billion-dollar Government deficit will create a surplus because the Government will get back so many more of the cheaper dollars in taxes. The Government is now budgeting on this theory.

Along Wall Street and Main Street this has been interpreted to mean that you can protect yourself against the disadvantages of inflation and reap its rewards simply by buying real estate or common stocks. After all, if inflation has become a "way of life," how can the stock market go any way but up?

These articles of faith rest upon two assumptions. The first is that the inflationary process can be endlessly repeated with the same stimulating effect. The second is that the effect will be more jobs for labor and more profits for business.

This, of course, was the effect in the first years of the postwar inflation. The war years not only brought huge increases in the supply of credit dollars but they also left the country with an enormous pent-up demand for just about everything. So from 1946 to 1950 inflation and rising profits for business did go hand in hand.

For one illustration, in 1946 the earnings per share of the stocks in the Dow Jones industrial average amounted to $13.62. A bare four years later, in 1950, they had doubled, to $30.70. Here, or so it seemed, was proof positive of the doctrine. And so the country continued in the decade after—through Democratic and Republican Administrations—a policy of inflationary deficits. The public not only accepted this from the politicians, it encouraged them.

But the effects were quite different. Although the monetary inflation continued, with both wages and prices rising, the number of unemployed steadily increased and the profits of business increased hardly
at all. Look at the earnings per share of those same companies that
make up the industrial average: In 1950, $30.70 a share. In 1960,
$32.21 a share.

Or consider the case of one of our biggest industrial companies,
which has lately been in the news, U.S. Steel. The first postwar inflation shot its earnings from $1.22 a share to $3.65 a share. But in 1960,
after 10 more years of inflation, it could raise its earnings to only $5.17
a share. And the following year its earnings dropped below what they
had been a decade earlier.

This being the case, why did the stock market take off on the biggest boom in history? For it did. During the same decade, the Dow
Jones industrial average shot up from the 200 level to the 700 level.
The market price of U.S. Steel itself rose from $20 (adjusted for
changes in the number of shares) to $100.

The explanation can be found in another statistic. In 1950, for the
shares represented in the industrial average, the market price was
about seven times the per-share earnings. In 1960 this price-earnings
ratio was more than 21. On U.S. Steel stock, to choose a particular
example, the price-earnings ratio skyrocketed from less than 9 to more
than 27.

In short, for stocks having roughly the same earning capacity a
decade apart, people at the end of the decade were paying many times
the price for those same dollar earnings as at the beginning of the
decade. They did this largely under the spell of the gospel that continued inflation was a guarantee of more economic growth in everything, including profits for business.

This gospel never made much sense; at the very most it expressed
only a half-truth. Conceivably if the inflation of the monetary supply
could spread its effects evenly at all times throughout the economy,
profits measured in dollars might have increased. Of course this would
still give only an illusion of greater prosperity because the dollars would
be worth less. But in practice even this did not happen. The costs of
doing business—particularly labor costs but also taxes—rose far more
rapidly than prices for the end product. At the moment wage costs are
still rising; prices are not.

Thus the cost squeeze, dramatized most recently by the steel industry. Its wage costs went up another ten cents an hour. It could not
raise its prices.

But it's not only in the stock market that the boons of inflation have
proved a delusion. By almost any standard you choose for measurement—unemployment, our economic position in world trade, the

strength of the dollar, as well as business profits—a decade of almost continuous monetary inflation has simply not produced the wonders that the economic managers promised in their prospectus.

We don't know, really, why anybody ever thought it would.

VERMONT ROYSTER

May 7, 1962

Mercantilism's Mirage

Santayana said those who don't remember history will be condemned to repeat it; and all the debate over "economic growth"—a new phrase about an old idea—suggests the United States is in danger of repeating one of history's most alluring and devastating errors.

For those who call for rigid (usually 5 per cent), more or less forced, annual growth rates—who emphasize the public sector in the American economy—are strangely reminiscent of the powerful Mercantilist school of economic thought in England and on the Continent in the 16th, 17th, and 18th centuries. And those who stand for free, unregimented, natural economic growth—who emphasize the private sector in the American economy—are close to the Classical and Neo-Classical schools of economic thought of the 19th and early 20th centuries. In 1960 only the names have changed, possibly to beguile the innocent. Some 200 years ago Mercantilism was opposed to liberalism. Today, however, the neo-Mercantilists parade under the "liberal" label.

So the debate between the Mercantilist enthusiasts for government intervention and the Classical enthusiasts for free enterprise is being repeated in the current debate between the forced growth and natural growth schools.

The parallels are striking.

For example, Walter Lippmann, a forced growther, declared in a recent column that Senator Kennedy is "committed to the public needs"—meaning, one supposes, a larger public sector. Then Mr. Lippmann goes on to say that the Democratic nominee cannot afford another round of inflation and is bound to "face the truth and tell the country that when prices and wages are fixed by monopolistic corporations and unions, the public, through the Government, must have a say." In other words, some sort of wage and price controls.

But controls were old hat to the Mercantilists. Listen to Dunoyer, a contemporary French historian of the period: "The State exercised over manufacturing industry the most unlimited and arbitrary jurisdiction. It disposed without scruple of the resources of manufacturers; it decided who should be allowed to work, what things they should be permitted to make, what materials should be employed, what processes followed. . . . Not the taste of the consumers, but the commands of the law must be attended to. . . . Machines were broken, products were burned, when not conformable to the rules. . . . There exists a decree of March 30, 1700, which limits to 18 towns the number of places where stockings might be woven."

Or take another example. Democratic Senator Joseph S. Clark of Pennsylvania, another growth five-percenter, has hit the "tail-fin road," decrying such things as liquor and cosmetics as wasteful.

But the Mercantilists had their Puritans, too. And although there were no tail-fins over the rear carriage wheels of the day, cosmetics were attacked as debilitating of national strength. In 1770, a bill was introduced in the British Parliament to curb the use of cosmetics. The bill declared: "That all women of whatsoever rank and profession, or degree, whether virgins, old maids, or widows, who shall impose upon, seduce, and betray into matrimony any of His Majesty's (George III's) subjects by scents, paints, cosmetics, washes, artificial teeth, false hair, iron stays, bolstered hips, or high-heeled shoes, shall incur the penalty of the law now in force against witchcraft. The marriage resulting from these usages shall be null and void."

Then there's the matter of inflation. Inflation is implied in the 1960 Democratic plank against the "tight money, high-interest policy" of the Republicans. Moreover, the forced growth school's insistence on a 5 per cent growth rate and a heavy public sector also implies inflation. It spells a $100 billion Federal budget; and it spells a policy that whenever the private sector lags, the Government should pour out money to keep the economy growing 5 per cent each year no matter what.

The Mercantilists were overwhelmingly of the cheap money persuasion, too. Sir Josiah Child, for example, believed the way to bring about an industrial boom was to lower the cost of interest, and many Mercantilist economists believed prosperity was merely a matter of swelling the money supply. John Law, a Scottish economist, for example, wrote in 1705: "Domestick Trade depends on the Money. A Greater Quantity employes more People than a lesser Quantity. A limited Sum can only set a number of People to Work proportion'd to it, and 'tis with little success Laws are made, for Employing the Poor or Idle in Countries where Money is scarce."

Not long afterward, Law, though a roué and a gambler, talked his way into setting up a central bank based on paper money in France and eventually into becoming the Royal Controller General of the Finances, virtually prime minister of France. Law pumped out more than a billion paper livres, and a boom overtook recession-and-inflation-wracked France. But now it was inflation with a vengeance. The boom was short-lived; the ruination complete. For in 1720 the "Mississippi Bubble" burst; a hard depression ensued; and Law fled the country.

It was on this long chaotic forced-growth Mercantilistic scene that Adam Smith's epoch-making, *The Wealth of Nations* appeared. The year was 1776—the same year as our Declaration of Independence—a new dawn of both political and economic freedom. Smith stood four-square for economic growth, though he simply referred to it as the increase of national wealth.

His prescription: free trade, free enterprise and sound money—no controls, no inflation. Every country that tried it, especially England and America, experienced tremendous growth in contrast to previous Mercantilist marking time or worse. The historian Buckle said Smith has "contributed more toward the happiness of man than has been effected by the united abilities of all the statesmen and legislators of whom history has presented an authentic record."

So natural growth won out and forced growth lost in the great growth debate some 200 years ago. Whether that denouement will be repeated in the current debate remains to be seen.

WILLIAM H. PETERSON

April 4, 1961

Big Bad Word

It's ironic that "big" used in connection with business has become such a "bad" word that even businessmen don't like to refer to their own companies as big. As Birny Mason, Jr., president of Union Carbide Corporation, said the other day, it is now the fashion to use terms such as "diversified, integrated, and growing—and perhaps even large." But not "big."

There are, to be sure, several reasons why "big" is so assiduously avoided. It may well be, as Mr. Mason suggests, that "an instinctive aversion to big business without any clearly defined reason" has clouded and confused Government and public understanding of our system of enterprise and of the climate it needs to maintain healthy growth. In addition, the big business image has been burdened by the myths that it is inherently monopolistic, cold-hearted, ruthless, and so on. And there always have been plenty of people around willing to keep such myths alive.

But as Mr. Mason observes further, it is a distortion of the true nature of our business society to characterize it either as big business or small business. The size of any business is "clearly a function of the size of the job it has to do."

Where markets are small, businesses are small. But where markets get bigger they clearly require larger business operations to supply them. From this Mr. Mason concludes that bigness in business results primarily from human, or consumer, needs and the competitive forces of economics. And, further, that "bigness itself is simply the result of growth."

To put it another way, you can't have growth without somewhere along the line getting an increase in size. Thus to set an arbitrary limit on the size of a business, as some people would like to do, is one way to stifle growth. Moreover, it would suppress any incentive to grow.

Were there a better understanding all around of the relationship between bigness and growth, there might today be more growth and less talk about the need of it.

COWL RIDER

October 17, 1962

The Economic Mugwump

Besides the traditional political mugwump, a species of economic mugwump is now abroad in the land. This phenomenon perches awkwardly on a fence between fields of plenty and a dreary vision of national austerity.

The economic mugwump, to be sure, is also highly political. But his chief identifying trait is this: he talks out of one side of his mouth about the need for much greater sacrifices on the part of everyone, and out of the other side promises more goodies for everybody.

So it is that by now we have had months of talk, mostly from Democrats but also from some Republicans, about the sad state of our national life. We waste our substance on gadgets, we think low, if at all, and live high. While we luxuriously vegetate, the dedicated Communists are on the move.

Our values, in short, are all wrong, so we are told. Instead of steeping ourselves in luxury, we should pull in our belts so that we (meaning Government in this case) can spend much more on the public needs for schools, roads, et cetera. In Senator Kennedy's words, we must sacrifice.

Certainly it is anyone's privilege to talk that way and to try to persuade the rest of us of the validity of the argument. It might even be a valid argument—except for the obvious fact that this country has the best schools (in terms of quantity), roads, hospitals, housing and what have you in the world today and in all history.

What is less easy to grasp is that the people who are demanding austerity are simultaneously promising much more of the good old materialistic things of life. Senator Church symbolized the contradiction particularly well when he deplored America's horrible decline and at the same time proudly declared that America is the marvel of the world. Senator Kennedy did the same thing when he called for sacrifice and in the same speech applauded the Democratic platform which promises more money and more recreation and more everything for everyone in the country.

How, you may justifiably wonder, can anyone with a straight face offer the people both austerity and luxury? But the question doesn't particularly faze this brand of economic mugwump; he thinks he has the answer—the magic key, in fact, to the resolution of all human problems. The key, of course, is Government.

In this view, if we will but consign ourselves and our goods to Washington, then Washington will "rationalize" life for us. At first, with much of our discretionary buying power removed, there would be austerity. But then the Government would go on a glorious bender to build all those gleaming new schools (to teach still more teenagers how to date and how to baby-sit and how to look at movies) and all those other things of which the nation is in such desperate need.

Thus would "public" luxury be created. And because the frenzy of Federal activity would be so great, the whole economy would be whirled into a euphoria in which everyone would have everything his heart desires.

Politically, this program may or may not have appeal. Certainly a similar one appealed to the Germans in 1932 (the poor Russians didn't have a chance to be tempted; they just got it). But economically, whether in Nazi Germany, Communist Russia, or would-be-collectivist America, it is hogwash.

A government can, indeed, create austerity by grabbing the bulk of the nation's resources for its own purposes through monstrous taxation; that is a swift avenue to national decline. Alternatively, a government can create the temporary illusion of lush prosperity by unbridled inflation; that is an even faster road to decline. The one thing no government can ever do is match the productive power of free private economic activity.

That activity is the source of the abundance which provides also for public needs. If the decriers of American life really want more schools and all the rest, the way to get them is to expand the area of economic freedom. And if the economic mugwump were capable of that reflection, he would jump off his fence into the limitless fields of individual liberty.

JOSEPH E. EVANS

August 2, 1960

———◆●◆———

MOVING TARGET

We moved in long enough ago
That just from habit now we know
Right where to find each thing we need
And life once more runs smooth indeed.
So smooth, indeed, that now my spouse
Has time to hunt another house!

—HERBERT WARFEL

Price of Indulgence

We've arrived at that unhappy age when the price of a brief indulgence at the dining table is many days of fasting, and when we must pay with that dragged-out feeling for an evening's celebration. Thus does experience teach its painful lesson.

Unfortunately, it's not a lesson easily learned any other way, which no doubt explains why some of the slight stabbing pains recently felt in the nation's economy, in the stock market and elsewhere, have come as a bit of a shock. It's been a long and wonderful party and nobody likes the sobering thought that it may not go on forever.

But it occurs to us that these little nagging pains—the recent drop in stock prices, the squeeze on profits, the sagging of the dollar in world markets—could be a blessing in disguise if the country will just heed them. Serious trouble is likely to come only if we all forget that the indulgence in economic excesses, like any other, has its price that must be paid, sooner or later.

Take the stock market. At first glance it may seem a paradox that the market has been sliding at a time when other signs point to a good business year. In fact, some of the companies whose stocks have fallen the sharpest have enjoyed earnings in the last two quarters higher than in the same period a year ago. Yet the same issue of this newspaper which notes that earnings are up may also report that the price of the company's stock is down.

Or look at another seeming paradox, in our balance of trade and the gold outflow. As Government trade officials have been pointing out, our balance of trade (that is, our excess of exports over imports) seems to be healthy. Yet in one recent week the outflow of gold in response to demands from foreign creditors hit a near record.

But these paradoxes are only seeming. The stock market is simply paying the price of an excessive valuation of the boom of the past 15 years; it's not that a recession has hit us now but simply that formerly people got too exuberant in what they were paying for tomorrow's possible earnings. The pressure on the dollar, of which the gold outflow is but one symptom, is not so much the price of present as of past indulgence.

And so it goes. Ever since the end of World War II we have treated ourselves to the pleasure of almost every kind of economic foolishness. Year after year, under Democrats and Republicans, the Government has spent not like a wise uncle but like a profligate nephew, piling debt upon debt.

Billions of these dollars were poured all over the world as if they were limitless. At home, business managers, or all too many of them, operated on the theory that inflation made things easy for them; why worry too much about rising wage and other costs if inflation was going to raise prices also and wash out any mistakes? It is the same psychology that operated in the overblown stock market.

What are being felt now are the twinges of indigestion. It is a healthy sign if people are taking some second looks at some of the ridiculous price-earnings ratios in the stock market, if they are beginning to pay attention to the "squeeze" on profits and to be concerned about the gold outflow and its related problems. Healthy, that is, if the pangs are recognized for what they are.

If they are recognized as warning signs, then sobriety can return in good time. One of the reasons why we have avoided more serious difficulties during the long postwar boom is that, at periodic intervals, some corrections have been made. There is nothing incurable now in the cost squeeze; nothing in the trade position of the United States to cause any collapse of the dollar; nothing in the basic economic situation at home to herald a depression.

But the warnings we have had, in the stock market and elsewhere, do mean that business managers will have to become more cost-conscious than they have been in 15 years. The stock market public will have to disabuse itself of the idea that there's some magic that will keep airy bubbles from bursting. And above all, the Government will have to recognize that after its long spending binge there has come the moment for sobriety. Otherwise there's sure to be real trouble.

At any rate, in a long life we never heard of anybody who found a way to avoid paying the price of indulgence.

VERMONT ROYSTER

May 17, 1962

The Price of Ignorance

President Kennedy's victory over the steel companies was certainly a convincing display of Government power. But it was also an equally convincing demonstration of the Administration's lack of economic knowledge.

For one thing, any business, be it U.S. Steel or the corner drugstore, must continually weigh its income against its outgo if it is to survive. No company can go on indefinitely paying increasing amounts to its employees and suppliers without increasing its income. At the end of that road, as any schoolboy should know, lies bankruptcy.

Wage costs of the steel industry have risen four times since the last price increase, in 1958. U.S. Steel's profits have been heading downward. In the circumstances, what could have been more normal than to test the market with a price increase?

U.S. Steel, of course, knew that the price increase might not stick. Competition in its industry was—and is—strenuous. Some smaller, newer companies in the industry, such as Inland Steel, have on the average more modern, more efficient plants than U.S. Steel, and thus are feeling the profit pinch less severely. Other companies, such as Armco Steel, rely on higher priced specialty steels for much of their volume, and it is these items that have been most affected by import competition.

So it's possible that economic factors alone could have forced U.S. Steel to back away from its price increase. But the Government seemed not to understand the power of such factors, for it refused to let them even be tested. Indeed, it seemed to argue that these competitive forces did not exist, and that the big steel companies were displaying "monopoly power."

Mr. Kennedy's excuse for forbidding any test of the steel market was that he was fighting inflation. This is a word that the Government seems to misread completely. Whatever Mr. Kennedy may think, it is the Government, and the Government alone, that has been inflating the supply of money and credit. So it is the irresponsible fiscal and spending policies of the Government, and not the "irresponsible" steel executives, that are to blame for inflation.

In the wake of the industry's cancellation of the price boost, there was fresh evidence of this lack of understanding of inflation. A Kennedy aide was quoted by this newspaper as saying, "The Administration's attitude is, 'Let's forget it happened and get on with the main job of keeping the economy growing without inflation.' "

The trouble is that the Administration seems to think one sure way to promote growth is to increase Federal spending. Even before the steel debacle, Government officials were worrying about the speed of recovery and talking of the possible need for a new "stimulus" from Federal spending. And last week in Omaha a Budget Bureau aide told an audience of economists that the public's feeling about the budget— that it's a good thing to have it balanced—may "constitute a significant barrier to the achievement of sustained full employment and vigorous economic growth."

"Vigorous economic growth" requires not a fast-spending Government but a vigorous private economy. Businessmen must be developing new products, pushing into new markets, creating new jobs. Government can only retard such growth by levying excessive taxes to support its excessive spending and by creating a climate of fear in the business community.

And there is no question businessmen now are fearful. As a Kennedy lieutenant says, "Everyone is going to be very reluctant to try to pull off what steel tried." The shock absorbed by business confidence could be felt for a long time. No businessman builds a new plant or launches a new product unless he believes it will return a profit—a profit based on prices in reasonable relation to costs. But the Government seems unaware of the importance of business confidence.

The smashing impact of the Administration's economic power now is evident to all. We can only hope the nation will not have to pay too high a price for economic ignorance.

LINDLEY H. CLARK, JR.

March 17, 1962

Who Gets the Profit?

A reader has asked for elaboration of a recent comment we made in passing. It was that not even a Communist economy can run without profits.

Before getting to communism, it might be noted that the most primitive economy imaginable must have a profit base. Even a one-family economy would have to have a surplus—a profit, as it were—over

immediate consumption, even if only in the form of seed corn to provide food for the next year.

Surpluses are also essential for the slightly more sophisticated but
still primitive barter economy. The farmer who trades wheat for shoes
must have a surplus and must think it more profitable to get the shoes
that way than to make his own; the cobbler reasons the same way
about the wheat he acquires. That is how a money economy develops,
to facilitate exchanges for profit.

Now, to take a notable example of a Communist economy, the Soviet
Union not only has a money economy, its government needs lots of
money. It needs it to finance the huge military establishment and the
costly space program and the fifth columns abroad and all the other
activities of that government and that party, including the lavish living
of the elite classes.

Though the Soviet Union has gone in for inflation at times, it can no
more simply print money endlessly without disaster than can a capitalist
economy. So it must get its money out of profits, no matter how much
Communists like to portray themselves as having abolished the "evil"
of the profit system.

And the profits are tremendous. As in our country, they come in
large measure from the difference between production costs and sales
prices, with the rather important difference that there the profits go to
the State.

More specifically, a big portion of Soviet profits derives from a series
of taxes at each stage of the manufacturing and distribution process.
Personal income taxes are relatively low, but that blessing is more than
offset by the size of these so-called turnover taxes, which are tanta-
mount to sales taxes ultimately paid by the consumer when he buys
clothes, appliances or whatever.

These taxes—the government's profit—account for the extremely
high Soviet prices in relation to income. Red officials are reluctant to
reveal production costs, but the cheap labor and inferior materials
show that the costs are low and that the mark-up between costs and
prices is huge.

In a nation where even fairly skilled workers earn less than the
equivalent of $100 a month, people must pay prices like these: shoddy
shoes, $20 and up; a poor-quality suit for around $70 and a better-
quality one for about $140; a pound of butter for $1.50.

Herein lies the real meaning of the common observation that Soviet
military strength and space progress are possible only by depriving the
consumer. His belt is kept tight both by the scarcity of consumer goods
and their high prices—and those high prices help pay for whatever
the Communist party bosses want to do.

In the United States, thank heaven, things are very different. We pay taxes for Government activities, but what profits are left in the private economy after taxes go for the benefit of the people. They are used to expand and modernize plant and equipment, to pay the 17 million shareholder-owners of industry for the use of their capital, to provide employee pensions and the like. The consumer is not the least beneficiary; in our kind of profit system the consumer is a sovereign instead of a serf.

And that is why we think the recurrent attacks on profits by many Americans are so misguided, if not worse. They talk as though ours were a profiteering instead of a profit economy. They seem not to understand that the more you curtail profits, the more you curb economic growth and work against the interests of employees and consumers. That the more you divert profits to Government, the more your economy tends to resemble a Communist one.

But whatever anyone thinks of their system or our own, no one should be under the delusion that somehow the Soviet system is not a profit system. They are among the biggest profiteers of all time, if not the biggest. It's great for the rulers but not for the people.

And the real question in any economy is not whether there are profits. It's who gets them and what's done with them.

JOSEPH E. EVANS

August 23, 1962

Teaching Economics

RIDGEWOOD, NEW JERSEY—"When father works and brings home money, what do we call that?"

In a sunny second-grade classroom in the modernistic Glen School in this New York City suburb, five hands go up in response to teacher Nancy Cook's question.

"Income!" says a proud seven-year-old boy, and Mrs. Cook carefully writes the word on the blackboard.

In the course of the next half hour Mrs. Cook, carrying on the discussion in the same vein, adds such terms as "advertise," "salesman," "consumer," "retail," and even "gross profits" to her list of "new words." The youngsters know what retail means because they've recently made a field trip to a near-by supermarket. And they know what a salesman is because one of the children's fathers, who is one, came in and described his job to the class.

With teaching techniques such as these, a small but growing number of schools around the land are seeking to implant the rudiments of economics—usually considered a difficult, elusive subject—as early as the first and second grades. Only by starting early, many educators say, can the schools produce an economically "literate" future generation. Despite its deceptive simplicity and "classroom fun" aspects, they argue, teaching such as Mrs. Cook's forms an essential building block on which more sophisticated instruction can later be superimposed.

"The important thing is that the seed has been planted," declares Harold Shafer, director of instructional services for the Ridgewood school system.

Only 5 per cent of the nation's high school graduates have ever had an economics course, and school men have largely written off the present adult generation as far as economic literacy is concerned. But the outlook for the next generation is improving. Five years ago, only 27 high schools in California offered a separate economics course. Since then the number has grown to 144, or over one quarter of the Golden State's public high schools. In Connecticut, the most economics-minded state, a separate course is now offered by over 50 per cent of the high schools.

The obstacles to expanded economics teaching are still extremely formidable. Nevertheless, the experience of some schools suggests that even the most awesome difficulties—the controversial nature of the subject and the dullness of traditional teaching methods—can be overcome.

The organization which claims to have made the most progress against these obstacles is the Joint Council of Economic Education. A non-profit organization based in New York City, the council was formed in 1949 explicitly to promote the teaching of economics in the United States. Initial funds came from the Committee for Economic Development, a nonpartisan group of businessmen and educators influential in shaping public policy. Since then the Ford Foundation has become the principal benefactor, currently supplying about three-fourths of the council's $217,000 annual budget.

With a small staff of educators and economists, the Joint Council coordinates the activities of 45 state and local "councils on economic education" that have sprung up in recent years with its encouragement. It has organized workshops in which 17,000 social studies teachers who never took the subject in college, including Ridgewood's Nancy Cook, have acquired some instruction in economics. It has agitated for more economics courses in teachers' colleges, and has helped local school districts devise experimental teaching methods.

Mindful from the outset of the hazards of promoting a controversy-ridden subject, the Joint Council has hewed to two basic tenets. First, it claims to be scrupulously nonpartisan. Its 65-man board includes business, labor and farm leaders, but educators—instead of interest groups with axes to grind—control half the seats.

At the local level a second tenet is stressed: broad public support. School districts interested in teaching economics, the Joint Council advises, should first consult community leaders of all shades of opinion and get their help in formulating a program. "When you're dealing in the area of economics, you're dealing in a very sensitive area," says M. L. Frankel, director of the council. "Unless the leaders of the community are involved, you're not playing fair with the individual teacher, who may find himself out on a limb."

The Joint Council has tried to make economics teaching more interesting for youngsters. The subject's reputation for dreariness is due in large part to the heavily abstract or "pure" economics approach used in college teaching. College economists, who have influenced what little there is of grade-school instruction, not only are scornful of injecting "value judgments" on whether the American system is basically "good" or "bad," but disdain the "applied" approach, which puts more emphasis on how the system works. All of which makes for dullness.

Therefore, some highly experimental approaches have been necessary, school men say, and more are needed. The Tulsa, Oklahoma, schools, with the Joint Council's help, prepared an economics course for ninth-graders which tries to make the subject exciting by tying it in with a history of the cattle industry in the Sooner State. In a textbook entitled *Cowboys, Cattle and Commerce,* some fairly sophisticated concepts, such as the elasticity of demand, are included along with range wars and gunsmoke.

In the senior high schools, economics of necessity moves closer to the abstract, college level. But even here, the presentation must be lively and closely related to what the student knows about life. This problem, as it relates to high school textbooks, has been the main concern of another organization active in economics education, the Council for the Advancement of Secondary Education. CASE, as the group calls itself, was formed by a unit of the National Education Association with the cooperation of the National Better Business Bureau. To date, it has spent seven years and $700,000 trying to develop high school texts capable of holding the interest of the average student.

In one CASE booklet called "American Capitalism," football is used to help explain the rather abstract principle of opportunity cost— the cost of using limited economic resources to perform a task, expressed in terms of the most desirable alternative use of these resources. A football coach, the book relates, lacks a good supply of linemen and decides to put his backfield star in at tackle. Keeping him in the back-field might seem wiser, it says, "but without a good line your backfield would be lost . . . the cost of shifting such an indispensable lineman to the backfield could be the victory."

The CASE book on capitalism gets hip-deep in value judgments at times. "Our competitive market and price system," it tells high school students, "based upon the right of private property and upon profit motivation, is one of the sources of our freedom and progress. . . . The foundations of free enterprise are also the foundations of a free society."

Some progress is being made in other areas, notably the lack of textbooks and qualified teachers. Traditionally leery of publishing high school texts on economics, several commercial publishers are either entering the field for the first time or are attempting to enliven the relatively few existing textbooks. These include Harcourt, Brace and World, Incorporated, Ginn and Company, Macmillan Company, Doubleday and Company, McGraw-Hill Publishing Company, and a new company, Curriculum Resources, Incorporated, of Minneapolis, formed expressly to develop economics texts.

As a gap-filler in teacher preparation, the CBS network next fall will present a televised 32-week elementary economics course. Most of the $1,335,000 needed for the course has already been raised from corporations and foundations. One of the principal fund-raisers is Roger Blough, chairman of U.S. Steel Corporation. Sponsored jointly by the American Economic Association, the Joint Council and Learn-ing Resources Institute, the course will devote roughly four-fifths of its program time to economics as such and the remaining portion to the vital problem of how to get the subject across to youngsters.

How much economics can elementary and secondary school pupils absorb? Schools in Kalamazoo, Michigan, claim they are successfully introducing the concept of capital investment in the second grade. In Indianapolis, high school seniors are taught such advanced topics as how the Federal Reserve Board's open market operations expand or restrict the money supply. In some areas such as New York City, voca-tional school students are now rated as capable of grasping the subject. Until three years ago, economics was required only for college-prepara-tory students.

Concepts such as "inflation" and "productivity" are as important for working-class people as for white-collar workers, educators say. "How many rank-and-file people in unions know what they're bargaining with management about?" asks Dr. Frankel. "Yet they're called upon to vote on a strike."

Meanwhile, in Ridgewood, they're even using classroom skits to introduce some concepts. A few weeks ago Anne, a pupil in Mrs.

Cook's class, set up an ice cream stand and "sold" cones for five cents. Later Debbie, a classmate, set up a rival stand and offered her "product" at the same price. Something had to give. Anne decided to win back business by painting her stand. But this didn't help, so she cut her price to four cents.

"What were they having?" Nancy Cook asks the class. Answer: competition.

Edmund K. Faltermayer

July 2, 1962

"That's it—sneak off to work!"

Changeable Consumers

MUNCIE, INDIANA—Here in the heart of Midwest America, talks with consumers and businessmen point up this precept: keeping up with the changing tastes of American consumers can be a mighty trying ordeal.

"On my last vacation, I spent $1,200 for a jet trip to Austria," observes Bette Ashcraft, a comely, brown-haired secretary in the local offices of Warner Gear division of Chicago's Borg-Warner Corporation. "It was quite a change from the short fishing trip the family used to take every year. I visited Beethoven's home in Vienna and watched people float lighted egg shells down the Danube. This summer I'd like to bicycle across Europe, providing someone will lend me the money."

"Secretaries and factory hands are booking passage for Spain, Hawaii and Acapulco without batting an eye," says an awed travel agent, Jim Leak, who is a partner in Muncie Travel Service. "Fifteen years ago, a Muncie man who vacationed in New York City was considered footloose, and the most popular honeymoon spot for Muncie folks was Indianapolis."

The sharp changes in consumer vacation habits and the other alterations in spending patterns, here as elsewhere in the nation, stem heavily from higher wages, which have roughly doubled since 1946. The cost of living has increased far less, so consumers have a considerably greater number of dollars left after paying for such essentials as food and housing. This higher income, teamed with effects of wartime travel, new products such as television, growing leisure and more education, has wrought many changes in the way consumers spend their money.

Consumer spending trends are of vast importance to a wide variety of American businesses, of course, and the changes noted in this Hoosier town are probably typical of those taking place over most of the nation. Muncie was the subject of two "Middletown" books, detailed sociological studies of a typical American town, some three decades ago.

Pleasure boating is one activity that has benefited from the sweeping changes in consumer buying trends. This Indiana town, once the hunting grounds of the Munsee Indians, is a dry land area a hundred miles from sizable bodies of water. But it is enjoying a boating boom, nonetheless. Five boat dealers in the Muncie area now do a brisk business, while there was no obvious effort to promote the business aggressively at the end of World War II. "We sold 70 boats in 1961, with prices ranging up to $5,400," comments Robert Smith, the owner of Delaware Marine Company, a boat retailer. "We're shooting for 100 this year and we're confident we'll make it." He estimates there are more than 1,000 boat owners in the Muncie area, three to four times the number in 1945.

The gains, while partially attributable to vast improvement in the product, stem mostly from new desires of consumers. Comments Marshall Staggs, a black-haired six-footer painting fenders in the Silverthorne Autobody Shop: "A few years ago I would have bought a new car with my money but I decided I would have more fun with a boat. I've got $3,000 in it and I have to drive 120 miles to put it in the water but I think I'll own a boat for a long time."

Women also are enjoying sharply increased leisure and there are equally sharp changes in the way they spend it. At a local bowling center, for example, some 200 women are gathered to try their hand at the sport. "I took it up about two years ago," recalls Mrs. Joyce Atkins, a trim woman in white sweater and black slacks. "With appliances to do most of my housework, I got bored sitting at home."

Consumers' changing whims have put quite a dent in some long-established businesses. Says Hugh McLachlan, state supervisor for Y and W Management Corporation, Indianapolis, operator of 18 movie houses, "About the only movies that will pull customers into the houses any more are the family pictures like *101 Dalmatians* and racy stuff like *Splendor in the Grass*. People can get the Westerns and detective stories on television."

Much of the movie houses' unhappy plight does stem from television, of course. There are only three indoor and two drive-in movie houses in the Muncie area now, compared with eight movie houses as recently as 10 years ago. Nationally, there are roughly 13,000 indoor motion picture theaters now, down from 18,719 in 1946.

While shying away from indoor theaters, consumers have taken happily to a convenient, informal substitute, the drive-in movie. For instance, in the darkened Muncie Drive-In, farmer Carol Morgan, his wife and three wide-eyed youngsters are munching hamburgers and watching the huge screen.

"Used to be he wouldn't get out of his easy chair after dark," comments Mrs. Morgan. "But since they built these fancy outdoor movies, he takes us out most every Saturday night." The nation's drive-in movies have swelled to 4,800 from less than 100 in 1946.

Families also are demanding bigger homes. "From 1946 to about 1950, two-bedroom houses represented about 40 per cent of our market," says Fred Bartel, vice president of Bar-Tel Company, a local building firm. "But in 1961 only 2 of the 40 we built were that small. More people want family rooms for casual living and dining rooms for entertaining guests." Bar-Tel built homes ranging from $8,000 to $9,000 in the years immediately following World War II. But in 1961 homes ranged from $14,000 to $60,000, reflecting the firm's steady shift to meet the biggest local market.

Hotels also have felt the impact of the consumer's critical eye. "Muncie boasts only two first-class hotels now," says Howard L. Fager, 56, who for 34 years has worked at the clerk's desk of the Van Orman-Roberts Hotel. "Two hotels have been torn down in the past few years."

The major problem of Muncie hotels, which they share with others around the nation, is exemplified in the new 150-room Holiday Inn Motel built recently on the edge of town. "Their prices are about the same as ours and the customers like new accommodations," reflects Mr. Fager unhappily. A dozen fancy new motels have sprung up in the area in the past decade, the hotel man says.

The fickleness of consumers has wrought other changes in this Indiana town. The little white-fronted "Ma and Pa" grocery operated for 18 years on West 11th Street by James and Dorothy Bailey is closed, forced out because customers preferred the big gleaming new supermarkets. There are only about 15 little family groceries in the area now, a third of the number around after World War II, but big supermarkets total about 20, double the number 16 years ago, a local supermarket executive estimates. Several are in shopping centers, which also are taking business away from stores in downtown Muncie.

Browse through the old Sears, Roebuck and Company farm store here in the heart of the agricultural Midwest and you'll find only such items as camping tents, riding horse saddles and snow removers. "We cater to suburban farmers now," comments Leroy Cotton, the farm store manager. Sixteen years ago the store carried such farm items as corn planters and plows. Only 4 per cent of the residents of Delaware County, in which Muncie is located, now make their living on the farm.

Not all of the consumers' affluence is coming out of the increased incomes, however; the traditionally frugal Midwesterners are showing a growing affinity for buying on the cuff. Outstanding consumer credit at Muncie's American National Bank and Trust Company, for instance, is roughly 40 times what it was in 1946. "Americans have become extremely willing in recent years to mortgage their futures," notes H. E. Woods, white-haired president of American National.

The dog-eared yellow section of the 1945 Muncie telephone book, compared with the crisp new 1961 version, gives ample evidence of other changes wrought by consumers over the years. There were no pizza stands then but the town has seven now. Absent in 1945 were car rental and tool rental shops, while four firms now advertise cars for rent and five offer tools. Coal dealers and ice delivery services are disappearing.

While Muncie folks would appear to enjoy their lively new way of life, it has produced some side effects. Some 200 per cent of the prescription sales of Rotz West Side Drugstore, for instance, now come from tranquilizers, compared with about 3 per cent in 1946-47. "The tempo of living is fast these days, even in Muncie," says John Rotz, the owner. "But people no longer fight their anxieties and their tensions—they subdue them with tranquilizers."

Even the old status symbols are almost gone. "It's becoming increasingly difficult to tell at first glance whether your new neighbor works at the factory or owns it," observes Dr. John Hannaford, social science department head at Muncie's Ball State Teachers College. "A great number of workers have taken on the trappings of position, such as big cars, fur coats, boats, hi-fi sets and expensive wines. But at the same time many of the moneyed families are making an attempt to keep down with the Joneses, in a conscious avoidance of display."

Whether or not you can tell a consumer's status in life by the things he buys, chances are good nowadays that he will have changed his spending habits by the time you make up your mind.

KENNETH G. SLOCUM

May 14, 1962

Evolution of Moneylenders

The moneylender, long the favorite of the law if not of society, has had the tables turned on him. For the law and the lawmakers now seem more concerned with protecting the borrowers.

This change was pointed up the other day when President Kennedy called for a Federal law to require lenders to spell out credit charges for consumers. If such a law is adopted, it will find its place atop a growing mound of Federal and state laws regulating lenders' activities. These laws are often overlapping and sometimes contradictory.

There is, however, at least one consolation for lenders: Though their relative legal position has deteriorated a bit, their social status has improved immeasurably over the centuries.

Credit is probably as old as trade; it certainly antedates the money economy. In early societies credit was introduced to make barter more flexible. If one party to a bargain agreed to let the other wait a bit before completing his side of the exchange, credit had been extended. And if the debtor eventually gave more than he had received, something approximating interest had evolved.

The creditor's social popularity has always been precarious, because he sometimes has to press for payment. In ancient Mesopotamia, a slave dealer named Ilabras once found he had to write to a customer: "May Shamash and Marduk keep thee! As thou knowest, I had issued a note for a female slave. Now the time to pay is come."

Lenders, of course, were placed in the same general category with merchants and traders, professions that in most ancient societies were considered things the better people avoided. And the introduction of interest tended to push lenders down even further.

In ancient times, as now, there were some lenders who charged fees regarded as exorbitant, and there were some legal efforts to curb such practices. But any interest at all had a hard time winning social and religious acceptability. The Old Testament makes an effort to draw a line: "To a foreigner you may lend upon interest, but to your brother you shall not lend upon interest."

All along, however, the weight of the law continued to be on the lender's side. The sanctity of contracts generally was upheld by the courts, whatever the public—and the borrowers—might think of the contracts. In Elizabethan England, a court's thwarting of Shylock's contract for "a pound of flesh" was still such an unusual idea that Shakespeare was able to make dramatic use of it.

In many countries, a man might count himself lucky if he was only thrown into prison for failure to pay his debts. In many cases, he and his wife and his children could be sold into slavery for failure to pay obligations.

By the early 19th century, however, this situation was beginning to change. Governments were becoming more democratic, giving the people—and hence the borrowers—more to say about the laws of their countries. The concept of human rights was on the ascendancy, and it was beginning to limit contractual rights.

In the middle of the past century, many countries passed laws that in most cases barred imprisonment for debt. Debtors in a few cases still go to jail, but it's now so unusual that it often draws wide news attention.

The fact that debt no longer was regarded as so heinous a crime may have had something to do with a growing public willingness to plunge into it. In any case, the 20th century ushered in a swift expansion of consumer borrowing. And as the debtors' numbers have grown, so has their political power—and the politicians' desire to protect them.

The consumers' rush into debt began earlier and has proceeded farther in the United States than in most other countries. And, as in other societies, some lenders have helped to sharpen the politicians' protective instincts by engaging in all kinds of excesses. One group in the late 19th century was known as the "salary lenders." Their tactic was to get borrowers to pledge future wages as security for loans; loans ranged from $5 to $50 and carried interest rates of 10 per cent to 40 per cent a month.

A refinement of this practice was known as "salary buying." A lender, for example, might agree to buy a worker's forthcoming $25 weekly paycheck for $22.50. This was equal to an annual interest charge of more than 500 per cent, an exorbitant rate by anybody's standards.

But the real expansion of consumer debt stemmed from purchases of consumer goods, and the first major push came from development of the automobile. Although a practical automobile was on the market before 1900, it took Henry Ford's Model T to push prices down within even the borrowing power of most consumers. And as refrigerators, washing machines and other new consumer goods came along, the consumers' wants—and their borrowing—expanded.

Credit demand would have been meaningless, of course, if there had not been lenders to meet it, and both the number and diversity of such lenders expanded rapidly. There were small loan companies, industrial banks, sales finance companies, credit unions and others to supply loans for the purchase of consumer durables.

Banks were slow to get into consumer lending. They were deterred in part by concern over the relatively high cost of lending small amounts to large numbers of people, as compared with the cost of lending large amounts to small numbers of borrowers. And partly, too, the prospects of repayment seemed uncertain to many bankers.

In 1928, the First National City Bank of New York established a personal loan department, and this is generally considered to have broken the wall of banker tradition against consumer lending. While only 16 commercial banks had small-loan departments in 1927, the number had risen to 65 in 1929 and to 277 in 1931.

The great new interest in consumer loans obviously created a fertile field for the regulators of the lenders, and the states and the Federal Government have long been active in the area. An extensive, if confusing, system of regulation for banks has long been in existence, of course. State-chartered banks are regulated by the state, but also come under the purview of the Federal Reserve System and the Federal Deposit Insurance Corporation, if they happen to be members of those organizations. Nationally chartered banks are regulated by the Comptroller of the Currency, but, like the state banks, may be subject to control by the Federal Reserve and the FDIC.

A number of states have set maximum rates of interest that banks can charge on consumer loans. These states also set maximum rates for other types of lenders. But state regulation does not stop with maximum rates.

In New York, state law sets the maximum loan that each type of institution can make; banks are permitted to make bigger loans than small loan companies, for example. The state sets the maximum additional charge that a bank can make if a borrower misses a payment or defaults on the loan. Under the law, the application for the loan must clearly state the interest charge.

If a lender insures the life of a borrower, the cost of this may be added to the cost of the loan. A bank may collect interest in advance, but a small loan company cannot. When a small loan firm makes a loan, it must give the borrower a copy of the section of the state banking law governing its operations. A pawnbroker is not permitted to sell any borrower's security until a year has expired and, even then, he must give the borrower written warning of the sale—and publish a notice in the newspapers.

Though the ethics of the lending fraternity generally are high, few lenders would quarrel with the need for regulation of their industry. After all, such regulation does cull out the occasional loan shark who reflects discredit on legitimate lenders. And if some lenders occasionally fret about the complexity of the laws wrapped around them, they may console themselves with the thought that most of them now are pillars of their communities, not pariahs.

LINDLEY H. CLARK, JR.

March 27, 1962

------◆◆◆------

KEY QUESTION

To every manuscript preparer
Having but a little time to spend,
Why does every hopeless typing error
Always have to ha½pen near the end?

—JANE HERALD

Are Installment Buyers Imbeciles?

Hillel Black's *Buy Now, Pay Later,* an extended examination of on-the-cuff living as it affects the American people, is a book that should be approached with some wariness.

On page 211, in a summing up, Mr. Black says he is no enemy of debt. He admits that if Americans were not allowed to buy cars on time there would be a 50 per cent reduction in the number of cars manufactured. There would be 8 per cent less steel, 24 per cent less malleable iron and 31 per cent less synthetic rubber. The resulting unemployment would touch off a depression to make the dip of 1960–61 look like a galloping boom.

With such a tribute to the prosperity-inducing factor that is involved in the use of consumer credit, it would be logical to look for at least a few kind words about installment purchases in the earlier parts of Mr. Black's book. But if there are any kind words, the reader will remember none of them by the time page 211 has been reached. At times Mr. Black even seems to be an enemy of check money, so avid is he to make out a case for cash.

The author begins with an old dodge. He invents a fictitious couple, Ralph and Alice Homer, who wend their way through the book behaving like imbeciles. Ralph is a rising young executive in a growing company. This ought to be a guarantee that Ralph has at least a residue of mother wit, but the sad truth is that our "rising young executive" doesn't know enough to come in when it rains. He lives in a Cape Cod house which he can't afford. When he meets his wife for lunch, he pays $15.80 for it with his all-purpose credit card. He buys his cars on time, without bothering to figure whether he is paying 12 per cent, 18 per cent or 36 per cent for the finance money.

Possessing an "instant money" checkbook, Ralph at the end of a hard day settles his overdue garage bill without reflecting that he has not even a minimal balance at the bank. Thus getting his car out of hock, he takes Alice back to their heavily mortgaged home to sit on their still-to-be-paid-for furniture and listen to the mortgaged murmurs of the washing machine and the dryer in the kitchen.

As the washing machine sings to itself, Alice also hums a happy little tune. She has just "saved" the Homers $53.55 by spending $117.45 for "bargains" at the stores, utilizing her revolving credit to load herself up with unneeded dresses, shoes and a lush smoking jacket for

Ralph. The payments on the revolving credit will necessitate forking over 18 per cent in "true annual interest" on the "declining" balance at the stores for a year.

In brief, the Homers are a couple of dopes. Hillel Black, making a quick jump from his description of an "average" modern couple's day, goes on to lament that "currently about 100 million Americans are participating in the buy-now, pay-later binge." Query: Is the reader supposed to gather from this juxtaposition that 100 million Americans are just like Ralph and Alice Homer?

Mr. Black does not really believe, of course, that his Homers are at all typical. A superb reporter when he is not trying to make the reader's flesh creep, he does a good, solid job of describing the origin and growth of such institutions as the Diners' Club and the Credit Bureau of Greater New York. He does a good job, too, when he is busy exposing the methods of loan sharks in states like Alabama and Texas.

When everything has been said and done about Ralph and Alice Homer, for whom 10 years each in debtors' prison would be altogether too light a sentence, it turns out that Mr. Black has only one real gripe about installment credit as such. The gripe centers on its concealed cost. Most people don't realize, he says, that they are actually paying 12 per cent and 18 per cent in "true annual interest" when they are nominally paying much less.

If a man borrows $100 at 6 per cent for a year and pays it off in monthly installments, he is not getting the use of that hundred dollars for the entire year. At the end of six months he will have the use of only half the sum he has originally borrowed. Averaging things out, the simple annual interest on the $100 will be 12 per cent, not 6 per cent.

Mr. Black thinks that borrowers ought to realize that car finance charges run anywhere from 11 per cent to 17 per cent, "true annual interest." They ought to realize that revolving credit at the stores costs them 18 per cent. He would like to see a law passed making it mandatory that all dealers in consumer credit state their true annual interest charges on every "package" of debt. Senator Paul Douglas concurs with this idea in an introduction; indeed, he has offered such a bill in the U.S. Senate.

Could be that Mr. Black and Senator Douglas have got hold of a good idea. But it would be an even better idea if people would learn some arithmetic for themselves.

JOHN CHAMBERLAIN

May 31, 1961

Error of Money Tampering

Money, historically fought over, debated over, much loved but little understood, is the subject of Elgin Groseclose's *Money and Man: A Survey of Monetary Experience,* a rewrite and expansion of this Washington economic consultant's earlier work, *Money: The Human Conflict,* published in 1935 by the University of Oklahoma Press.

The new version is a penetrating look not only at money but at the human race and at the persistent and tragic Governmental confusion about money and wealth, a confusion seen in the alchemist's bedazzling plan: Transmute lead into gold—multiply money and, presto, you multiply wealth, a plan not essentially different from that of the counterfeiter. At any rate, the history of money turns out to be, pretty regularly, a history of inflation.

Dr. Groseclose, formerly a university professor, financial editor of *Fortune,* and treasurer-general of Iran (by appointment of the Iranian Parliament during World War II), argues persuasively that the soundness of a nation's money is a fairly reliable indicator of the soundness of a nation's government. Indeed, civilizations seem to rise and fall on the quality of money. Why might this be so?

St. Paul described the love of money as the root of all evil. Dr. Groseclose describes money as the root of all trade. Trade, meaning all commerce and industry, prospers when the value of money is stable, calculable, when cost-price relationships can be seen clearly, depended on, risked in—when, in other words, money serves not only as a medium of exchange but as a lasting store of value and a yardstick of economic measurement.

The courses of money and trade, accordingly, are intermingled and highly interdependent. Money makes possible the fantastically complex system of international trade, transcending national borders. A Chinese miner wrests a handful of cassiterite from the alluvial deposits of Malaya to be smelted into tin in Singapore, which in turn is coated over a thin sheet of steel in Ohio, shipped to Alaska, where as a can labeled in paper manufactured in Canada and financed in Britain, it is used to package a morsel of salmon to be transported to a nitrate worker in Chile.

If any link in the money chain binding this system breaks, men on three continents could be thrown out of work. Thus money oils modern economic society, and therefore its mistreatment can be disastrous.

Certainly the progressive breakdown of Rome, one of many historical cases cited, seems to be tied to the progressive breakdown of the imperial coinage. The denarius issued by Augustus (described as the Roman penny in the New Testament) was, save for a bit of hardening alloy, pure silver. Yet by the time of Nero, who came into power in 54 A.D., the silver content of the denarius had slipped to 94 per cent; by Vitellius, in 68 A.D., to 81 per cent. By the time of Marcus Aurelius, in 161 A.D., it was down to 68 per cent; By Elagabalus, 218 A.D., to 43 per cent; by Alexander Severus, 222 A.D., to 35 per cent; and by Claudius Victorinus in 268 A.D., to 0.02 per cent.

From practically pure silver to practically pure copper—that was the history of the denarius as the Roman economy deteriorated. When Emperor Diocletian assumed office around the turn of the 4th century, the treasury was empty, agriculture prostrate, industry demoralized, foreign trade at a standstill, and in the Eternal City itself little economic activity but a maddened, consuming, almost parasitic speculation.

Diocletian vowed a halt. But like rulers before and after him, in fact right down to the present day, he attacked symptoms and not causes; he attacked sellers, those who presumably set prices, and not those, as he himself, who were bloating the money supply. In 301 A.D. he issued his famous price-fixing decree and in it nicely washed his hands and those of his predecessors of any blame for the spiraling of prices, completely ignoring the enormous expansion of the Roman currency. It was the merchants and other "gougers" who came under the emperor's lash and bloody punishments for infractions of the price-fixing law. Said the decree in part:

> Who is of so hardened a heart and so untouched by a feeling of humanity that he can be unaware, nay that he has not noticed, that in the sale of wares which are exchanged in the market, or dealt with in the daily business of the cities, an exorbitant tendency in prices has spread to such an extent that the unbridled desire of plundering is held in check neither by abundance nor by seasons of plenty.

Yet despite all the blood-letting, prices persisted on their upward flight, now surreptitiously, now openly, soon here and there officially. Finally, after a few years, a disillusioned Diocletian put aside the sham of fixed prices and banished the black market by shelving the decree. *De facto* inflation became *dejure* once more, until the Germans swarmed in and the Roman Empire was no more.

Other inflations, creeping and galloping, are noted—inflations in the Italian city-states, in England, France, Spain, Holland, Denmark, Germany and America.

The emergence of the printing press and central banking was, historically speaking, not calculated to enhance the value of money. Accounts are given of the fate of such famous paper currencies as the French assignat and the American continental and greenback and such famous banks as John Law's Royal Bank of France.

Inflationary roles in the history of central banks, including the Reichsbank, the Bank of England, the Bank of France and the Federal Reserve Bank, are seen in terms of the monetization of the national debt. And the background of President Roosevelt's proclamation of January 31, 1934, officially devaluing the dollar to 59.06 per cent of its former value in gold, is thoroughly reviewed.

Dr. Groseclose makes no bones over his suspicion of managed money. To him, money ideally is not paper but something with a ring to it, something hard and durable, and yellow or silvery-white in appearance.

WILLIAM H. PETERSON

May 22, 1962

THE NEW BEHEMOTHS—
BIG GOVERNMENT . . .
BIG UNIONS

Speaking of Payola

Payola, as everyone realizes, can be applied to a lot more than disc jockeys, and a splendid candidate for its further application is feather-bedding. Paying people for not working is simply a bribe employers have to pay powerful unions for the privilege of getting any workers or any labor peace.

The issue is important in the railroads' contract disputes; it is also emerging as a major issue in forthcoming negotiations between trucking firms and Mr. Hoffa's Teamsters. Here are some of the practices, as reported in this newspaper the other day, which the companies are finding it increasingly difficult if not impossible to continue living with:

Paying drivers nine hours' wages for six hours' work. Paying drivers additional wages for other work done during the minimum driving period. Paying drivers for the miles on an old route even when they are actually traveling a shorter route.

Thanks to such deals, one carrier figures its drivers get some 6,000 hours—more than $15,000—of unearned wages a month, or about 12 per cent of the monthly wage bill for drivers. In addition to Teamsters' payola, there is the business of paying four dock workers to unload trailers that two could easily handle.

Such arrangements, paralleled in greater or lesser degree in numerous industries, are obviously building high-cost rigidities into the American economic structure. They are therefore a direct threat to the greater economic growth so many politicians claim to want.

Essentially, however, the practices represent a moral problem. It is useless to appeal to the conscience of a Hoffa. But this growing feather-bedding, payola, bribery or whatever you want to call it ought to begin weighing on the conscience of Congress, for Congress alone has the power to restrain the union power from which immorality inevitably flows.

JOSEPH E. EVANS

April 13, 1960

"*If the mess is ever cleaned up here, you know who will do it.*"

The Public Be Damned

It was a long time ago that one of our leading tycoons, questioned about the public interest in a private decision he had made, was quoted as saying, "The public be damned."

Nonetheless, the phrase has passed into history as a symbol of arrogance and ruthlessness on the part of private power over the public weal. It is usually encountered in school books under a Nast cartoon portraying the stereotyped "robber baron" of the turn of the century.

Yet the Goulds, the Fisks, the Vanderbilts, the Rockefellers and all the rest had in their day not so much power all combined as one or two men each now holds in their little fingers. And just the other day, one of these men, Jimmy Hoffa, told us how he might use that power, though he later promised not to use it right now.

Mr. Hoffa, the durable boss of the Teamsters' Union, envisioned one solitary strike throughout the United States to tie up all the employers of the nation at one time. And his threat was given a rousing endorsement by William Bradley, president of the International Longshoremen's Union.

Now the cause of all this is the fact that the Congress of the United States is considering legislation to regulate labor unions. In one much-discussed bill the regulation is so mild it would hardly affect Mr. Hoffa's power at all; even in another form it would seek only to apply to the conduct of some labor unions the same legal restrictions, such as the anti-trust laws, that apply to other types of economic organizations of people, such as shareholders in a business.

But Mr. Hoffa disapproves. So does Mr. Bradley. Disapproving, they are prepared to show employers a thing or two. And the Congress. And the public. For a general strike is a strike against everybody, big employers, little employers, housewives and employees everywhere who may not share the Hoffa views but who are put out of work just the same.

Technically speaking, the Messrs. Hoffa and Bradley may not be able to order the steelworkers or the bakery workers not to work. But they can order the longshoremen not to load cargo and the truck drivers not to carry it, and when the members do as they are told it will not be long before there is no steel in the shops and no bread in the stores.

Now the disturbing part of all this is that under our present laws no one can say "nay" to the Messrs. Hoffa and Bradley. Or to Mr. Mc-Donald if he wants to shut down all the steel mills. Or to Mr. Reuther if he wants to shut down all the auto factories.

And the shocking part of it is that the public has not only let this power grow but seems to be apathetic about its continuance. People can get excited when some labor official, as many have, dips his hand in the union till or has somebody knocked in the head. Very few show concern about the power of unions to knock the country in the head.

Perhaps it's just one of those cases where people ignore a threat until it becomes a real disaster; a *Mein Kampf* always seems too arrogantly fantastic to be true. If so, no one ought to be surprised if one day a Jimmy Hoffa says "the public be damned"—and the public finds that it is.

VERMONT ROYSTER

May 21, 1959

Freight Train Featherbedding

ABOARD "RED BALL 67"—Wheels clacking over the rails, the big Missouri Pacific Railroad diesel locomotive heads south from Dupo, Illinois, dragging 111 boxcars, flat cars and piggy-backs. At speeds up to 60 miles an hour, the freight train styled "Red Ball 67" heads for San Antonio, 948 miles and 32 hours away.

Affecting every minute of the freight haul, and each one like it on Mopac tracks, are sets of work rules and labor agreements that for the most part are unchanged in years. The two paradoxical concepts—the modern diesel locomotive and outmoded labor and work agreements largely dating from the era of steam power—have spawned much of the "featherbedding" that is at the root of the threatened railway strike.

Before "Red Ball 67" reaches San Antonio, 37 men in seven different crews will be aboard to run it, for distances ranging from 90 to 191 miles. The railroad believes many fewer are required, and is specifically asking changes in the work rules that would have six crews totaling 24 men running this train.

The 37 men will earn different sums individually, but they will collect a total of $1,103. If, as the railroads claim and the railroad workers officially deny, 37 men are dividing the wages of 24, economic waste is evident. If, as the railways hope, such waste were eliminated, there would be a substantial easement of the carriers' fiscal pinch. Presumably there would be more pay for the surviving workers. An average engineer in Mopac's freight service draws about $8,800 a year, a brakeman $7,700.

Specifically, the railroads would like to do away with three main things which constitute "featherbedding" in their view. They estimate the saving at some $500 million annually. But for a close-up look at these practices in action, and at the situations which surround them, ride along in the cab of Engine 374, the first of four diesel units generating 6,400 horsepower, as "Red Ball 67" roars out of Illinois through Missouri and Arkansas into Texas.

Meet white-thatched Joseph Love sitting tall in the engineer's seat on the right side of the functional but comfortable cab. He will be at the controls for the first 191 miles from Dupo to Poplar Bluff and will be on duty for seven hours. But for this he will receive pay for 1.9 days —a situation behind one of the railroads' three major complaints.

This pay-time system also applies to firemen and brakemen. Why do Mr. Love and his other crew members get almost two days' pay for their seven-hour stint?

On the Mopac this "dual basis of pay" system has its origins in 1885 when the railroad and engineers' union signed a one-page agreement that specified a run of 100 miles, or ten hours' work, as a "day's" labor. In 1885 it was a feat for a freight train to travel 100 miles in anything like ten hours; physical labor was hard, some engines were still fired by wood. The only real change in this system of computing a day's work came in 1916 with Congressional law requiring an eight-hour day.

By contrast, today's diesel is nearly as automatic as the family auto. In his enclosed, heated compartment, Mr. Love has five controls—a throttle, two air brakes, a drive-wheel sander plus the dead-man's pedal that will stop the train if he lifts his foot from it.

By 1922, the engineman that had a hard time making 100 miles in 10 hours was traveling the distance in 6 hours and 35 minutes to get his day's pay. It took Mr. Love 4 hours and 35 minutes of running time, with most of the rest of his seven hours on the job gathering additional fringe payments. So what the railroads want to do is boost the mileage for a day's work to 160 and get some of the time benefits from the more efficient diesel equipment.

Naturally, Mr. Love doesn't like the prospect of a pay cut which he figures at about one-third if the railroad gets its way. "These diesels are fine," he declares as his train thunders through the night, "but we didn't ask for them so there is no reason why we have to take a pay cut because they go faster."

But diesels not only go faster; they have no steam boilers to fire or water to tend. If the railroads seek a saving from the one, what about the other?

Meet Fireman D. R. McCord, nattily attired in highly polished black leather shoes and pink and gray sports shirt as he climbs into his seat and spreads a clean gray cloth to spare his dark blue slacks. In another of their major complaints, the railroads say they must pay unneeded personnel, including firemen on diesels who are all but useless. The carriers want to abolish the fireman's job on diesels at an annual saving of $230 million of the $500 million.

Mr. McCord is one of eight firemen who share this particular run of "Red Ball 67"; his tour of duty is some 146 miles from Little Rock to Texarkana. Just what does he do? Like the others, he sits on the left-hand side of the cab, peering ahead and calling out the signals along the right of way to the engineer who, of course, is also peering ahead. Mr. McCord has no controls on his side of the cab, except for a heater and windshield wiper. When the train rounds a curve bending leftward, he leans out of the side window and looks back along the train for signs of smoking brakes or hot boxes at the wheels of the freight cars. In addition, he usually makes two or three routine checks of the engine compartment, taking four to ten minutes. There he checks fuel injection gauges on each 12-cylinder engine, indicators which show oil, fuel and air pressure, and large six by four-foot panels of relay switches.

Mr. McCord's union, the Brotherhood of Locomotive Firemen and Enginemen, says that the fireman, while he may appear to be doing little, is thus actually performing a vital safety function. In addition, he can take over for the engineer if need be. The union likens the fireman to a copilot on an airliner (copilots help the plane captain cope with several hundred instruments, assist with engine control on some planes, make some of the landings and takeoffs and are qualified to replace the captain); if something happens to "Red Ball 67's" engineer, the "dead man's" pedal can of course stop the locomotive.

And on this run Mr. McCord does face an emergency, the only one of the eight firemen to do so. Crossing the Arkansas River and tackling a long upgrade, cab warning lights and bells set up a clatter. Mr. McCord scampers to the engine room and the noise stops. He returns, shucking his soiled gloves, and reports: "The automatic shuttle valve on the air cooler on the engine in the first unit stuck. I put it on manual."

Suppose Mr. McCord hadn't been there? Engineer O. D. Whitsell says he would have had to stop the train, go back and find the trouble and fix it. Since the train would have had to halt on a grade, he says a pusher engine would have been needed to get the freight up the hill and some 30 minutes would have been lost. The company says Mr.

Whitsell properly should proceed to the top of the grade, halt, make the adjustments and proceed.

What does Mr. McCord himself have to say about firemen on diesels? Shoving his light gray cap back on his head, he comments: "We'd have lost 30 minutes if I hadn't been aboard—you have to be an electrician, mechanic and general handyman to be a fireman. A lot of the old engineers, who learned their job on the steam locomotive, don't know the diesel and they need a fireman." Mr. McCord, after 16 years with Mopac, has been officially promoted to engineer, but rigid seniority requirements will probably prevent him from becoming one for another five years.

This sort of rigidity doesn't particularly bother Mr. McCord but other rigidities in railroading bother railroad managements plenty. And these are the third big area of "featherbedding" they seek to abolish.

In this area are an array of payments for fringe services railroaders render, largely in connection with their main job of running "Red Ball 67."

Meet J. D. Mitchner, engineer on the run from Poplar Bluff to Little Rock. He had $4.88 added to his paycheck for 1½ hours of time added to his 4½ hours' running time for "hostling."

This task dates back to the 1880s (the term originally concerned caring for horses at inns) and the language in Mopac's contract with the union dates from 1885. The work consists of bringing the engine from the roundhouse to the freight train it's to haul. Engineer Love also collected such a fee as part of his 1.9 days' work. Many engineers and firemen do, though at some terminals there are special crews assigned to the job.

"Red Ball 67's" crew received another type of special payment when it halted at Newport, Arkansas. It cut a car of potatoes out of the train and each crewman earned 47 cents. There were also payments for delay in leaving terminals, in the case of Mr. Love's run due to a faulty brake. At the end of "Red Ball 67's" journey, engineer E. B. Smith collected ten minutes' special pay for moving half his train to an adjoining track.

And special state rules and laws added to the featherbedding load carried, along with crated Rambler cars, auto parts and a long list of merchandise, by "Red Ball 67."

In Texas, the engineers received 52¾ cents at each of three crew-change stops for inspecting the engine—though no inspection was evident to the traveler at the two stops where he disembarked with the engineer. All across Arkansas the crew was swelled from five men to six; an extra brakeman must be carried because of the state's "full crew" law, even though there is almost nothing for him to do.

There are other similar rules by agreement between the railroad and union. For example, on the "long" 191-mile run from Dupo to Poplar Bluffs, firemen must be changed—so "Red Ball 67" had eight different firemen by the time it reached the end of its trip, but only seven different engineers. But because 191 miles is considered a long run, the engineer and crew, except the fireman, were served a free lunch of two sandwiches, pie and coffee.

These then are samples of what the railroads call "featherbedding," as seen on one trip on "Red Ball 67." In their drive to change the basic time-distance pay system, eliminate such "unnecessary" personnel as firemen, and eliminate arbitrary and special payments like those for "hostling," they face the task of changing things that have grown up over the history of railroading under widely differing conditions.

FRED STANNARD, JR.

December 21, 1959

LEGAL NOTE

The small print usually means you'd better read it.

—F. P. JONES

How Not to Run a Railroad

Time was when men went on strike for higher wages. Nowadays, as often as not, unions call strikes in order to tell management what to do.

Consider the demands of Mr. Michael Quill's Transport Workers Union and System Federation 152 of the International Association of Machinists. These two unions have shut down the Pennsylvania Railroad, the nation's largest, grossly inconveniencing scores of thousands of riders in 13 states, the District of Columbia and the New York City metropolitan area.

The unions would, to be sure, like higher wages, but in three years of "bargaining" never got around to discussing this matter; the strike came on other issues.

Issues like this: Mr. Quill's TWU demands a so-called scope rule that would define jobs in such a way as to diminish the company's flexibility in job assignments. The company says further concessions of this sort would force it to support unneeded jobs and men and so run it into the red.

Mr. Quill also demands, among a lot of other things, a ban on the letting of contracts by the road to outside concerns for maintenance and construction work. Thus the union is trying to tell the company it cannot sell or lease properties, consolidate or coordinate with another railroad, or rent equipment unless the union does all the maintenance work.

No one has to accept the company's word that the demands are wildly out of line. These and other issues were submitted to a neutral referee, whose findings were accepted by the company and rejected by both unions. They were also submitted to a Presidential fact-finding board; it made the same recommendations, which the company accepted and the unions rejected.

Wiser union leaders of an earlier time knew it was bad business for labor to try to take over managerial functions; a union's job, they figured, is higher wages. The soundness of that approach is emphasized in this strike. For, considering the disastrous managerial notions of Mr. Quill, the country can be thankful that so far, at least, he and his friends have not been running the railroads.

JOSEPH E. EVANS

September 6, 1960

How to Run a Monopoly

Nearly two decades ago, the late Professor Henry Simons warned that the growing power of labor unions was a danger to everyone, even a threat to our form of government.

That was strong talk, then as now, but the words were not those of an anti-labor polemicist. Professor Simons, a highly respected University of Chicago economist, was merely considering unionism in terms of an old-fashioned liberal's principles of freedom and equality. On that basis, his quarrel was not with unionism itself but with the monopoly power explicitly granted unions by Congress.

Simons' warning is worth recalling now as the Government intervenes increasingly in the private economy to try to deal with some of the results of union monopoly power. What are these results? First, how have the workers themselves been affected?

Unions take greatest pride in the fact that their power has enabled them to push up wage levels in most industries, often on a basis of industry-wide equality. But this has not been an unalloyed blessing for workers.

To some extent business has offset higher labor costs by raising prices. But business, unlike unions, is constantly exposed to competition and thus cannot always pass along higher costs in its prices. So businessmen, to stay in business, have been forced to find new ways to turn out more goods with fewer workers. This has not only limited their demand for labor but changed it; the unskilled employee finds fewer and fewer places in modern industry.

To strengthen their monopoly power, unions have introduced the element of compulsion. Any good monopolist knows that a prime need is control of product, in this case workers' services. So workers are forced to join unions, to pay initiation fees, to pay dues—if they want to hold on to their jobs.

To control his product effectively, the monopolist must avoid change, for change may shake his grip on a market. Thus unions, with their stress on seniority, develop a built-in bias toward older workers. Labor organizations lose interest in bringing in younger workers as members or in training them in apprenticeship programs.

The effective labor monopolist not only must control the workers themselves but also their work. So the unions draw up complex work rules, often specifying just how much a worker can do in an hour or a day. Any worker who exceeds those limits may run the risk of union-imposed fines.

This leveling tendency benefits the incompetent and the indolent, who earn more than they would if they were offering their services in a system of free competition. But it penalizes the workers who are capable and industrious.

All of this leads to real troubles for the economy. Workers are constrained from switching from a declining industry to an expanding one. "Featherbedding" work rules make it difficult for business to benefit from advancing technology. New businesses, which could provide jobs for some of the unemployed, are frozen out by inability to meet union-imposed standards. Higher prices resulting from rising labor costs are making it increasingly difficult for American businessmen to compete abroad.

Moreover, unions have acquired the capacity to put whole segments of our economy out of action, with resulting damage to the nation. Union leaders at the flick of a finger can shut down the steel industry, the auto companies, the railroads, the airlines.

The dangers of all this are apparent even to our pro-union Administration, for otherwise it would not feel compelled to step in between companies and unions in an increasing number of industries. In steel, in railroads, in airlines, it has tried to deal with union monopoly power by "suggesting" contract terms and putting pressure on unions, as well as companies, to accept them.

A sounder approach would be to subject unions to the same kind of competitive pressures that confront other groups. For, as Professor Simons warned 18 years ago: "A community that fails to preserve the discipline of competition exposes itself to the discipline of absolute authority."

By now, this prospect should be worrying union officials as much as it does businessmen.

LINDLEY H. CLARK, JR.

July 16, 1962

"If they ever cut his work week to twenty hours, I'll go out of my mind."

Hoehengefahrenzulageausfallsentschaedigung

Americans are abundantly familiar with featherbedding, short work weeks and other devices for getting money without really trying. But it may be some European unions are more progressive.

The UPI reports from Austria that workers on Europe's highest expressway bridge are getting various pay premiums, such as for danger and for working in a high place. That's all right, but it seems the workers at the base of the bridge felt cheated.

So they demanded, and what is more they got, a "compensation for the lack of danger from working in high places premium," or as we say in German, a *Hoehengefahrenzulageausfallsentschaedigung*.

We are sure their American brethren won't want to miss that one, with all its endless applications. And we doubt that even language will prove an unbridgeable barrier.

JOSEPH E. EVANS

December 4, 1962

Union Warning

As a young economist for the United Steelworkers of America in the thirties and the early forties, Harold J. Ruttenberg was a self-confessed enemy of the rich.

He wanted to make them pay through the nose for what they had presumably done to keep the steelworker in chains before there was any CIO to free him.

As time went by, Mr. Ruttenberg changed his status. He got a wider vision of things working for the War Production Board in 1944 and 1945. After the war he blossomed out as a steelmaster on his own account, running the Portsmouth Steel Company for Cyrus Eaton. Quitting that job with some money in his pocket, he acquired a business of his own, the Stardrill-Keystone Company, an outfit which makes well-drilling equipment for sale in countries as far away as Iran and Indonesia.

All of this might be of little moment in a fluid country that binds no man to his past. But Mr. Ruttenberg believed so fervently in the education which he had absorbed from his variegated experience that he decided a year or two ago to sell out his drill-rig business to get time to finish a book that was gnawing at his mind. Published as *Self-Developing America*, the book is remarkable not for its views on America's "mission" in the world (Mr. Ruttenberg has an all-too-touching faith in foreign giveaways, which he dignifies by the name of "feedbacks"), but for its views on the place of unions in modern industrial society.

To his old Steelworker friends, it may well seem that Mr. Ruttenberg has "sold out" in his refusal to back the bargaining tactics of the present leadership of the steel union. But this is certainly not the case: as a tremendously impassioned sermon, *Self-Developing America* is sharply critical of people on both sides of the bargaining fence. He still argues that the Steelworkers were justified in the big strikes of the thirties; after all, he says, it sometimes takes *force majeure* to remind an entrenched interest of its "essential humanity." Using a special lingo of his own, Mr. Ruttenberg speaks of the enforced "humanation" of Big Ownership, which may seem something of a euphemism when one recalls such things as union violence in the days of the Flint, Michigan, sit-ins. But the union aims of the thirties, so Mr. Ruttenberg insists, are not germane to the sixties—and *Self-Developing America* warns the Steelworkers Union that the shoe is now on the other foot. It is the leadership of the union that now needs to be reminded of its own humanity.

What the union has done, says Mr. Ruttenberg, is to forget that the "cow" (i.e., the steel industry) must be fed before she can be milked. From 1956 to 1959, "steelworkers enjoyed the special privilege of having their wages insulated against the erosion of higher living costs. . . . Each time wage increases not justified by productivity were followed by price rises, the union was robbing those Americans who live on fixed incomes—exploiting them."

Even when he was a union economist Mr. Ruttenberg had a special interest in productivity. He had talks with the late Philip Murray, first head of the steel union, on the possibility of linking wage increases to a productivity index. But Murray, as Ruttenberg recalls it, thought it was "premature" to champion any such linkage.

Mr. Ruttenberg is both glad and sorry to see that steel management, in suggesting that wage increases be measured by productivity, has gotten ahead of the Steelworkers in "anticipating" the future. By refusing to accept a non-inflationary settlement of differences in the 1959–60 strike, the steel union obviously won its battle. But, says Mr. Ruttenberg, steel management, in losing the battle, has very probably won the war. The consuming public, he says, will not put up with another inflationary wage agreement in 1962. Henceforward, productivity will control the course of collective bargaining no matter what political party is in possession of the White House.

As part of his "co-development" thesis, however, Mr. Ruttenberg turns once again to lecture management. It must, he says, be prepared to grant an annual wage wherever it is practicable. Since people eat 52 weeks in the year, they must have an income to cover each one of those weeks. Management might very well argue that the annual wage, in addition to being uneconomical, is unnecessary as long as there are unemployment insurance benefits to which industry contributes. But Mr. Ruttenberg is not convinced. Moreover, he thinks the union leaders can make the annual wage palatable to management by some concessions on their own.

The annual wage, so Mr. Ruttenberg reminds the union leaders, is not compatible with time-and-one-half for overtime. And in return for a guarantee of 52 paychecks a year, union men must inevitably take on a responsibility for the continued solvency and profitability of their employers.

If they want the annual wage, "labor leaders will have to roll up their sleeves and go back to work. They will have to go out and teach their union members that the employer is not a cow to be milked dry, but a humble goose who has to be fed with hard, steady and better labor to produce eatable eggs."

In the forties another Steelworkers Union economist, Joseph Scanlon, quit Pittsburgh to take a job at the Massachusetts Institute of Technology, where he gave courses in methods of encouraging union-management cooperation in cost-cutting. Scanlon had despaired of getting his own program of productivity-sharing accepted by his union. Harold Ruttenberg shows no such despair; he thinks he has the future on his side.

While his precise formulations may not be the ones that are finally adopted in the course of future collective bargaining, Mr. Ruttenberg's book has a hard core of common sense. And it is of special interest owing to its source, for Mr. Ruttenberg knows what it is like to sit on each side of the bargaining table.

JOHN CHAMBERLAIN

December 22, 1960

Socialism in the Sky

If along about the turn of the century some dreamers had come forward with a plan to put one of these newfangled telephones in every home and hook together every city and hamlet, they might well have concluded that this was beyond the resources of private industry.

After all, as late as 1880 there were only 34,000 miles of telephone wires on the whole continent. There were a host of little telephone companies, many using different kinds of equipment. Some cities had two or more telephone companies that couldn't connect. Nowhere in sight was there the capital necessary, nor the organization, to carry out such a fantastic dream.

Only government itself, so it might have seemed, could take on a job of such magnitude in money and planning. Indeed, in a great many countries the job was taken on by governments and, to this very day, the telephone systems are run by the government, like the postal services.

But fortunately this country lagged behind the rest of the world in socialistic economics; our telephone system was allowed to grow in free soil. And it would be laboring the obvious to point out that here the dream has not only come true but has been surpassed. The contrast between our phone system and those operated by governments is a dramatic one to anybody who has spent even a few vacation weeks abroad.

Yet, curiously, we are being told now that further expansion of this communications system, using relays in the sky, is too formidable a job for private enterprise. Its magnitude in money, planning and effort is so great that we must have it done by government.

Thus there is a concerted campaign under way in Washington to get President Kennedy to reverse his very wise decision in favor of private development of the satellite system for intercontinental communications. All manner of arguments are marshaled. At one and the same time it's said private industry would create a great monopolistic combine and that it's too big for private industry.

Most of these arguments are window-dressing. Private capital is not lacking to build and operate a communications satellite; nor does it involve insurmountable operating difficulties. As for the "combine" threat, there are workable proposals to make it a cooperative effort of many companies, large and small, with adequate regulatory safeguards to protect the public interest.

What has actually happened is that in socialistic economic philosophy Washington is no longer laggard. As in the public power arguments, the bias is simply that such enterprises "ought" to be Government enterprises just because they "ought." That being the basic attitude, the so-called practical arguments are made to fit the bias.

For instance, it's said there will be a "fatal delay" in waiting for private enterprise. But why is there any delay at all? Simply because government delays final authorization. Again, if it's pointed out that the danger of a combine is resolved by having many participating companies, the reply is that this opens a "Pandora's box"; it would "splinter" ownership. How is anyone to grapple with such slippery reasoning?

There is only one way. That is for the President to realize that such arguments are irrelevant, and to stick by his original decision because it is the right one.

The point here is not merely that private enterprise capital will save the Federal Government large sums of tax money, though that is no small consideration. It is, rather, that a private system will simply give us a better communications system, more economically operated by the very demands of making a private profit and more efficiently operated by the absolute necessity of satisfying the customers.

If you doubt which system is the better—government or private—pick up the telephone, phone your local postmaster and ask for more mail service. And see how far you get.

VERMONT ROYSTER

September 13, 1961

*"While we're at it, how about medical care
for the middle-aged?"*

A Matter of Growth

A friend of ours reports that when the Federal Government moved from Philadelphia to Washington in 1800, the jaunt was by stage-coach.

It didn't take a great many stagecoaches, either. According to some estimates, the whole Federal Government in those days employed only about 150 civilians.

Matters are very different now; for example, if the Federal Government decided to move back to Philadelphia and locate all its scattered employees in the City of Brotherly Love, it would take the railroads some time to move them; today the civilian employees number about 2,387,000.

Now, before somebody jumps on us as a 19th-century reactionary who would like to see all Federal employees tossed off the payroll, we want to say that we know very well that the country is bigger and richer than it was in 1800 and that furthermore a population of 180 million people needs more Federal employees than an 1800 population of 5.3 million could possibly need.

But it's the ratio of growth that interests us, and we think it might interest you, too.

And the ratio shows that while the number of people has increased about 34 times since 1800, the number of Federal employees has increased nearly 18,000 times.

A Merry Christmas, one and all.

WILLIAM H. FITZPATRICK

December 22, 1959

Strange Twist to an Old Dream

One of the self-evident truths that led to this country's founding is the right of every man to pursue his happiness in his own way so long as it doesn't wrong his neighbors.

And one of the ways happiness was pursued was to try to lay aside enough so that, when the evening of his labor neared, a man might rest.

Thus when one reads that 22 farmers in Wisconsin, whose average age is 58, have decided to retire it reads like the old American dream come true.

Well, perhaps, but with a twist. These 22 farmers, this newspaper reported, retired by retiring their land in the Government soil bank conservation reserve program. This means that nothing can be grown on the land and that the farmers will get paid for not working it. One farmer will receive, over a 10-year period, $30,000 for taking his 160 acres out of production. Another explains why he's retiring: "The money will come in steady every year. It won't ever freeze, a drought won't hurt it and you don't have to work to get it."

That sounds a little different from what the Founders had in mind. They would have considered it strange for any able-bodied man to be supported by other men, and they would have considered it outrageous for anybody to suggest that the taxpayers, through Government, should do so.

But troubles like the farm program, outrageous as they are, can't be blamed on all farmers or on just farmers; the farm problem is only chief witness to a national trend. There are lots of other people who would like to have the Government pursue their happiness for them so that they don't "have to work to get it."

Government, though, cannot guarantee happiness. And the country would be far better off if it came again to see what was once a self-evident truth—that pursuit of happiness meant a man's right to seek it and not a Government responsibility to provide it. When we come to see that, we will see also what a strange twist has been given the old American dream.

WILLIAM H. FITZPATRICK

April 10, 1959

Art and Freedom

In recent years, especially since World War II, there has been a cultural upsurge in the United States of extraordinary proportions, with seemingly the majority of the populace, if not painting, writing or performing, at least paying close heed to those who do.

This burgeoning of artistic interest, in fact, has moved Secretary of Labor Goldberg to note: "America has some 5,000 community theaters—more theaters than radio and television stations. There are better than 500 opera-producing groups—seven times as many as 15 years ago. Symphony orchestras now total 1,100—twice as many as only 10 years ago, and 50 in the suburbs of Los Angeles alone. . . . An era of unequaled achievement may well be upon us."

Strangely, in the face of this partial listing of America's cultural statistics, Mr. Goldberg chooses to enter a plea for Federal aid to the arts, reasoning that such tax support is required exactly because the arts have shown such tremendous vitality. The Secretary believes that since some of the performing arts groups are having a difficult time making ends meet, it follows as the night the day that Washington must provide the solution.

Well, for 30 years now, looking to Washington for answers to all problems has been a reflex action for some people. But even putting philosophy aside, it's hard to see how the arts can be improved by tying them to politics.

The off-Broadway theater, for instance, has never been more active and, while the quality of the productions may not always suggest genius at work, it's unlikely that the mere act of pouring in Federal funds would make a turkey look any less like a big fat bird.

And the same is true for the symphony orchestras and opera companies throughout the nation. Certainly they would all enjoy having more money to work with, but thus far they've not only gotten along very well but their numbers, as Mr. Goldberg points out, are constantly increasing. Private and municipal monies have succeeded in supporting the performing arts to the advantage of hundreds of communities, and they have proven that recourse to the Federal Treasury is totally unnecessary.

This is not to say that some artistic groups don't have trouble balancing their finances. But what's the reason for these tight budgets? Mr. Goldberg might find one answer in the weird work rules which unions, especially the musicians', have used to hobble the performing arts.

These rules include paying musicians who don't play, forcing the hiring of more performers than are needed, and generally keeping the management of performing groups handcuffed by nuisance rules and high labor costs. It is remarkable that such groups can thrive at all.

But more importantly, we should remember the one work rule which art itself rightly demands. Art must function in an atmosphere of unquestioned freedom if it is even to fulfill Tolstoy's basic definition as "a human activity having for its purpose the transmission to others of the highest and best feelings to which men have risen."

The Federal obligation is quite the opposite. The Government, if it is to be responsible for its actions, must assure itself that Treasury money is being spent in a Federally approved fashion. Thus the artist could not escape accountability to Washington.

Indeed, Mr. Goldberg himself cites the danger of Government manipulation of the arts: "The issue of Federal support for the arts immediately raises problems. Many persons oppose Federal support on grounds that it will inevitably lead to political interference. This is by no means an argument to be dismissed. . . . In an age in which a third of the globe languishes under the pathetic banalities of 'Socialist realism,' let no one suppose that political control of the arts cannot be achieved."

With the risks of political involvement in the arts so great, then, and so unnecessary, the plea for Federal subsidies is certainly a strange one.

Art, whatever else it may be, is a grace of life that springs solely from whatever resources a man may have within himself. And that is something no Government can instill.

EDWIN A. ROBERTS, JR.

December 21, 1961

Chronic Distress

In the days when Charles Dow was editor of this newspaper, at the turn of the century, Leadville, Colorado, was a boom town. When the present editor visited it a few years ago it was a quiet, pleasant place living mostly in the past.

In the years between, Leadville had often been a distressed area with chronic unemployment as the lead mines which made it boom closed down. It was not unique in this.

All across the country there are other towns and whole areas which have had their days of distress as the economic pattern of the country changed. When we were young, there were many such areas in the South; only recently have some of the New England states begun to emerge from their own unhappy times.

Some of the old boom towns have disappeared entirely. Some have settled down to a different gait as people moved away to other opportunities. Some towns and areas, as in the South and in New

England, have revitalized themselves by finding new bases for prosperity. One way or another, the people have made their adjustment to change.

But we can't help wondering what would have happened if there had been a commission of the Government, along about the turn of the century, to "help out" these distressed areas, such as the commission appointed the other day by President-elect Kennedy. For the temptation of a Government commission to look into the problems of distressed localities is to "do something" to keep things as they were. To subsidize the lead mines, or the coal mines, or the factories, or the farms, so that people will not have to move away or the area change.

Well, perhaps if the Federal Government had stepped in fifty years ago some of those vanished towns would still be with us, still threatening to relapse again into chronic unemployment if the supporting hand of Government were removed. Other areas, perhaps, would also be thriving beyond their present state from the influx of Government money, drawn from taxpayers elsewhere in the country.

But none, we feel sure, would have made the adjustment to changing times. Even those areas once more booming would not have felt the spur of fortune to do what they did do, being sheltered by the hovering commission of the Federal Government.

There is nothing, we suppose, that more nags at the kindness of men than the plight of an area seemingly fallen into chronic distress. But that relief is no kindness which relieves men of the necessity for moving on, and for changing, and so makes their distress truly chronic.

VERMONT ROYSTER

December 7, 1960

Benicia's Rebound

BENICIA, CALIFORNIA—"When I first heard the news I thought we were ruined," recalls gravelly voiced James Lemos, mayor of this town of 6,300 persons. "Now I think it was a blessing in disguise."

The news that has swayed Mr. Lemos' sentiments so sharply has had serious repercussions not only in this small town but in several other communities around the country. It was the announcement slightly more than a year ago by the Defense Department that 52 domestic military establishments in 25 states would be closed or curtailed.

While most taxpayers may have applauded the cost-cutting move, the Pentagon was immediately stormed by outraged citizens from many of the affected communities who protested the loss of vital payrolls. Certainly the cries of anguish were strong from Benicia. It faced the "phase out" over three years of the only sizable "industry" it has, the Army's big Benicia arsenal. But the Pentagon stuck by its order; indeed, defense officials have made many other communities uneasy by warning that additional defense facilities are being eyed for disposal.

So the efforts by Benicia to cope with its potential economic catastrophe, as well as its newly found optimism, perhaps assume more than limited interest.

Tucked away along a languid stream which feeds the north end of San Francisco Bay, Benicia is probably one of the more likely candidates that could be found to become a ghost town. A cluster of squat, shabby buildings form Main Street's business district for four blocks, then the road turns to dirt among boarded-up shacks at the water front. Along tree-lined side streets, paint peels from many houses which stand in weed-filled lots.

Nothing much has bothered Benicia's torpor for a long time, say residents. The word that the arsenal would be closed was perhaps the first shock the town has experienced since the heady days of 1853 when it became the state capital—only to see the government move on to Sacramento a year later.

Loss of a facility like the Army arsenal would be no small thing for any community, much less little Benicia. Dozens of machine shops, warehouses and other facilities stretch out along the Army's 2,200-acre preserve. In recent years the arsenal has provided steady employment for 2,300 workers. It has poured $21 million a year into the region's economy in payroll and purchases. Now employment has dropped to 1,700. By June 30, it is slated to fall to 1,200. By 1964 the Army will be gone for good.

By then, though, Benicia is confident the old arsenal will be humming with new industry. And in cooperation with some private developers the town has worked out a plan to bring about its hopes.

After receiving assurances from the Government that the town will get first crack when the arsenal is put up for sale, local officials started scratching around for capital. Their search led them to Stanley Hiller and Joseph Coney, San Francisco real estate developers. A deal was made.

Messrs. Hiller and Coney have agreed to give the town funds to buy the arsenal. In return, the town has agreed to lease the arsenal property to the developers for 50 years for an annual sum equal to the tax rate on the land. The developers will then set about to convert the arsenal into an industrial park, with the town retaining a veto over the type of industry that may be established. It's hoped that industry can be phased in at the arsenal, perhaps by next year, while the Army phases out. The military says it would be willing to turn over its facilities piecemeal.

"It looks as though we can do a job on this property," enthuses Mr. Coney. "We'll have the Army's deep-water wharf at the site and there are any number of possible industries that could be located here."

An elderly Benicia merchant remarks: "We've lain dormant for a long time, but now we're going to go."

To be sure, there are uncertainties which could still disrupt Benicia's big plans. Most importantly, the Government has yet to set a price on the arsenal; the General Services Administration is just starting an appraisal. Messrs. Hiller and Coney understandably remain mum on the price they would be willing to pay. The developers can back out of their contract with Benicia if they consider the price too high.

But even if Benicia's attempt to put industry in the arsenal should prove futile, the town has other projects perking. A separate deal has been concluded with Messrs. Hiller and Coney whereby they have purchased 170 acres of water-front land from the city for $75,000. The purchase contract stipulates that industry with an aggregate value of not less than $1 million, employing at least 500 persons, will be placed on this land. And, to the surprise of many townspeople, another firm has purchased some 6,000 acres for residential development in the town environs.

All this has led to talk of boom times in this seemingly tired old town. There's even talk along Main Street of sprucing up the business district. "Some people laugh at me but I think we will have a population of 60,000 here in 10 years," declares John A. Bohn, a local lawyer.

If things now look bright for Benicia, it doesn't mean the turn for the better came without pain.

For six months the town stubbornly sought to keep the arsenal to maintain the *status quo*. Employees at the arsenal chipped in $2,400 to send a delegation to Washington to argue the town's case. When that attempt failed, appeals were made to Congressional armed services committees. Only when every door in Washington was closed did the town give up.

Indeed, rancor still runs deep in Benicia over the loss of the arsenal.

Many families have had to move when wage earners were laid off. One long-time resident speaks bitterly of the Pentagon's "cold-blooded" closure order.

Yet many ex-arsenal workers have found employment in near-by towns and have stayed on in Benicia. Those that have left have been replaced by newcomers, possibly lured by generally low home prices within commuting distance of other towns. With an air of wonder, Quentin Babcock, a local real estate man, reports that "there aren't more than six vacancies in town."

This old state capital clearly has a lot of work to do before it transforms itself into a prosperous and diversified industrial city; so far, the new plants are only hopes. But the most important change already has taken place; it's the intangible air of bustling optimism which came when Benicia finally faced up to the loss of its Government payroll and decided to do something about it.

NORMAN C. MILLER, JR.

May 15, 1962

Definitions in Non-English

722.2 Definitions. As used in 722.1 to 722.51 and in all forms and documents in connection therewith, unless the context or subject matter otherwise requires, the following terms shall have the following meanings and the masculine shall include the feminine and neuter genders and the singular shall include the plural number. . . .

That splendid bit of prose is from "Cotton MQ Bulletin 1, Handbook 5-CN (Revision 3)," which itself is but a fragment of the reams of literature the farm planners in Washington pour out for the benefit of farmers' county committees throughout the land. As Mr. Carley explained in an article in this newspaper the other day, these committees are supposed to help the Agriculture Department administer its programs.

It is truly awesome to think of someone, or perhaps a group, actually sitting down to write a non-English passage like that "Definitions" one. It is even more so to contemplate the countless rules, equally confusing, that fill these handbooks. The Department's solicitude for the farmer is so exquisite that he had better not make a move without double-checking the regulations, if he can understand them at all.

If he can't, retribution can be swift and terrible. One farmer, with a bachelor's degree in economics, thought he was following the rules to the letter in planting 315 acres of cotton; the county committee thought so, too. But it turned out his rows should have been 96 inches apart instead of 76 as he had planted them, and now he faces a $16,000 penalty for his egregious error.

In addition, this impenetrable bureaucratic maze provides endless opportunities for deliberate deception. The Billie Sol Estes case has amply demonstrated what can be done with such valuable items as cotton allotments.

Much has been written about the farm program, its cost, waste, scandals, confusions and complexities. But we think these homely examples of bureaucracy at work give an idea not only of its absurdity but of the real meaning of the regimentation Secretary Freeman is so eager to intensify.

That is one definition, at least, that any subsidized farmer can understand.

JOSEPH E. EVANS

August 20, 1962

Effective Bureaucracy

Up until a few days ago, Mrs. Earl Gundrum owned and operated an upstate New York nursing home that had been cited by state officials as "a shining example" of what such an establishment should be.

Explaining why she closed down the home, Mrs. Gundrum declared: "It was just impossible. There were 18 state and Federal agencies putting forms, questions and statistical requests across my desk. Medical reports . . . census figures . . . Social Security . . . unemployment insurance . . . workmen's compensation . . . withholding taxes . . . daily sheets . . . work plans . . . It was just one darn thing after another."

Mrs. Gundrum said the situation had gotten so bad she was often forced to spend 18 hours a day at her desk just handling the government-required paper work covering only 21 patients and 14 employees.

And, while this nursing home was being put out of business by the tangle of bureaucratic red tape, the Federal Government was announcing that several of its departments were hiring hundreds of new employees to administer their still burgeoning thicket of rules and regulations.

Well, this being the trend, we don't blame Mrs. Gundrum a bit. The situation is vexing enough to make anybody lose interest in a nursing home—at least as proprietor.

EDWIN A. ROBERTS, JR.

August 22, 1962

"Colonel, you know *any proposal to cut red tape has to go through channels!"*

The Tangled Growth

The sad story of the Rutland Railway is, among other things, a comment on the difficulties with the Government's present regulation of business. The small Vermont line wants to go out of business, and it's been having a tough time trying to do it.

Rutland was struck back in September of 1961. Three months later, it asked the Interstate Commerce Commission for permission to quit. It took the ICC a full year of mulling before it finally decided that the permission should be granted. But the unions have gone to court in an effort to keep the railroad operating, and the whole wrangle may yet wind up in the Supreme Court.

Doing business, under the Government's rules, can be even harder than stopping. Washington abounds with horrible examples of "regulatory lag" and other ills afflicting the 100-odd independent or semi-independent commissions, boards and agencies, many of which have judicial as well as administrative functions.

A White House study group, after looking into the problem for the past two years, finds that the average ICC time to decide a transportation rate case is one and a half years. The average for the National Labor Relations Board, on an unfair labor charge, is 350 days. The Civil Aeronautics Board has only now finished an airline subsidy proceeding ordered in 1954.

Nor is it only a question of delay. A profusion of vague and confusing laws, subject to strange interpretations by the regulators, leaves the businessman often groping in a legal jungle. There is little uniformity of procedure among the agencies, and there are large questions of fairness. For example, a "black list" circulates among them, containing names of companies to be barred from Federal contracts with no reason given.

All this adds immeasurably to the cost and complexity of doing business in these United States, and the Administration is well aware of it. The worry, as Mr. Kohlmeier reported in this newspaper the other day, is that over-regulation may hold back the whole economy at a time when economic growth is a prized goal.

One official sums it up: "A year's unnecessary delay in a license to build a hydroelectric project or a gas pipeline can have effects all down the line, on constructing, the hiring of operating personnel and ultimately consumers."

So the question is what to do about it, and it is not at all clear that the Administration is taking the best possible tack. In effect it wants Congress to create a super-agency to preside over the others; it would have a chairman, a "board of directors" and an assembly. The hope is that such a setup might be able to bring about procedural reforms leading to less delay and greater equity. And such improvements are indeed devoutly to be desired.

Yet surely the existing troubles themselves point to another approach. The way to deal with the problems caused by over-regulation is to reduce the whole scope of the regulation. Why should business be so minutely controlled that it is under constant harassment no matter what it does? Why should there be scores of official entities in on the act?

Some of these bodies go far back in our history, but a number of them flowered in the thirties, under different economic conditions and attitudes. Then there was widespread suspicion of the American economy as something that had to be tightly controlled if it was to be made to work.

In the intervening years the economy, in war and peace and despite all obstacles, has shown again its tremendous productive power. Today there is much greater realization that sound growth depends not on holding it back but on increasing the opportunities for invest-ment, production and employment.

If much of the prevailing regulatory philosophy and practice is out of tune with the times, then the need is to weed out some of the agencies, make others more responsive to public opinion, and revamp the outmoded laws. Perhaps a super-agency could help, but no one should forget that what is really required is a direct attack on the bureaucratic jungle's tangled growth.

JOSEPH E. EVANS

March 22, 1963

WINDOW ON THE WORLD

Struggling Against History

Other nations have gone through convulsions comparable to South Africa's, but in that country the outlook seems hopeless indeed.

For there, a small white minority, and particularly a small white Afrikaner minority, is struggling to remain supreme over a black majority, and trying to do it on the basis of force. There is no apparent willingness to compromise, to let Bantus develop to the point of sharing economic and political power. Such a struggle is a struggle against the forces of history.

We do not say that the tide which is sweeping independence into Africa and Asia is necessarily good. Indeed, the prospects for real democracy are dim, as some of the newly independent states are already proving; an independent native government can be just as tyrannical as the worst colonial regime, and is likely to be tyrannical when the majority is poor and illiterate.

The point is simply that this nationalist sweep is happening, and at an accelerating rate—who would have believed, a few years ago, that the Belgian Congo would be independent by the summer of 1960? And as a generalization, the white nations or groups that have come out best are those that have made their peace with the realities. Britain's departure from India, and its high esteem in that nation today, is a notable example; in contrast is the mess in Algeria.

In South Africa, of course, there is no external rule; the white minority and the black majority are both natives and that makes it worse, for if the whites are forced out they are forced out of their homeland. It may be possible for the extreme nationalist Afrikaners to hang on for quite a while yet, if they resort to total repression such as the Communists used in Hungary.

But even if they are temperamentally capable of doing that, they will run into still another force—the not so nebulous force of world opinion. It is one of the stupefying ironies of our time that the Communists, whose whole purpose is the destruction of liberty, can be treated like respectable people, while any nation in what is loosely called the West is the object of unlimited abuse when it errs.

Conceivably, the force of nationalism and international opinion will serve to moderate the policies of the white extremists in South Africa, and the United States is not out of line in deploring the violence. But there is a limit to what this or any other country can do. The real tragedy is that the outlook is likely to remain hopeless until the Afrikaners themselves realize that they are struggling against history.

JOSEPH E. EVANS

April 12, 1960

"I concede the election."

Anti-German Bias

BUDAPEST—"When Khrushchev pushes the Berlin button, he is doing the thing which wins him the most support in the satellites. The Germans left a residue of hate here which will last at least through this generation."

So says one West European diplomat here in the capital of Hungary.

That appraisal is supported by a tour of satellite countries. People in Eastern Europe are worried about chances of war over West Berlin. But they endorse any Soviet action that may guarantee a split Germany, or that might reunite the two Germanys into one weak, neutralized country.

Satellite citizens remind you that West Germany has not renounced claims on any of the lands taken from her in World War II settlements. They fear that as a free-world-oriented West Germany grows stronger, it may press not only for reunification of East and West Germany as presently constituted, but for all the old German lands as well.

"Will there be a war?" the porter on the Prague-Budapest express asks a traveler as the car rocks and sways over clicking rails.

"That depends on Mr. Khrushchev," says a visitor.

"No!" the porter retorts. "It depends on the Germans. They are always ready for war."

"And we are ready for them," adds a Polish traveler in the next compartment. He thrusts a hand beneath his shirt to show the religious medal strung around his neck, and adds: "Catholics or Communists, we are together against the Germans."

It is 16 years since the German collapse in World War II. It may seem surprising that the residue of hate for Germany should linger so long here. Then a visitor remembers that even in Britain, which was not occupied by Germans, anti-Teutonic sentiment still is strong in some quarters.

East Europe was not only occupied for a good part of the war, it was systematically looted by Hitler's armies. Hungary, a country which now has a population of about 9.5 million, lost 400,000 to 500,000 people. Poland was literally overrun, cities were destroyed and tens of thousands slaughtered. All through Eastern Europe there are vivid, livid memories of the German occupation.

"Part of my family was murdered by the Germans," one elderly university professor in Budapest says quietly. He adds: "Germans are not popular here."

In Prague, light-haired, broad-shouldered Dr. Miroslav Uxa, 47, a physician now working under Czechoslovakia's socialized medical system, avoids any political discussion as he sits in his plain office, except to say he is a non-Communist. But he grows articulate on the topic of Germany.

"I was studying medicine at the University of Prague when the Germans closed the university in 1939. Only those students who were German could go on to school and they had to go to Germany to complete their educations."

Dr. Uxa spent six years in a factory, working in the plant safety department, before he could pick up his education. Now he regards Germans with bitterness.

In all the satellite countries, Communist governments constantly fan this anti-German feeling with heavy doses of propaganda. As the Berlin situation has heated up, this propaganda has mounted.

In Czechoslovakia, the government recently published alleged secret Nazi documents covering a ruthless German policy in Eastern Europe from 1939 to 1945. Whether or not the publication is accurate, the fact remains that many people in the satellites are willing to believe the worst about the Germans.

East Germany, which of course is composed of Germans too, is accepted by some as a satellite ally. But East Germany has publicly endorsed present boundaries in Eastern Europe. So it is on West Germany that the residue of hate is centered.

If this hatred sometimes seems illogical, one must remember that in a Communist country people are fed whatever propaganda the government wishes to dispense. In Eastern Europe the comeback of Western Germany is presented in a different light than it is in the Western world. The West sees this as an economic miracle. In Eastern Europe, the German renaissance is presented as a rebirth of Prussian militarism.

Moreover, Poland and Czechoslovakia carved chunks from prostrate Germany at the end of World War II. It is easy for people in these countries to imagine that a powerful Germany might seek to rectify the boundary situation. Therefore, it seems logical to many people that Germany should not be allowed to become too powerful.

After the war, Czechoslovakia deported between one and two million Sudetenland Germans from their homes in what now are western areas of Czechoslovakia. Some of these refugees settled in West Germany. They formed cultural and nationalistic groups which still agitate for return to their homeland. Any time any such rallies are held in West Germany, they are widely publicized in the satellites.

One Polish trade official attending a Prague meeting shows only lukewarm feelings about Communism before launching into a diatribe about the Germans. First he gives his feelings about the Russians:

"You know that expression about doing as the Romans do. Well, if you're in Warsaw you do as the Russians do. If you're in Cracow, you do as the Russians do. And when you're in Hell you'll do as the Russians do, too, because that's where they will all be."

Then he switches conversation to Germans and his native city of Kostrzyn, Poland, a city only 40 miles from Berlin on the placid Oder River. Gruffly, he says: "The Germans are all gone from the land east of the Oder-Neisse. We don't want them back, either."

He is speaking of the nearly 40,000 square miles of old German territory taken over by Poland following World War II. Here in this section you find such names as Freiburg, Heidersdorf, Sonnenburg and Rothenburg. Old castles and mansions with German gables sit amid groves of trees.

Before the war this area held a population of about 11.5 million Germans. Most fled before the advancing Russian armies near the end of World War II. Those remaining were expelled. About seven million Poles then moved onto the vacated lands.

Now Poland, certainly not the most pro-Red country in the satellites, is violently opposed to any revision of its present Oder-Neisse border. Even non-Communists would take up arms to defend it, say Western diplomats behind the Iron Curtain.

Most of the Germans who once lived east of the Oder-Neisse line also are now living in West Germany. Thus, including the refugees from East Germany, probably one in every four West Germans once lived in land now occupied by a Communist regime. This is what makes it difficult for any West German politician to admit that it may be hopeless to pine for return of one-time German lands.

Meanwhile, the agitation of these displaced Germans—even though becoming weaker as the years go by—continues to fan fears in Eastern Europe about revival of Prussian militarism. It is this fear which brings Khrushchev support from the satellites when he rails against West Berlin and West Germany.

RAY VICKER

October 13, 1961

Peking Analyzes the U.S. Economy

TOKYO—Among the many nations of the world that scrutinize and comment on the workings of the American economy, Communist China now feels impelled to deliver some distant judgments on "the crisis of capitalism" in the United States.

More in China, perhaps, than in any other Communist country does Marxist ideology, fabricated around the notion of impending collapse of the capitalist system, regulate and obfuscate economic analysis. Political rigidity, in part, has also heavily damaged Red China's own food-short chaotic economy. But, curiously enough, the hard Peking line occasionally rubs elbows with conservative American economic thought in a full-circle turn. For instance, across a vast political gulf and starting from vastly different assumptions, Red Chinese and respected U.S. economists both cite the perils of high U.S. Government spending.

To some extent, Chinese discussions of the American economy reflect a frustrated desire to know what is really going on in the United States, which no Red Chinese official ever visits. One gathers, from perusing Chinese essays on the American economy, that nearly all facts and figures are gleaned from official U.S. Government reports and articles and books by U.S. economists, much as American reporters piece together developments in China by examining Red Chinese publications.

With the wide spectrum of economic opinion available from such sources, one is hardly surprised to find the Chinese eagerly pouncing on a theory that U.S. unemployment is actually far larger than official statistics portray and branding a suggestion to the opposite effect as "absurd raving." But the Red regime puts even heavier blinkers on its economists. So attempts to analyze what some Chinese writers call the "deathbed struggle of the capitalist system on the eve of its extinction" make pretty amusing reading.

For instance, Chinese economists not long ago gathered at a forum in Peking to discuss "the shortening of the interval between American economic crises from about ten years to three or four years."

Comrade Wu Ta-kun, as reported in Peking's *Kuang Ming Daily,* addresses himself to the issue in fairly straight economic terms. Mr. Wu tells his associates that the "frequent U.S. crises" are the result of renewal of fixed capital, in other words, expansion or improvement of plants. Citing the U.S. Internal Revenue Act of 1960, Mr. Wu says that the five-year depreciation for tax purposes allowed firms producing for export encouraged reinvestment in such intervals in order to avoid taxes, "even when the equipment has suffered no breakdown." Such frequent investment, he continues, leads to excess production over consumer demand.

Economist Wu closes his remarks on a plaintive note. He admits that Chinese research is "incomplete" and that it is difficult to gain a complete understanding of the current U.S. crisis.

So much for Mr. Wu's attempt to explain U.S. economics. But now it's the turn of the critics who castigate Mr. Wu for leaving out some vital doctrinal points in his analysis.

Hsiang Chung, an economist who has obviously done his Stalinist homework, slams his associate for failing to "expose the connection between the dollar crisis and the policy of aggression and war which U.S. imperialism has consistently carried out." The gold flow, declares Mr. Hsiang, is "an evil fruit brought on by the frantic indulgence of U.S. imperialism in foreign aggression and expansion" after World War II.

Sun Chih-chung, another economist who quotes Marx liberally, says that Mr. Wu has it all wrong; that crises cause U.S. investment in new plants, not the other way around, and "stepped-up exploitation of workers to lower production costs." True, he goes on, this will lead to new consumer demand in primary goods industries where employment will rise, but later it will result in excess capacity and overproduction.

Furthermore, the measures to relieve crisis, such as more Government spending, he says, only aggravate the crisis and through taxation "laboring people are thus robbed further of their purchasing power and the contradictions in the economy grow more acute."

Summing up his arguments, Mr. Sun declares that militarization keeps the U.S. economy running, that American foreign aid merely encourages dumping of inferior quality products, that such anti-recession measures as highway construction, for example, are really only preparation for atomic war and that expanding domestic credit simply means additional usury.

"All this is done to tighten the belts of workers to starvation and to insure the capitalists higher profits," he concludes.

Though these invective-laden judgments may satisfy Red China's ruling politicians, one wonders what impression they make on other educated Chinese, not to speak of the broad masses who have yet to gain the basic amenities of life.

Surely the notion that the American economy is headed for collapse because it produces too much of everything must be greeted with some baffled skepticism. And one may suppose that among the impoverished

Chinese millions, at least some are reluctant to believe that capitalists can make profits without selling goods to the "downtrodden" American worker. Yet, since the debates on U.S. economics are published in Chinese periodicals for domestic consumption, the regime apparently does hope to convince its subjects that such, indeed, is the case.

The Chinese analysis, though, is considerably more convincing as evidence of the ideological wall insulating the Chinese Communist rulers from the realities of the outside world.

IGOR OGANESOFF

September 17, 1962

Franco's Hold Unshaken

MADRID—His critics at home and abroad may have been attracting more attention than usual lately, but the regime of Generalissimo Francisco Franco is far from crumbling.

This, at least, is the overwhelming opinion of responsible diplomats, informed Spaniards and foreign businessmen with long experience in this enervating, oven-like capital. What's more, add many of them, including some who are hardly admirers of the Caudillo, the strength and stability of the dictatorship is probably all for the best just at this time.

"Spain has a lot of problems to solve in the next few years," remarks a representative of one friendly foreign government. "The move back toward Europe, especially the application to go into the Common Market, is going to mean some difficult adjustments. It will be all the harder if it should all get mixed up in a political squabble, too."

An American businessman who is outspokenly in favor of the government's policy switch of the past three years sees an even more positive benefit in Franco's status. "Once he makes up his mind which way the country ought to move," he says enthusiastically, "he can really get things going. That's the best thing about having a big boy like that up there."

There is no question that General Franco wields an immense degree of power. Chief of state, chief of government, leader of the country's only legal political party and head of all armed forces, he combines in himself more undivided and unchallenged authority than any other dictator now on the scene. This is not to say, however, that his power is unlimited.

"He's no absolute monarch by any means," insists a political specialist in a Western embassy. "In fact, one of the real keys to his success, I think, is that he has always gauged accurately how far it was safe for him to go. That's why there have been no serious challenges to him."

The actions of the Spanish leader during the events of the past few weeks are a case in point in this man's view. While on the surface there appears to be a contradiction in Franco's rather tolerant attitude toward the striking coal miners in Northern Spain and his harsh crackdown on leaders of the political opposition who had attended a Munich conference with exiled anti-Franco leaders of the past, this theory rather neatly squares the two.

In the first instance it was clear that public sentiment was largely with the strikers (to the degree those not in the immediate area could learn about the walkout under the rigid press censorship). Spanish workers are among the lowest paid in Europe, topping only those of neighboring Portugal and perhaps Greece. In recent years their impatience with their lot has been growing.

"To have taken a tough line with the strikes would have alienated the workers, who have been generally pro-Franco over the past decade or so," explains a diplomatic analyst. "And, perhaps just as important, it would have stirred up the unions and socialist politicians within the Common Market and might have ruined Spain's chances of ever getting in."

An entirely different set of factors was involved in the political flare-up. One suggested by a number of diplomats is simply that General Franco—possibly unaware of the Munich meeting until it took place—exaggerated its importance and the degree of political opposition planned there. But even if his assessment of the conference was entirely accurate, others declare, the circumstances involved in such a strictly political dispute were far from those in the strike.

"To begin with," explains a veteran Western intelligence expert, "it's extremely doubtful that the men who took part in the Munich meeting enjoy any really significant support inside Spain. Of course, it's impossible to be certain of such things, the way everything is controlled, but all we know indicates very few people are even aware of such people as Gil Robles and Prados Arrarte. And a lot of those who do know them are inclined to dismiss them as people who had their chance back in the days of the republic—and failed."

General Franco, moreover, had hardly anything to fear from outside reaction to his crackdown on his political enemies, this man believes. Such a move was no more than Franco's foreign critics expected and merely confirmed them in their hostility. Inside the country and out, in other words, the politicians lacked both popular support and powerful allies—but the strikers had both.

Finally, say those who watched recent events closely, it was probably a little more than either General Franco or his army backers could stomach to take two humiliating blows in succession without lashing back. "He just couldn't let the politicians get away with it after the strikers had," says a long-time observer of Spanish affairs.

If they had, this man goes on, it would not only have appeared an obvious sign of weakness but would have encouraged the disparate and frequently warring elements of the opposition to join in a common program.

But if there is no serious political threat to force changes in Spanish policy, it appears to many here that economic realities are slowly forcing the dictatorship to make concessions in the political realm as well as in those of business and labor.

"There's just no overestimating the importance of this move toward the Common Market," asserts one economic specialist here. "A country like Spain simply can't fit into the framework without granting a degree of freedom that doesn't now exist. The right to strike, which is denied formally but now certainly recognized tacitly, is a good example. And there will be more all the time."

Adds a business consultant who has lived in Spain for years: "I learned long ago that you can't get anywhere with a Spaniard by telling him bluntly he's wrong and trying to force him to change. He won't argue about it as a rule—he's much too polite—but he'll get his back up and then you can't budge him. What you have to do is give him full credit for whatever good he does and enourage him to go on from there. We've been beating them over the head for years about democracy and it hasn't worked. But if they begin to see that it's all for the best I think they'll come around."

DAN CORDTZ

June 29, 1962

— ◆ —

RECIPE

Instant coffee, instant cake
Are agreeable to make.
Instant doughnuts, instant pie
Also may be reasons why
Instant marriage in our nation
Often leads to instant separation.

—MARGARET FISHBACK

Igor's Forbidden Fruit

Igor Alexandrovich's most beloved possession is a new Moskvitch car which cost him $2,600 cash. Yet Igor's salary as manager of a Moscow variety store is only $35 a week.

We had met Igor, a 34-year-old bachelor, at the Moscow circus where he and a girl friend had box seats next to ours. Now, sitting in his car, he was explaining how he could afford such luxuries.

"You have to understand our economic system," said Igor. "In Russia, everything is Socialist property. And what is Socialist property? Is it my property? No. Is it my neighbor's property? No. Is it anybody's property? No. So naturally, everybody steals it. And with a clear conscience.

"Except it is not really stealing. It is what we call here, having a little business on the side. In Russia, everybody has a little business on the side."

Igor unlocked the trunk of his car and displayed several large boxes. "In these," he said, "is some rare merchandise that came today to my store—some radio tubes, and color film, and some nicely made white shirts. Such things do not come often.

"These I do not put on sale. If I put them on sale, there would be long lines and much confusion in the store. Instead, I put them in these boxes and later tonight I bring them to somebody else. He has a little retail business on the side. He also has a Moskvitch."

Igor feels that he is grossly underpaid, considering he is in charge of eight employees. So, when he thinks he deserves a bonus, he explained, he helps himself to a share of the day's receipts before they are picked up by a policeman for deposit in the Moscow Trade Ministry's account.

But what about the government inspectors, the auditors? "They also make a little business on the side," said Igor. "I told you—in Russia, everybody's got a little business."

Igor's activities may seem surprising, but they are by no means unusual in the Soviet Union. The tourist runs into many such examples. The truth is, the Soviet Union has been mightily unsuccessful in stamping out the acquisitive instinct—however illegal it may be in Russia, and however immoral some of its Russian manifestations may seem to Americans. Khrushchev himself recently noted activities by some of these Russian-style "capitalists" when he complained that half the corn crop in one area had disappeared, presumably into the Soviets' active though illegal free market.

Even university students often have "a little business." It usually is black-marketing in dollars.

In most countries where black markets still exist, the operators are rather sleazy, unshaken, unkempt characters who loiter on street corners, cigarettes dangling from their lips, murmuring under their breaths to passing tourists the hushed, heavily accented password: "Change money?" But in Russia, this is different.

In Red Square in Moscow, on the main street, the Nevsky Prospekt, in Leningrad, along the beach in the tourist resorts of Yalta and Sochi, you are approached instead by immaculately tailored young men wearing Saville Row suits, Italian shoes, Swiss shirts, American stretch socks, French neckties and (in one case) a tie clasp that said, "Souvenir of California."

These young Soviet gentlemen speak perfect English. Their approach is casual and confident. They talk with you, not surreptitiously, as a potential partner in an illegal enterprise, but as a friend they are trying to make feel at home in the Soviet Union.

In fact, it usually takes them five minutes or so to get down to business.

"Welcome to Leningrad" (or wherever the city) is their usual opening gambit, as they extend their hand in greeting.

"We Soviet people are always delighted to meet Americans," they continue. "With the world so troubled, better understanding between peoples is necessary to further peace and friendship."

They explain that they are university students, and ask about your profession, and how you like Russia, and after a while their voice lowers just a trifle.

"I would now like to discuss with you a little transaction."

And we found that we were being offered 30 rubles for $1—instead of the 10 rubles the Soviet government gave tourists. In fact, if we hesitated, we were usually quickly offered 35 rubles.

This transaction completed—generally around the corner on a less heavily trafficked street—your new friend gets down to other propositions.

Would we like to sell the suit we are wearing? For $150 (it cost us $69.50 new)? Or do we have an extra pair of stretch socks—for $5? Or that shirt we are wearing—$15?

Merchandise bought from tourists or provided by store managers goes into regular underground trade channels for sale to wealthy Russians—big bureaucrats, factory managers, scientists, et cetera—who get substantial salaries but can find little worthwhile in the shops to buy with their money.

And the dollars, one of our university friends told us, are all funneled to sailors. They take the dollars to West European ports, buy foreign merchandise, and bring it back to Russia with them, for sale.

"The customs officials overlook this trade," said our friend. "And both the customs officials and the sailors have a nice little business on the side."

It isn't only corn farmers among ruralists who also have a business. In the government food stores all over the Soviet Union, one can find only the wormiest pears and most moldy apples. Yet along the main highways in the fruit-producing Crimea and Ukraine one can buy luscious fruits—from roadside hawkers.

These privately sold fruits are all supposed to come from little family-held plots of land that the government permits collective farm workers to keep as their very own. But we were told that most actually come from collectives, whose workers will divvy up a good crop and hawk most of it privately, rather than let the government have it at low fixed prices.

Government housing is a very lucrative private business for those officials in charge of allocating that most valuable of all valuables in Russia—an apartment larger than one room. They expect sizable "presents."

As a result of the apartment shortage, factories have been going into the housing business. In a large printing plant we visited in Kiev, for example, we asked the director how he goes about obtaining new machinery. He said he applies to the Ministry of Culture.

"Do you get it?" we asked.

"Rarely. Mostly, the ministry says we should buy it out of our own profits."

"Do you?"

"No. We feel machinery is the ministry's job. So we use our profits to build apartments for our workers instead."

Waiters in restaurants catering to foreign tourists do a lively business buying meal coupons from them—at discount prices. To the restaurant, these coupons are as good as cash, and the tourist has to pay for them in advance before being given a visa to enter Russia. But they are good for more food than any normal human being can consume, and are non-refundable. So the waiter cashes in.

"It helps take the place of tips, which are forbidden as being a bourgeois custom," one waiter told us. "And there is really nothing wrong in doing this, because it is sanctioned by our restaurant manager. In fact, he even participates in the profits."

One of the most vexing problems of an automobile tourist in the Soviet Union is buying gasoline.

First, he must line up in an Intourist government travel bureau office to buy coupons. Then he has to hunt up the gas station, usually in some obscure out-of-the-way corner of the city. Then there is the lineup at the one or two pump stations before the attendant (usually a woman) hand-squirts gas into the car with a super-powered pump that generally showers half the gas onto the ground.

But this is only for the uninitiated. Said one Russian: "Smart Russian motorists who do long-distance driving never go to the gas station. We just hail a passing truck on the open road. The truck driver will fill our tank from his almost for free." He added that the going rate for truck-supplied gas was 20 to 25 per cent of list price.

The truck drivers not only make money on the direct deal, they also collect extra mileage pay by citing their high gas consumption as "proof" that they drive long distances. Naturally, they also advance their mileage gauges.

"Nobody really cares," someone said. "After all, everything here is supposed to belong to the people. And we're people, too."

All of these *sub rosa* activities are well known throughout the Soviet Union. Russians boast freely to foreigners about them, as if by participating in such operations they are staging their own little revolt, scoring a small triumph over a stupid and restrictive system.

Some Russians, of course, must engage in "business" to eke out a decent living. But others seem to enjoy such activity for its own sake, as the only way they can savor the forbidden fruit of "free enterprise."

LOWELL BLANKFORT

February 2, 1961

French Foreign Legion

ALGIERS—To many in this tense, sullen city, one of the saddest consequences of last week's army revolt against Paris is this: It may have brought to an inglorious end the proud history of the world's best known and most exaggeratedly glamorous military force—the French Foreign Legion.

"Les Kepis Blancs," as the Legionnaires are known here from their white caps, were the backbone of the revolt headed by the four French generals. It was the crack First Paratroop Regiment of Legionnaires who were in the van, and now the regiment is being dissolved. But that isn't the end of the question being debated in Paris of what to do with the Legion.

French law specifically bans units of the Legion from France. Mostly non-French mercenaries, they and France have long been considered better off at arm's length from each other. But the Legion has been for more than a century the darling of French North Africa. Organized in 1831, only a year after the French first took over Algeria, the Legion was the outfit that kept the North African territories subdued for years. It has always been associated with the vast Sahara Desert regions, as any teenager who has daydreamed over the story of "Beau Geste" knows, though Legionnaires have fought the world over.

Undoubtedly, there has always been a special "entente" between Legionnaires and French North Africa's Europeans, as well as a certain amount of animosity between Legionnaires and Moslem North Africans. Among the factors in the ready revolt of the Legionnaires is the fact that French North Africa and the Legion itself are the closest thing these hardened mercenaries know to "home," and when Algerian independence comes there would be a home for neither Legionnaires nor the Legion itself.

The Legion's permanent headquarters and training camp is at Sidi Bel Abbes, 30 miles south of Oran, and an estimated 10,000 retired Legionnaires and their families now make their homes in that region. All these century-old ties of the Legion and the North African French have been strengthened considerably in the past six years as Legionnaires bore the brunt of efforts to put down the revolt of Moslem nationalists against French rule in Algeria.

"They always give the Legion the toughest, dirtiest jobs," proudly declares a corporal who defiantly wears his identifying white cap and green-necktie as he strolls along an Algiers street crowded with hostile Moslems. "It helps keep the casualty figures down for the French troops and keep the people in France happy."

This explanation, which Legionnaires are fond of making, may be largely myth, but it has some figures to back it up. An estimated 10,000 Legionnaires died in the bitter fighting in Indo-China, and Legion casualties in Algeria include close to 1,500 dead—or more than 7 per cent of its estimated strength of 20,000 men.

Certainly France has had no more effective warriors during the bloody and losing battles it has fought since World War II to retain its far-flung colonies. The Legion's ability, its *esprit de corps* and the traditions it has built up account not only for its fame but for the influence it exerts—out of all proportion to its numbers—on the entire professional military establishment of France.

"Officers who have served with the Legion will frequently tell you, 'I've spent 23 years in the Legion,'" says a Western military adviser in Paris. "They may have had one hitch after they left St. Cyr and spent the rest of the time behind a desk at the Ministry of the Army, but they still wear the green tie and think of themselves as Legionnaires."

To a considerable extent the Legion spirit, like that of the U.S. Marines, is consciously and deliberately cultivated. Visitors—especially American journalists—are not welcome these days at Sidi Bel Abbes, but persons who have been there in the past say there is the same pride in pure toughness. Training involves unbelievable punishment and work and is regarded as not nearly rigorous enough if it does not weed out a substantial share of recruits.

The Legion becomes a substitute for family, for country, even for religion to the hard-bitten, cynical yet sometimes sentimental mercenaries who make up its ranks. One of the regular features of the Legion's annual April 30 fete celebrating the Battle of Camerone (canceled this year) is the display in a glass case of the wooden arm of the Legion commander in that ill-fated but gallant fight.

"It's just like a religious relic," remarks an American who has attended the celebration. "You can see these battle-scarred troops marching past the spot where it stands, saluting, with tears running down their faces." In the battle, whose centennial was to be observed in 1963, a force of 60 Legionnaires—outnumbered more than 30 to one by a Mexican army—held out for two days before the two survivors surrendered, exhausted and out of ammunition.

As its name implies, the Legion is composed entirely of foreign troops—although Frenchmen can get in by declaring themselves to be of another nationality. Currently an estimated 60 per cent of its enlisted strength is made up of France's old enemies, the Germans. Another 25 to 30 per cent are Spaniards or Italians, with most of the remainder Belgian, Swiss, Polish or Hungarian. Officers are all regulars and all are French—with the exception of the 3 per cent who have managed to rise through the ranks to a commission.

Traditionally, of course, the Legion has been a haven for some of the world's more desperate characters. A Legionnaire's true name, nationality and background are kept secret if he desires, and there is no question that many have left police records or other liabilities behind them in their home countries.

An American diplomat in Paris, for example, tells of an encounter he had in Asia some years ago with a Legion sergeant whose physiognomy and close-cropped blond hair proclaimed him as a German. In good, though heavily accented English liberally sprinkled with barracks obscenities, the Legionnaire recalled that he had been fighting at one place or another in the world since Adolf Hitler's troops first started shooting in 1939.

"Do you like the life?" asked the American. "What the hell, it's like any other life," shrugged the sergeant. "Well, why don't you do something else? You certainly could make more money elsewhere," observed the diplomat. "Huh," replied the Legionnaire with a contemptuous stare. "Who'd hire me?" And he rolled up his uniform sleeve to show, tattooed in the bend of his arm, the telltale letters: ss.

Such men are not particularly reluctant to accept the terms of Legion recruitment: a five-year enlistment at a beginning salary of about $5 a month. The typical Legionnaire will require that entire first hitch to make corporal and will then sign on for another five years. With his second enlistment he is permitted to marry, and many Legionnaires in Algeria do have wives and families. Promotion, however, is slow—three enlistments are usually behind every top-ranking non-com.

The lack of any real feeling for France, and the fanatical loyalty to its own officers are also two of the reasons why units of the Legion formed an important part of the generals' revolt against President Charles de Gaulle. Moreover, although it has now been established that only four of the Legion's ten regiments were involved, there is an astonishing disinclination on the part of those who remained loyal to criticize their brothers.

The Legionnaire corporal questioned here, for instance, has only sympathy for the members of the First Paratroop Regiment, which all but demolished its base at Zeralda before heading back toward Sidi Bel Abbes and extinction. "The Legion built that base," he says truculently. "Why should they leave it for anyone else?"

Members of that unit, as they drove away, were still chanting "*Algerie Française*" and their officers, separated and brought to Algiers for shipment to France and disciplinary action, sang a once-popular ballad called, "I Regret Nothing."

The French government has refused to say what it has in mind for the Legion, beyond the dissolution of those units proven to have been directly implicated in the unsuccessful revolt. But the old law which established the Legion and forbade its garrisoning in France during peacetime remains. There had been talk before the revolt in Algiers that the law might be changed, but significantly no one is suggesting that today.

Here in Algiers, where the past three years have clearly proven that few see the realities of French political life, there is disbelief that the Legion's days of glory may be over. "They'll never disband it," asserts a bartender in the Hotel Aletti's Cintra Bar confidently. But in Paris, where the decision will be made, no one is promising anything.

DAN CORDTZ

May 3, 1961

Russia's People

SOCHI, USSR—The night train from Tbilisi is a local which follows a westerly line for 150 miles through the Georgian countryside until it touches the Black Sea, where it bends to the north. The first few hours of the run are in daylight, or soft twilight, and from the car window the visitor gets new glimpses of the land and its peoples.

On the right side, not too far away, is the ridge of the Caucasus Mountains. To the left the land is flatter, showing at first the outskirts of the city, then a row of villages close together, until finally you reach more open country.

There the dreary apartments of the cities give way to separate houses, small, often unpainted, sometimes rather tumbling, but usually surrounded by a plot of land which supports a garden. More often, both house and garden have a well-tended look, with flowers around the doorway. The passing train, as everywhere in the world, draws the gaze of curious children, and a friendly wave is always answered.

The depot platforms, like the train itself, are crowded. There are soldiers, more often carrying babies than guns. Young girls in blouses and skirts. Older women, kerchiefed and shawled. Farmers in boots and tunics. Here and there a Western-style suit. And always boxes, bundles and the ubiquitous bulging net bags in which shoppers and travelers stuff their belongings.

From the car window a "hello" in halting Russian will bring delighted laughter and a hail of friendly chatter. If an interpreter is handy (and quite often one of the younger people on the platform will know a score of English words) you will soon have a little crowd gathered with whom to pass a pleasant time.

It is a leisurely journey from Tbilisi to Sochi—all Soviet trains go slowly—and it permits you to reflect upon all you have seen, the beauties of land and the simple niceness of the people.

Physically, the Soviet Union is an impressive country. Its cities are well laid out; its villages full of rural charm. In a few hours by jet you can sweep over farmlands like Southern Illinois, wheat fields as in Kansas, plains that look like Texas, deserts with the desolation of Death Valley, and mountains with the bleak grandeur of the High Sierras. It is an unforgettable experience to fly across the great plain of Turkestan, east of the Caspian Sea, crossing great gorges in the earth for all the world like the craters of the moon, over the edge of the Tien Shan mountains, and then drop down into the green and abundant valley by the city of Tashkent.

It is a land rich in resources. Much is said of Soviet wastelands, but its arable land is fertile indeed; in former times the country was an exporter of wheat and other agricultural crops. Mineral resources, including oil, abound. There are plentiful forests and great rivers. As a land the Soviet Union is as fully endowed as the United States, and fully as beautiful. A visitor has no trouble understanding the mystic feeling of the people for Mother Russia.

But the people themselves are perhaps the greatest resource. These are able people; patient, long-suffering, intelligent, wonderfully hospitable and full of vitality. The manager of the ball-bearing plant in Moscow, the director of the cooperative farm in Uzbekistan, the shop foreman in Pravda's printing plant, the electrical technician at Volgograd's great power plant—these are people who know their business. It is not their fault that the horizons of what they know are so narrow or that their abilities are confined by the system under which they live.

The same is true of the nimble-fingered girls who run the looms in the textile mill that is the Soviet's pride, or even of the husky women who have to dig a sewer line with pick and shovel; they too labor with energy. Everywhere you turn the air is full of vitality and eagerness— and a frustrated curiosity to know more.

These are outgoing people. Whenever the American editors in our group could slip away from our traveling Soviet hosts, we had no difficulty in starting conversations, and found no effort to hide inquisitive minds.

True, the conversations would begin with some such question as "Why did President Kennedy shoot off the atom bomb?" or "Why do you enslave Negroes in the South?" and it was futile to argue back; the people were not insincere, merely ignorant of what goes on in the world. Still, these were passing questions. Inevitably, our Soviet acquaintances would get around to asking about America, its techniques and its ways of living.

One evening in the square at Tashkent there were eight such talkative groups going simultaneously, each with its American editor surrounded by a score of local people. Do you have a car? What is a schoolteacher paid? How many rooms in your apartment? How much did that suit of clothes cost? Is it true that the masses have washing machines?

Sometimes, unfortunately, the questions would get too technical for poor journalists. A farmer asking questions about nitrogen fertilizer, a machine-shop foreman wanting to compare lathes, or an airline pilot asking about pounds-of-thrust in jet engines. But always an insatiable curiosity about America, and sooner or later the questions about wages, prices, employment and the whole standard of living.

These, of course, are the same questions the visitor also asks about the Soviet Union. And the answers always seemed (as no doubt ours did to our Soviet friends) complex and often paradoxical.

The minimum wage here is about 30 to 40 rubles per month, little more than the lowest relief pension. At the official rate of exchange, $1.10 to the ruble, this seems incredibly low. The average for fairly skilled workers is estimated at only 90 to 100 rubles.

But, wherever possible, Soviet wages are on a piecework basis and there is a complicated bonus-and-penalty system. Thus a linotype operator at Pravda is paid by the lines of type set; there the average printer will get over 100 rubles and some more than 150 a month. Collective farmers are paid by "working day units," each of which is worth (in Uzbekistan) 2.70 rubles plus 200 grams of rice and a half-kilo of potatoes; the average is 300 working day units per year, an income of less than $1,000.

The intangibles confuse matters further. The farmers, of course, have their housing and their garden plots which give them both extra food and some cash crops. The city workers also get their housing at a nominal "rent" (it's cheap but minimal housing) and side benefits depending upon their rank and status.

Rank and status are the most important things. Second-tier managerial people may get 250 to 500 rubles per month, top management up to a thousand rubles. But their main reward is in the "perquisites," priorities on cars, housing, recreation facilities and so on. If you are far enough up the ladder—party leader, manager, scientist or government functionary—you may have a car and chauffeur furnished, the privileges of household help and a host of things that money cannot buy.

For money here does not buy much except labor, the cheapest thing in the Soviet Union. A poor quality suit of clothes runs 70–80 rubles; a halfway decent one 150 rubles. The cheapest street shoes we saw were 25 rubles, many were 35–40 rubles and up. Yet it's not unusual among the new upper classes to see Italian and British tailored suits or imported broadcloth shirts. New York's "Bond" clothes (with two pairs of pants) are not uncommon among journalists and others who have had the privilege of visiting America.

It is different with the masses, and you only need to look at their clothes, their housing and their food to see that they live not only below the standard of working-class Americans but also below their counterparts in most of Western Europe. Still, prosperity and austerity are relative things. The people tell you happily about the improvement in their living standards over a decade ago, and still more proudly about what they hope for from tomorrow.

Tomorrow is a big word here. The government's propaganda, blared from every newspaper, billboard and radio, is not about what is but about what is going to be. Ask how many apartments were built last year in such-and-such a place and you will be told how many square meters of living space are called for in the current Seven Year Plan. Ask about the number of tractors on a farm, or how many people have telephones, and you will be told what it is supposed to be at the end of 1965.

The Seven Year Plan replaced the last Five Year Plan in midstream because the latter had gone askew. No matter; it keeps everybody's attention focused on the future. Thus, while much of what a Western visitor sees here seems so backward that after a few weeks he begins to feel sad for the Soviet people, still he cannot recall any sadness in the people themselves that is not matched by their faith in tomorrow.

And while they obviously have their share of lazy and shiftless comrades, most Russians work for that future as ably as they are allowed to. A plant manager's eyes brighten as he tells you of the new equipment he is going to get under the Plan. The young girl at the spindle who has set a production record displays her bright red pennant proudly, even if she is somewhat flustered at being fussed over before all these foreigners. Make no mistake about it. These people have vigor, a sense of purpose and an unabashed love of country.

Looking about that country it's not hard to see why. When morning comes, a train attendant brings you a glass of steaming tea, brewed at the end of the car in an old-fashioned boiler heated by an open chaircoal fire. You open the window curtain and sit idly watching a countryside that might have been America 50 years ago. A man digging in the earth, a woman washing clothes in a big wooden tub, two boys herding some cows on a dusty road.

But the air is warm, and here and there between the houses you catch glimpses in the distance of early morning bathers relaxing on the beach. And beyond, a jewel in any land, the Black Sea glitters in the summer sun.

VERMONT ROYSTER

August 10, 1962

"But they have always been poor, oppressed and downtrodden. Why should that upset them now?"

Chat with Dr. Castro

NEW YORK—"We either develop our own economy, or we ask a friend to give us a billion dollars a year," said the bearded traveler aboard his private railroad car as it rolled through the greening New Jersey countryside toward New York yesterday morning.

Sprawled full length on a bed in his drawing room in fatigue uniform and short, black boots, and puffing on the ever-present cigar, Fidel Castro goes on to suggest it is better for both Cuba and the United States that his country develop its own economy rather than lean on U.S. aid.

And Dr. Castro is chock-full of broad ideas on how he intends to develop the Cuban economy and wipe out Cuba's chronic unemployment which he says idles 20 per cent of the work force. "We are going to produce many products we now import," he assures his visitor perched on the other end of the bed.

Asked for specifics, Dr. Castro says Cuba imports much food which can be grown on the island. "We import now $150 million of food. If we grow that, we give work to our people. We also save $150 million which we can use to buy tractors, machinery, other things we need," the Cuban premier maintains.

He says Cuba also is capable of producing "cotton, paper and newsprint." He figures domestic production of these items could trim another $100 million off the island's current imports. Another Castro prescription: "Some tariff protection for our domestic industry."

It seemed quite clear in his mind that what Cuba needs is not necessarily a lower total of buying from abroad but a change in the composition of her foreign trade.

In his program to diversify industry and thus reduce Cuba's dependence on sugar (which accounts for as much as 25 per cent of national income in some years), the revolutionary leader offers some encouragement to American investors who have already poured over $800 million into Cuba.

He gives an emphatic "yes" when asked if he welcomes foreign investment to help trigger Cuba's industrial expansion. He assures his questioner that his government will continue to give new industry tax breaks and other incentives which date back to 1945.

While Dr. Castro demonstrates what some observers might consider a certain naïveté about the ease with which government can mold the economy to the form it desires, he also shows more awareness about economic matters than he is usually credited with.

Asked about his plans for expanding sugar production—a question which worries sugar producers the world over—Dr. Castro appraises his visitor for a second or two, smiles, and then says: "We are not showing our hand just yet. Let everyone worry for a while." But then he goes on to remark: "We'll do what is best for sugar and for Cuba. We would like to increase production if we can do it without disturbing the sugar market."

He also volunteers a significant remark about Cuban laws which forbid employers to fire workers, a restriction which has long rankled American investors in Cuba. Dr. Castro believes it will be impossible to change the laws as long as Cuba is afflicted with "worse unemployment than you had in your depression," because once a man is laid off he has little hope of obtaining another job. But he exudes confidence that his program will reduce unemployment drastically, and he leaves his visitor with the impression he then would consider no-firing edicts "unnecessary."

In contrast to the cheerful confusion prevailing elsewhere in his party (his car is loaded with bearded bodyguards and clean-shaven U.S. security agents mingling with Cuban cabinet officers and wives). Dr.

Castro seems cool and collected in the privacy of his drawing room as he continues to expound on his economic beliefs.

Casually flicking scraps of cigar onto the bed, he says he has no intention of confiscating Cuban Telephone Company, an affiliate of International Telephone and Telegraph Corporation, which has been operated for the past couple of months by a government "intervenor" who is looking into the utility's costs and rates.

Does the government plan to buy the phone company? "We have not talked about it; we have more urgent uses for our money," he says airily.

He claims further that people have misinterpreted a remark of his in a recent speech which indicated he intended to abolish both the lower and upper economic classes and put everyone into a level middle class. "We do hope to raise the standard of living of everyone to what the middle class now has," he says. But he insists he has no thought of taking money away from any wealthy individual who invests in industry. "Industry owners will still make money," he promises.

He is considerably less sympathetic, however, toward people who have invested in real estate and apartments. He defends vigorously his rent decree which slashed rents April 1 by 30 per cent to 50 per cent. He maintains Cuba does not need this type of "non-productive" investment.

Asked if his rent reduction hasn't frightened all investors, including those who might put up the industrial plants he wants so much, he concedes that many potential investors "are worried." But he claims manufacturers in Cuba "are happy."

He says further that investors who are worried will change their mind as the Cuban economy is stimulated by increased consumer spending—the theory behind the cut in rents. Of the frightened investors, he says, "It's all up here," pointing to his curly black hair in one of the sudden, forceful gestures he habitually uses.

Already, according to Dr. Castro, the Cuban economy is responding to the rent law. He claims retail business, which slumped badly in the first three months following the hasty exit January 1 of Fulgencio Batista, already has begun to bounce back since the rent decree put more money into the hands of consumers. He also credits a recent cabinet action in raising minimum government salaries to $85 a month (the old minimum was $65) with helping retail spending.

Dr. Castro predicts optimistically: "If investors don't believe in us now, they will in three months or six months." Calling on Treasury Minister Rufo Lopez Fresquet for confirmation, Dr. Castro says Cuba's gold and dollar reserves have made a modest recovery from a low point of about $100 million at the time the Batista government collapsed.

Government revenues are exceeding expenses, Mr. Lopez Fresquet insists, notwithstanding stories in the American press to the contrary. The Treasury Minister also boosted the amount of back taxes he expects to collect under Law 40. Under this law, taxpayers who offer to pay taxes they failed to pay under Batista's regime are excused from paying a portion of such levies. By the April 24 deadline, Mr. Lopez Fresquet now expects to receive $100 million, compared with an earlier forecast of $65 million.

Dr. Castro's much-publicized agrarian reform program, a move to distribute land to Cuba's desperately poor rural folk, is getting off the ground, the premier says. Land has actually been distributed to about 760 people, according to Dr. Castro.

He brags a bit about the $35 million "given by the Cuban people" to help finance the land-distribution program (owners of private land will get some payment for acreage the government will take). Asked about reports that he "suggested" a certain contribution from sugar mill owners to this fund, he retorts acidly: "Suggested gifts were what you had under Batista. This is all voluntary."

Despite the many anti-American statements made by Dr. Castro since he came to power, he insists he's a good friend of this country. He claims, in effect, that he has only been pointing out past "mistakes" in U.S. policy toward Cuba—from the Platt Amendment (which gave the United States some control over internal affairs in Cuba from 1901 to 1934) to support of Batista.

"I came here on this visit, didn't I?" he asks. "I took the initiative," he maintains, contending this is proof of his friendship. But he still exhibits great sensitivity toward American criticism of his execution of Batista henchmen. Without the subject being brought up, he launches into a fervent justification for the executions and an attack on American press coverage of the trials which he suggests has been a deliberate misrepresentation.

In regard to suspension of the writ of habeas corpus, a move which has disturbed many American observers in Cuba, Dr. Castro makes this promise: "We will re-establish the writ, as soon as we recognize the judiciary." Asked when this might be, he indicated it should be accomplished "within a couple of months."

ED CONY

April 22, 1959

The Role of Power

As American ships deployed to enforce the blockade of Cuba last night, the world felt the breath of nuclear war. So it is somewhat surprising, in view of past attitudes and the general fear of war, that the United States is getting so much support from the British, French, Latin American and other governments.

There are brickbats too, of course—demonstrations in London, criticism of the United States in foreign papers and conversation—and there may well be more. But it is entirely possible that President Kennedy's show of strength, the decisiveness which removes uncertainties, has helped produce the support of friendly nations.

In any event, it is significant that the President acted forcefully in the full knowledge that he would be accused, by some and perhaps by many in the world, of threatening the peace. He was prepared to act with or without external backing; this is a U.S. operation, undertaken with little fretting about "world opinion" or even the opinion of allies.

That puts the power struggle clearly where it always basically has been: a direct confrontation of the United States and the USSR. Too long and too often the United States has been kept from benefiting from its own might by an understandable reluctance to use power. At times it has almost seemed as if the United States had ruled out the use of force no matter what.

Yet, the world being as it is, the United States could not remain the bulwark of the Western world on that basis. John Foster Dulles, a man of peace, nonetheless found it necessary to ask the question: If force be ruled out of the conduct of foreign affairs, then what shall replace the use of force?

The plain answer is that there is not and never has been a substitute for force when a nation's safety is directly involved. Not all the parliaments of man have been able to replace it. Nor all the sentimental chatter about the need for world government. Nor all the talk that war is "unthinkable" because the new weapons are so frightful. It is not at all unthinkable; right up to and including this hour, war is an almost continuous fact of life.

The Soviet Union has always understood the role of force, far too well for our comfort. It has committed the most brutal deeds, in Berlin and Hungary and elsewhere, when it thought its interests threatened. It sponsored the Korean War when it thought it could get away with it. It turned Cuba into a nuclear base because it must have thought—what else?—that the United States had indeed ruled out force.

Just about every other nation has deemed it necessary to resort to force. Peace-loving India did not hesitate to conquer the Portuguese enclave of Goa. And how could the government of India maintain any self-respect, or hope to stay in existence, if it were not now facing up to the Chinese Communist aggression?

Obviously there are fundamental differences in the reasons for the employment of force in particular cases. We must not let any external denunciation of our Cuban policy confuse us about exactly what those differences are. The Communists are everywhere the destroyers, we the defenders of civilization. In Cuba as in Vietnam we use force only because others have forced it. If we must now also fight at Berlin, then that is the way it must be.

But there is a much more hopeful possibility in the agonizing decision at last to employ our power. If the U.S. Government follows through on the President's words, we may finally be beginning to put the Soviet Union in its place; that is, to make it realize it must stop its world-wide aggressions for the excellent reason that the United States has had enough and won't have any more. The considerable support we are now getting in the world improves that prospect.

Whatever happens, let us remember that it is easy for foreign individuals, groups and nations to criticize. In the last analysis, however, they are on the periphery of the struggle and we are at its center. While some complain, we play for keeps. That is the only way America can play. And it makes all the difference.

JOSEPH E. EVANS

October 25, 1962

*"They agree with our resolution!
What's wrong with it?"*

White Hunters in a New Africa

NAIROBI, KENYA—At the Muthaiga Club, the 50-year-old white settler stronghold on the bougainvillea-lined edge of town, members are arguing about whether or not the club should become integrated. The club is one of rambling verandas, white-uniformed African waiters and many red-mustached and red-necked clients. It seems to personify the old leisurely settler way of life, with its pre-breakfast morning tea, its myriad of "boys" for life's chores, and numerous drinks in tall glasses to end each day.

Now, even here, there is a growing realization that Africa's Bwana days are about over, going to join the pith helmet, the head porter caravans, and the stalwart district commissioners of yore. Many an old settler may be gone shortly, too, rather than face inevitable change. But there is one colorful character of an older Africa who may yet survive the transition from colonialism to independence. That is the white hunter, with the game safari which supports him.

"There is no reason why we can't continue operating here," says Sid Downey, slender and wiry partner in Africa's biggest safari firm, Ker, Downey and Selby Safaris, Limited, Nairobi. This firm was recently formed by merger of Ker and Downey with another old-line outfit, Selby and Holmberg Safaris, and now can put 20 safaris into the field at one time.

Over coffee in the New Stanley Hotel here, a tanned Mr. Downey adds: "We're having a bumper safari season this year, and bookings are coming in steadily for next year, too."

A few blocks away in an office decorated with hunting trophies, Colonel Robert Caulfield, business manager of White Hunters (Africa), Limited, second largest in the business, says: "We're remaining in Kenya. And why not? We're full up this year, and bookings are coming in fast for next year."

Confidence in the future is strengthened by an increased interest in conservation among Africans, a relatively recent development. This development raises hopes that the wild game of Africa may yet be accorded a place in the new scheme of things.

The fate of the white hunter, of course, may seem inconsequential in a fast-changing continent now preoccupied with the glitter of independence. Yet he represents a part of old Africa which is worth keeping, no matter what race occupies government offices.

His is the animal world of the clumsy, hump-backed wildebeest, the Roman-nosed hartebeest, the ever-alert Thomson's gazelle, the spiral-horned kudu and the flappy-eared elephant. If the white hunter disappears, it will be because the game has gone. And Africa's game represents a native heritage which is unique to this continent.

This is the Africa which is best known to America through Hemingway's virile stories and through countless Hollywood movies of derring-do amid East Africa's wild game. It is a world which most tourists—a considerable number of them Americans—look for when coming to Africa.

Those tourists spend money. And money is something that Africans need desperately.

Even today, after years of game poaching, East Africa offers more to animal-seeking tourists than does any other part of Africa. On almost any given day you can stand on the rim of Ngorongoro Crater in Tanganyika and see thousands of wildebeest, zebras and gazelles grazing below.

There still is abundant game in a few other parts of Africa, in reservations such as Wankie Park in Southern Rhodesia or Kruger Park in the Republic of South Africa, and in Mozambique and Angola. But nowhere is the safari business so well organized as it is here.

Contrary to the tales of some folk who know little about Africa, the game seldom is in competition with Africans for the land. Few, except migratory tribes, live in areas where game abounds. The soil is too poor. There isn't enough water for farming. Animals have been forced relentlessly into plains country which might compare with the Painted Desert of Arizona, or, as in the case of Uganda's Nile Valley, into swampy jungle which compares with Florida's Everglades.

Only a little bit of conservation is needed to assure continuation of the game. Water holes must be maintained. Hunting must be controlled. But above all, cooperation must be obtained from citizens.

Even that little bit of conservation seemed only a remote hope under an African government until recently. Most Africans saw game as meat on the hoof to be slaughtered indiscriminately. Conservation was viewed as a device of the white man to protect game for the benefit of a few rich hunters.

Now, Africans are beginning to show signs of a changing viewpoint. Some realize that controlled hunting may provide them with continuing meat sources, and that tourist dollars will continue to come only if the game is there as an attraction. Slowly, conservation is beginning to make sense to them.

Drive east of Mount Meru in Kenya to the Tana River in the land of Elsa the Lioness, and you find one of Africa's newest game reserves, one operated by the Meru tribe. At Leopard Rock Lodge several thatch-roofed huts wait for the tourists tribesmen hope will enrich their treasury.

In Kenya's far north, the Samburu tribe, a nomadic people of spear-bearing warriors, now is cooperating in another project aimed at conserving game in this dry wasteland.

"These are promising developments," says Sid Downey. "You can't have conservation unless Africans cooperate and they are starting to cooperate."

"My colleagues and I in the government see game as one of Tanganyika's great national assets," says A. S. Fundikira, the Tanganyikan government minister responsible for game. In Uganda, too, the government is backing a new conservation program.

"As soon as Africans find there is money in tourism for them, they are for it, and for the game which attracts the tourists," says W. J. D. Wadley, deputy general manager, East African Tourist Travel Association, Nairobi, a 37-year veteran of Africa, and retired Kenyan director of education.

"Tourism will one day be Kenya's major industry," enthuses Arvind Jamidar, Kenya's minister for tourism.

So, while die-hard white settlers may soon be leaving Kenya, the white hunter is digging in for a long stay.

RAY VICKER

November 15, 1962

Better Living Isn't Turning Czechs

Toward the West

PRAGUE—"Every fifth adult in Czechoslovakia belongs to the Communist party," says a Western diplomat here. "That's the highest percentage of party membership for any country in the world."

A simple percentage, of course, does not reveal why, or under what pressures, so many people here became party members. Nor does it reflect how many anti-Communists have been executed, imprisoned, reduced to penury or have fled the country. The old-time bourgeoisie hardly exists as a force the Reds have to reckon with today. Many of the new recruits to the Communist party are to be found among the working people the regime has tried to woo while rigidly ruling.

All the same, there are sobering implications in the diplomat's appraisal of Red influence in Czechoslovakia, where the standard of living is higher than anywhere else behind the Iron Curtain. A visit to this country quickly makes one aware that as a citizen gets better off materially, he doesn't necessarily lose interest in Communism.

This would appear to explode one pet theory of Western wishful-thinkers—that as Communists become more affluent, they automatically become more bourgeois, more interested in such things as individual freedom, and thus more susceptible to Western ideas.

"Bunk," retorts a Westerner who has spent many years behind the Iron Curtain. "The better off people become in the Communist world, the Redder they get."

Most available evidence seems to support this statement. Not only is the Communist party very strong here, but the Red Czech regime acts as if it possessed fervent missionary zeal. Aid to underdeveloped nations exceeds that dispensed by Russia, when figured on a per capita basis. Of course Russia coordinates all aid by its satellites and may be playing up Czech aid in hope of disguising its direct political penetration of underdeveloped countries.

Agriculture is being socialized to a greater degree than even the Soviets have dared attempt. And whereas anti-Red grumblings are often heard in Poland and Hungary, the Czechs seem to be somewhat better adjusted to Communist rule.

And there is little reason for doubting that people here do have the highest living standard in the Communist world. Reds took over a soundly based economy in 1948, with a well-developed industry and a solid core of skilled workers.

Today, Czechoslovakia's per capita output of steel is greater than Britain's, almost as much as America's, and 70 per cent greater than Russia's. With only a half of 1 per cent of the world's population, this country of 13.8 million people claims to account for 2 per cent of the world's industrial output. In 1960, its 2.3 million industrial workers turned out 6.8 million metric tons of steel, 132,000 refrigerators and 194,000 vacuum cleaners.

The government claims one million television sets now are in the hands of consumers. Evaluating the costs of a Moskvitch sedan against earnings in various countries, a visitor finds that the average Czech worker needs 22 months' work to pay for the car versus 30 months' work in Russia, 62 in Rumania and 76 in Poland.

At the six-story White Swan Department Store in downtown Prague, floors are as crowded as Macy's just before Christmas. Everything from needles to complete kitchens are on display, with most goods purchasable off the floor. Especially noticeable are such consumer goods as fly fishing rods, spinning reels, skin diving suits, rubber boats, and other products usually associated with an affluent economy.

A crowd collects before a cutaway model of a Skoda Octavia auto-mobile revolving on a first-floor stand. About 30,000 autos a year now are being delivered to Czech consumers, while 120,000 hard orders, accompanied by half the price of the car, wait to be filled.

As goods are made available, the government proclaims that all this is being made possible through Communism. Many young people now don't even remember any other system, so they seem willing to believe the propaganda.

"We find it difficult now to talk to our children in certain areas," one parent says, rather sadly. "They don't know what we mean when we use such words as 'landlords,' or 'profit motives,' or 'free speech.' So we must explain to them, and even then they don't seem to under-stand."

Cheap staple foods are coupled with low rents that seldom amount to more than 5 per cent of incomes, and with free medical care. Here again, Red propaganda constantly stresses that "socialism" is respon-sible for these gains, with the implication that the alternative is a system of high rents, expensive food and stiff medical bills.

"That's the sort of thing people are told throughout the Communist world as living standards rise," says one Western source. "If you kick a man in the pants and then tell him the kick is for his own good, he may not believe your propaganda. But, if you give a man a handout, and then pass out some propaganda, he may listen. This is so elemen-tary the mission churches have been using the idea for centuries. Still you hear this half-baked talk about an affluent Communist becoming less doctrinaire."

This isn't pleasant to hear, especially when one sees the heavy price in lost freedom charged by Communism.

In many ways the Red regime here is more orthodox in its Com-munism than is Russia's. Though it is the most Westernized of Red countries, it now is the Communist state with the fewest cultural ties with the West.

The civilian Union for Cooperation with the Army has attracted a million recruits. This para-military group, which stages parades and military-type drills, was formed to encourage "combat preparedness of the working people and to help form in our people traits and knowledge necessary to build a mature socialistic society," says a gov-ernment handout.

Czechoslovakia has become a favorite nesting place for various "peace" groups in the Red world. This summer, Prague played host to the Christian Peace Congress, a group of 700 delegates from nu-merous countries which passed a resolution to "take a stand against atomic war, cold war, colonialism and racism."

Prague has become the headquarters for training Communist labor leaders from all parts of the world. Today, this labor school is paying special attention to training unionists from Latin America and from Africa.

Some 2,700 students from 80 countries now are attending universities, language schools and technical colleges in Czechoslovakia. Most are holders of scholarships. More than half hail from Africa, Asia or Latin America.

With their educations they receive doses of Communist propaganda. One student winks slyly when asked if any of the propaganda is taken seriously. But, an engineering expert familiar with courses of study says:

"The aim isn't to convert every one of these students to Communism. If these students go back home thinking just a little better of Communism, that may be enough from the Red viewpoint."

In agriculture, Czechs are tightening the screws on holders of individual plots—the small holdings allowed for personal vegetable growing when farmers join collectives. Even Russia found it advantageous to allow peasants to hold such plots, though this idea conflicts with Marxist dogmas about agriculture.

As a foreign-aid giver, the Czech regime is the most openhanded in the Communist world. Up to the end of 1960, Czechs had spent $660 million in foreign aid to underdeveloped countries, or nearly $48 per capita. Russia, with 217 million people, had allocated $3.6 billion in aid, or about $16 per head.

These figures tell only part of the story. A lot of Russian aid has been in the form of long term credits, much of which still must be collected by receiver nations. Czechs have been much prompter. Moreover, Czechoslovakia has given almost as much aid to other Communist states as it has to underdeveloped countries. One Western intelligence source estimates the total Czech aid at $1.1 billion over the last four or five years, or about $80 per capita. This same source puts Russian aid at "over $3 billion" and Red China's at $1.5 billion during the same period.

Little Czechoslovakia now has the third largest Communist party in the world, running only behind Russia and Red China in total numbers and exceeding these countries on a per capita basis. The Czech party now totals 1.6 million, a rise of 280,000 in the last three years.

If Communists can continue to raise living standards here, this trend may well continue. There is no evidence here to indicate that the Communist, once "affluent," begins to favor Western ideals.

RAY VICKER

October 9, 1961

Letter from Abroad

DEAR MOTHER AND DADDY:

As you know there was quite a thing stirred up about that girl's postcard and so the Peace Corps has asked us all to be extra careful about what we write home about.

Well, we've gotten around quite a bit in Africa and nowhere is it more beautiful than here in quaint, unspoiled Lower Insomnia. It's not like West Hartford at all—that is, it's not exactly like West Hartford any more than West Hartford is like Fairfield. But it's very nice.

The first day I went with our P.C. group to talk to a certain tribe about democracy. The chief was very helpful and said that all his tribesmen were simply dying to learn about how representative government works. But when the chief himself heard how it works he got very angry and told us to leave. It was the funniest thing.

After that we went down to the local shopping center to see the native arts and crafts. You know how I've always loved arts and crafts, like that time in camp when I made those slippers for Daddy. Well, to tell you the truth, arts and crafts are a little different here. For instance they had these shrunken . . . er, what I mean is some of the things would make interesting conversation pieces, but we are going to try to teach the people to emphasize the functional, rather than the purely ornamental.

My girl friend, Hegira, has been sick to her stomach for five days but not because of anything she ate. She hasn't eaten anything since she got here. I think it's all in her mind myself. The riots at the airport just weren't that bad.

A couple of days ago we drove out to Lake Typhus, which is an all-year-round summer resort. Everybody for miles around goes to the lake for a swim, and not only people. What I mean is that there is an abundance of animal life and sometimes the animal life goes swimming too. The lake gets pretty crowded but since we've been here no swimmer has died of drowning.

The Minister of Health and Recreation invited us to go swimming but I thought the lake was crowded enough with all those . . . all those people. Anyhow I had to stay with Hegira who fainted when she saw the . . . well, I really don't know what made her faint but it could have been anything. You know Hegira.

The natives are very informal about all manner of things. You might say they're not an especially clothes-conscious people. Oh, but don't misunderstand, they wear something all right. At least they seem covered enough when they stand still, but when they run. . . .

No matter what you read in the papers back home, Lower Insomnia is not going Communist. Some of the boys in the Corps said they don't think it's going anyplace. I asked some people here if they planned to go Communist and they shook their heads. And that means no. I did notice, though, that they shook their heads to any question. It may be that their English is spotty.

The students here are a lot like students back home. They have pep rallies when there's a big game coming up and even when there isn't. They have so much school spirit about everything.

It's even more remarkable when you find out most of the students don't even go to school. Hegira says it all sounds very progressive to her.

I don't care what they may do in other underdeveloped countries, but in Lower Insomnia they do not cook in the streets. These people prefer to eat their food raw—undoubtedly they realize how cooking destroys valuable vitamins and minerals.

The housing here is different from what we have in West Hartford. The cottages are smaller and more rustic. They don't have windows or floors or furniture. But it's almost always warm, so why should they have floors? Windows are really unnecessary because the people would probably never bother to look out anyway. And without furniture you'd be surprised how much more room they have to move around.

Tomorrow we start teaching the local folks about farming, which I expect to enjoy. You remember how much I've always liked to take rides in the country and look at farms. Well, just imagine little me teaching how to make the land give forth its bounty, how to turn miles of trackless jungles into rolling fields of wheat, corn and grain.

In closing, let me say that the Peace Corps thus far has really been an enlightening experience.

Oh yes, please tell Hegira's parents that she's all right. For some reason the Peace Corps won't let her write any letters.

Love,
PENELOPE

EDWIN A. ROBERTS, JR.

October 24, 1961

WINDOW . . .

OUT OF THIS WORLD

———◆———

Call of Space

CAPE CANAVERAL, FLORIDA—Astronaut Glenn's dramatic earth-orbiting feat yesterday was more than a great accomplishment in scientific terms. It was a great human accomplishment that tends to underscore and yet make hollow the old debate about manned versus unmanned space flight.

True, most of the tasks performed by Lt. Col. Glenn could have been performed with at least equal precision by electronic instruments. But it was not the purpose of yesterday's shot to make scientific observations. Rather it was an engineering test of the space capsule and a medical experiment to give doctors an inkling of how well a man can function in the rigorous environment of space.

Whatever the astronaut is able to contribute, the concept of manned space flight is likely to remain one of the most controversial ideas in American science. With President Kennedy's announced intention of putting men on the moon "before the end of the decade," this controversy is assuming a new turn and a growing importance. Is it worthwhile or necessary to rush men to the moon as soon as possible or should the next several years be spent exploring the moon, the planets and space with unmanned scientific instruments, holding men back until the potentials of the instruments are exhausted?

Man, of course, has many skills that cannot yet be duplicated by machines. He can make judgments and has an ability to cope with the unexpected. Because of these abilities, one school claims, man would yield the most fruitful results in exploring space.

Yet instruments have made an impressive showing in the space program. Satellites and deep space probes have poured back volumes of new scientific information about space—the discovery of the Van Allen radiation belts that girdle the earth is already rated as one of the great scientific discoveries of the new age.

Satellites have demonstrated their capacity to gather weather information, relay intercontinental telephone and radio calls (and shortly television programs), serve as navigation beacons, take pictures of enemy military installations and detect missile launchings.

And there is more than enough on the drawing boards to suggest that machines in the future will be performing even more intricate tasks, probably even developing an intelligence.

There are other aspects to the debate, however. The effort to rocket men to the moon as soon as possible will cost, as Mr. Kennedy notes, $20 billion to $40 billion—an amount that will be spent within the next five years.

A program to spend the next few years exploring the solar system with unmanned instruments and delaying sending men to the moon until the 1970s would be far cheaper. The President's proposed 1963 budget gives only a hint of how much cheaper.

He proposes spending about $1.1 billion next fiscal year on the manned space program. The unmanned space program, however, will run less than half this amount and will include landing instruments on the moon, sending instruments into the vicinity of Venus and deep into planetary space, as well as a host of earth satellite experiments.

Intertwined in the debate is the question of why there should be any exploration of the moon and the planets at all. So far no one has come up with any concrete military or economic reasons for going to the moon with either men or instruments, and arguments that such feats will impress the "uncommitted peoples of the world" seem dubious. Almost anything would impress the uncommitted peoples, including firecrackers.

Scientists, however, can make a strong case for wanting to go to the moon and the planets.

A study of the moon's surface and interior—the amount of radioactivity, the stuff it's made of, and whether it once had a molten core or not—should provide significant clues about the origin of the earth and the solar system. Such information, in turn, would help us understand the earth much better.

More exciting, perhaps, is the chance to look at living organisms that may have developed under conditions different from those on earth (a remote possibility on the moon but highly likely on Mars). Too, a study of interplanetary space should provide highly important answers on how the sun affects the earth's weather and its radio communications.

It is difficult if not impossible to put a dollar value on such research. But almost since the inception of the space effort, scientists have left no doubt that they believe it well worth a major effort to explore the

moon and the planets with scientific instruments and eventually, after
the possibilities of the instruments have been exhausted, to send man
to the planets. Fewer and fewer of these scientists seem willing to
justify the sharp step-up in the manned moon program on a purely
scientific basis, however.

As early in the space program as March, 1958, for example, the
President's science advisory committee put the major emphasis for
lunar and planetary exploration on unmanned scientific instruments.

"Remotely controlled scientific expeditions to the moon and near-by
planets could absorb the energies of scientists for many decades," the
committee noted. "Since man is such an adventurous creature, there
will undoubtedly come a time when he can no longer resist going out
and seeing for himself. It would be foolish to try to predict today just
when this moment will arrive. It might not arrive in this century, or
it might come within one or two decades. So much will depend upon
how rapidly we want to expand and accelerate our program. According to one rough estimate it might require a total investment of a
couple of billion dollars, spent over a number of years, to equip ourselves to land a man on the moon and to return him safely to earth."

Whatever the early estimates of the program, Mr. Kennedy's sudden
step-up of the man-to-the-moon effort is now playing havoc with the
scientists' carefully laid plans for a thorough exploration of moon and
planets by mechanical means before attempting to send men. The
contracts for the Project Apollo manned moon flight, for instance,
are now being let although the United States has failed so far to put
even a small instrument on the moon.

As a result, researchers don't know whether the moon's surface is
covered with a deep layer of fine dust or whether it is rubble. Hope-
fully, the second Project Ranger later this year will televise back some
pictures to give them an idea.

Another unmanned moon project, called Prospector, is now hanging
in limbo as a result of the stepped-up manned-vehicle program. This
project was to have put a mobile, heavily instrumented device on the
moon in 1966 or 1968, the target dates for sending a man to the moon.

But whatever the status of various unmanned space projects, there's
no challenging the fact that achievements like Lt. Col. Glenn's stimulate man's lust for adventure.

The situation was summed up recently by Dr. Leo Stag, manager
of General Electric's space science laboratories near Philadelphia.

"As far as unmanned exploration is concerned, I can make a very
good case on economics. I can show that you will turn over the investment shortly in terms of weather and communications satellites. I can
also make a very good case on political principles. But as far as manned

exploration is concerned, when all is said and done and all the arguments are heard, we will probably go exploring only because we want to."

And that, of course, was also the reason man finally left the cave for good.

JERRY E. BISHOP

February 21, 1962

STUCK

I pulled all the pins
From my brand-new shirt,
And yet my poor skin's
Badly scratched and hurt.
Oh! Seldom one wins,
When all's said and done.
For I pulled all the pins,
As I've said—except one.

—RICHARD ARMOUR

Man in Motion—

From Cart to Capsule

When the human species finally closes up shop, the cause may be man's inability to come to terms with his own colicky disposition. But whatever his fate, the record will show that this fragile biped did not bow out before learning to transport himself at speeds of five miles per second.

John Glenn's ride on the celestial whip, its scientific implications aside, tends to stir the philosopher in all of us. With the Wright brothers' success at Kitty Hawk not yet a lifetime behind us, man is already soaring through space at 30 times the speed of sound.

To even the least contemplative soul, this extraordinary acceleration of technology is as stunning as the fact of space travel itself. After so many ages when man was solely dependent upon human and animal muscle for transport over land, the world was suddenly rocked by an explosion of invention. In the last century the steam and internal combustion engines replaced the horse and the sail; in the last decade nuclear energy and jet propulsion revolutionized transportation again; in the last year rocket power lifted three Americans into space; in the next decade, the U.S. Government plans to send a manned expedition to the planets.

Technological progress in the 20th century has become a brakeless bobsled, but the thrill ride was a long time coming.

The first breakthrough, of course, was the wheel. Nobody knows who got the big idea but the cart is known to have existed in Sumer about 3500 B.C. The first wheels were solid, made by slicing up a tree or by fitting three triangular pieces together and rounding the outside edges.

Next came the spoke which permitted lighter, more maneuverable vehicles. These appeared before 1800 B.C., and they were soon hitched to horses which had a more favorable gear ratio than oxen. At the outset there was some trouble figuring how to hitch up the narrow-shouldered animal to a cart, and more than one ancient teamster found he had strangled his horse.

The wheel, wonderful as it was, meant little until roads were built and the early civilizations recognized the need. Egypt, Mesopotamia and Crete went so far as to pave a few freeways. But even in Rome.

where great roads were built as avenues of conquest, the animal-drawn wagon couldn't compete with the relative efficiency of the sailing vessel.

Land travel, in fact, remained a cumbersome business until the advent of the rail, which occurred in the 17th century when German miners fixed a peg underneath a truck to guide the vehicle along a groove in a plank and thus keep the front wheels on a straight course.

But even then, with only gravity or brute strength to provide the motive power, little headway was made. The world awaited the steam engine.

It is a real wonder that the steam engine was ever invented, inasmuch as the leading scientific lights of a few hundred years ago knew little more about gases than did the ancients who proclaimed air an "element." Finally, Galileo's pupil, Torricelli, hit upon the fact of atmospheric pressure. It then dawned upon the scientific community that if a simple means could be found of repeatedly creating a vacuum, atmospheric pressure could be used as a source of power.

After much preliminary experimentation with "atmospheric engines" of dubious value, James Watt brought some of the basic principles of this device to the steam engine. It was in 1776 that Watt's first two steam engines were put to work, and the era of mechanical power really began. In 1807, Robert Fulton stuck a Watt-built engine in the hull of a paddle-wheel ship and chugged from New York to Albany.

Paralleling the development of the steam engine was the internal combustion engine. Among the early pioneers of this invention were Gottlieb Daimler and Karl Benz, a couple of Germans who eventually adapted their motors to the horseless carriage. But it was for an American, Henry Ford, to make the automobile popular.

Although the flanged wheel on the steel rail did more than anything to improve land travel, it was always clear that if man could somehow fashion a heavier-than-air vehicle to stay aloft, the speed advantages would be extraordinary.

Orville Wright's 40-yard flight from a North Carolina sand dune got very few people exercised, even though the invention was to change transportation as no invention had changed it since ships were first fitted with sails. The airplane emptied the oceans and flattened the mountains. Man could at last roam the air and outer space was at hand.

Under the stimulus of war and, in the last 15 years, under the stimulus of the Communist challenge, technology advanced on countless fronts. But the free world, which was taking its own sweet time about exploring space, needed the dramatic prod of Sputnik I to get its rocket research moving.

Oddly enough, the rocket—the reaction engine—predates the steam and internal combustion engines by many centuries. The earliest known rocket engine was put together by Archytas of Tarantum, a Greek philosopher and scientist, around 400 B.C. This invention used a jet of steam to propel the figure of a bird through the air, but outside of scaring the daylights out of a lot of Greeks, the device was never put to significant use.

The Greek mathematician, Heron of Alexandria, built a steam rocket that spun on an axis but he couldn't think of anything to do with it. Sometime later, however, Heron's invention was modified into the lawn sprinkler of suburbia fame.

Next came the Chinese who were manufacturing gunpowder-propelled skyrockets 1,000 years ago. The Chinese soon found that an arrow fastened to a tube of gunpowder made a wonderful weapon. And it was a Chinese also who first saw the connection between rockets and space travel around the year 1500.

This early astronaut, named Wan-Hoo, fastened a seat between two kites and 47 gunpowder rockets astern for motive power. When Wan-Hoo climbed aboard, his servants, presumably after an appropriate countdown, ignited the rockets. When the dense clouds of smoke cleared, no trace of Wan-Hoo or his spaceship could ever be found.

The first genuine rocket expert was a British lawyer, Sir William Congreve, who developed a war rocket with a range of 2,000 yards. In 1807, 25,000 Congreve rockets were used to destroy the city of Copenhagen. Soon after that, rocket corps were organized by most European armies. Incidentally, those rockets in the "Star-Spangled Banner" were after the Congreve model.

In the latter part of the 19th century there were many designs for rocketships, the best known of which was thought up by Hermann Ganswindt, a German. Ganswindt wanted to go to Mars and imagined that the best way to break away from the earth's gravity was by combining the action and reaction characteristics of a rocket. He figured that by filling large cylinders with dynamite, steel balls could be fired against the inside of the ship, while escaping gases would provide additional thrust as well.

Russia got into the space race (it wasn't called that then) in 1903 when Konstantin Ziolkovsky, a schoolteacher, proposed the use of liquid fuels in rockets. Ziolkovsky also made important studies of friction on the skin of spaceships and it was none but he who first used the term "sputnik" (fellow-traveler) to describe an artificial earth satellite.

The man who is known as the "Father of Modern Rocketry" was an American named Robert H. Goddard, a physics professor who proved in 1919 that it would be possible to send an 11-ton rocket to the moon and to set off a charge of magnesium powder which would be visible to observers on earth. In 1926 Goddard launched the first liquid-propellant rocket and, in succeeding experiments, he fired an 85-pound rocket to an altitude of 7,500 feet at a speed of 700 miles an hour. It was Goddard, too, who invented a gyroscopic guidance device with which to control the missile in flight.

Meanwhile, a rocket craze had overtaken the scientific community in Germany. In 1933, the German Rocket Society (which included a young man named Wernher von Braun) built a passenger-carrying rocket designed to send a human cargo a half-mile into the air and return him by parachute. But for some reason (perhaps a shortage of astronauts) the rocket was never launched. The Germans continued their research through World War II and came close to turning the tables on the Allies with their V-2 rocket, a weapon that traveled at 2,000 miles an hour with a range of almost 200 miles. A transatlantic model of the V-2 was in the works when the war ended.

The United States and the Soviet Union continued to work on the German rocket designs after the war, but it was not until the first man-made earth satellite, put aloft by the Russians in 1957, that the average man became aware of the possibilities. And it may be said that it was not until John Glenn's voyage last week that Americans were sure they would not always be getting their eyebrows singed by Russian exhaust.

In assessing the great technological strides of recent years, it is at once clear that the main booster has been the historic hostility of man to man, or at least of nation to nation. If there were no need for new and better weapons, the advance of rocketry would have moved at a comparatively sluggish pace. Fear has been the prime mover.

For all that, the accomplishment has been, one might say, unearthly. It took 4,000 years for man to progress from the horse to the automobile, and only 66 years after Henry Ford built his first car a human was sent into space and brought safely back. Moreover, before a child born today is ready for kindergarten, there could well be a man on the moon.

It's a little like riding the back of a tiger—invigorating but risky. Yet there's nothing for us but to hang on and let the great cat run.

EDWIN A. ROBERTS, JR.

October 12, 1962

*"Some chalk company wants me to endorse their
product."*

Exploring Space—
Too Much Too Fast?

WASHINGTON—The exploration of space touches on questions
of the most fundamental kind. In the end they are metaphysical questions, and so perhaps unanswerable.

The argument of the proponents of the specific programs embarked
on by the National Aeronautics and Space Administration boils down
to this: it is the nature of man to explore what he can. Space is there
and we have a rapidly growing capability for exploring it. The effort
will pay big economic dividends, in industrial and commercial applications. Finally, and possibly most important, if we don't do our best,
the Russians will get ahead of us.

"It would not be a becoming international posture for this country," says one high space executive here, "to announce in effect that we have the capability for space exploration but we just don't care to do it." Historically, he and others contend, power rides with the most efficient peoples. And this being the age of science and technology, space is the logical target for our efficiency. Otherwise, the Soviets might be able to enslave the world with or without war, through their mastery of the sciences needed for space work.

Thus stated, the thesis seems all but unarguable. But it does not satisfy some people, including some scientists. Their concern centers on these areas: the enormous cost, especially the farther we try to go in space; the inevitable neglect of other problems urgently clamoring for attention; the danger of using space as a vehicle for an unprecedented growth of Government power, even to the point of direction of labor. "A cosmic boondoggle," one critic recently declared.

Right now, of course, most of the publicity is about the attempt to land a man on the moon by the end of this decade; Scott Carpenter's flight is one step in that direction. This is an incredibly complex and costly undertaking, on which somewhere between $20 billion and $40 billion is expected to be spent. Yet it is only one of innumerable space projects, and it is far from the most startling one in the planners' minds.

Space officials rather vehemently deny that the lunar landing is some sort of stunt. If you are going to explore space, they observe, the moon is a likely initial objective. Later, there is every intention of visiting other bodies in our solar system and, if science and technology permit, in other galaxies.

We are beginning, then, an enterprise that dwarfs history and the comprehension of most men. "After all," says one questioner, "regardless of what Columbus thought he was doing, his voyage was inescapably finite. But space, so far as anyone now knows, is infinite."

If you may have forgotten some of your high school astronomy, here is a brief reminder, in the words of James J. Haggerty, Jr., editor of *Aerospace Year Book:*

The barrier to the exploration of the universe lies in the distances to the stars, distances so great that it is difficult for the human mind to grasp them. Even a billion miles is too puny a measure of distance in outer space; we must employ the light year, or the distance light travels in one earth calendar year. Light moves at a velocity of 186,300 miles per second, so a light year is . . . almost six trillion miles. . . .

As a portion of the universe, our entire solar system is infinitesimally minute. Proxima Centauri, the star nearest our sun, is four and one-quarter light years away. These two stars—our sun and Proxima Centauri—are members of a galaxy we call the "Milky Way," a grouping of an estimated hundred billion stars. The Milky Way is so immense that it would take a spacecraft moving at the speed of light 100,000 years to traverse its length. . . .

And in the universe there are uncountable groups of galaxies, at distances so vast that even the light year becomes an inadequate measurement.

Yet, according to currently accepted scientific theory, the speed of light is a limit beyond which no particle can be accelerated. Even if such a velocity were possible, it would take almost nine years to make a star.

Or, as Pascal summed it all up in a sentence centuries ago, "The silence of infinite space terrifies me."

Scientists do not know whether it may eventually be possible to exceed the speed of light. In any case, the cost of future space activity is obviously beyond reckoning. Space is not going to bring anyone any profits any time soon.

The space men do insist, however, that it is bringing economic rewards now and will bring many more in the years ahead. Such as which?

One clear case is the Tiros weather satellite, which has saved lives and property by its ability to forecast storms. Another instance is the communications satellite, versions of which have been developed by both AT&T and NASA; this opens up the prospect of instant worldwide telephoning and television, among other advances. Legislation now in Congress would permit the public to buy shares in a new communications-satellite corporation.

But an expert in this field at NASA's Goddard Space Flight Center near Washington has a word of caution for investors. "We still have a long way to go," he says. "And this thing has got to be economical. People are not going to use it simply because it exists."

In addition, the crash-program nature of the space effort means the rapid development of new industrial processes, new materials, new metals, a host of electronic advances, and whole new concepts of propulsion which conceivably could have earthly applications in time. All this spells, space officials claim, not only economic benefits but a guarantee that our military establishment has the most advanced science and technology at its disposal, even though NASA is a civilian agency and space may never be a theater of war.

"In fact, it's like a war effort," says one official. "World War I practically gave our chemical industry a big shove. World War II gave us atomic energy and major electronic advances. Frankly, I don't know what all will come out of space work, but I am sure it will be a great deal."

The question nonetheless remains: Why space rather than some other scientific focus? "If you ask me why the United States doesn't spend this money and effort on curing cancer," replies another official, "then I say this country is rich enough to do both."

That surely is the weakest of all the relevant arguments. For precisely one of the fears is that we may endanger the financial underpinnings of the economy—not by space as such but because the U.S. Government refuses to limit any other spending in order to devote all these billions to space.

Besides, there are other scientific areas that deserve attention, and not necessarily the ones usually mentioned, like curing cancer or cleaning up the cities or feeding the hungry of the world. One of the least explored phenomena in the universe is man himself—man who creates wars, who retains a medieval penological concept, who concocts uncountable other evils. What is the future of man under the increasing influence of the doctrine of individual irresponsibility, of something for nothing, more pay for less work? What profit to gain the universe and lose man's soul?

No sensible person seriously supposes that billions of dollars and a crash program alone would make us understand and improve the nature of man. But who is to say it would not produce important insights? And that if it were done, it would not put us farther ahead of the Russians than space can? Anyway, nothing has altered Kant's perception that the two most astounding things are the starry heavens and the moral law in man.

The space officials observe that they are of necessity exploring man, at least how he reacts in space. More importantly, they suggest there could hardly be a better hope of improving man than this concentrated attempt to push back the frontiers of knowledge. It benefits all science; for the first time, they argue, we are getting interdisciplinary science; that is, a real interaction of the basic sciences involved in space. For many of them, this, the advancement of human knowledge, is the whole point of our voyage into the unknown.

Still, nothing is without its price. Suppose we are eventually able to go beyond our solar system into other galaxies. In infinity, where do we stop? Will there be any rational justification for sending people on years-long trips through the black night of space? And, since many scientists suspect there is intelligent life somewhere in other galaxies, will we be inviting more trouble than ever dreamed of on this poor little sphere?

Infinity, if that is what it proves to be, means that space work could become so gigantic that the Government would take over the lives of all of us in pursuit of it. If that were ever to happen, space would be not only a cosmic boondoggle but the instrument for the destruction of the free society.

Only fanatics, to be sure, contend that we should not be in space at all. We are in it, both because our science and technology have been moving that way, and because the Russians are in it. Only the insensate could fail to be proud of the achievements the nation has made in a few short years—and, so far as can be judged at this moment, our scientific space work is well ahead of the Russians'.

The reasonable questioning, rather, is along the line of whether it is too much too fast, to the possible detriment of other work and other values. The fact that there do not seem to be satisfactory answers is no excuse for not asking the questions. Space, with all its wonderful and frightening possibilities, both earthly and unearthly, is far too important to be accepted uncritically from the mouth of Government.

JOSEPH E. EVANS

June 1, 1962

THE BUSINESS OF WORDS

Confidentially Yours

NEW YORK—Newsletters, periodicals typically plain in format, fancy in price and confidential in tone, are bulking larger in the publishing world.

An array of Washington newsletters purport to give businessmen and others the lowdown on politics and government each week. "Newsette," also out of Washington, aims at women with items on such topics as the population explosion and Jackie Kennedy's hairdo. "International Art Market" keeps collectors and dealers posted on the prices of art and antiques, while "Party Line" tips off public relations men as to the types of material magazines and newspapers are looking for. There is a newsletter especially for dentists with tax problems and another for private secretaries with boss problems.

All told, according to Gale Research Company, a Detroit publisher of reference books which is assembling a directory of newsletters, there are now about 1,000 newsletters, double the number five years ago. These are all paid-circulation periodicals, and do not include the thousands of house organs and other free publications often called newsletters.

Newsletter circulations, usually all mail, range from a few hundred to the more than 150,000 claimed by the "Kiplinger Washington Letter." Because a majority of newsletters deal in some way with business topics and trends, executives comprise the largest group of subscribers.

Four to eight pages of short, to-the-point items, with no advertising or photographs, is the usual newsletter fare. Some of the smaller letters are put together by one man working in his spare time and relying mainly on other publications for his information, but many are issued by sizable organizations. The weekly Kiplinger letter, which costs $24 a year, boasts a staff of 12 reporters who dig for Washington news useful to businessmen.

Highly specialized newsletters aimed at people in a particular field account for much of the recent growth in the number of newsletters. Prentice-Hall, Incorporated, of Englewood Cliffs, New Jersey, a book publisher, issues 14 of these specialized newsletters, including the one for dentists concerned about taxes and others for lawyers and company treasurers.

"Our job is to give people the tools to do a better job," says John G. Powers, president of Prentice-Hall. Typically, a recent number of the $36-a-year tax letter for dentists explained how a dentist can cut his tax bill by selling his professional building to a member of his family and then leasing it back.

The "Gallagher Report," which covers advertising and publishing and delights in needling newspapers and magazines, is one of the better known of the specialized newsletters. Its publisher, gray-haired, nattily dressed Bernard P. Gallagher, claims considerable influence for his letter. The "Gallagher Report," he says, was the first to mention Matthew J. Culligan last spring as a possible new president for Curtis Publishing Company, and Mr. Gallagher himself first brought Curtis and Mr. Culligan together. Mr. Culligan was named president July 9.

Not all Mr. Gallagher's reports are so non-controversial. His October 29 newsletter stated that Time Incorporated had decided to "unload" *House and Home,* its monthly magazine for the home building industry. Time Incorporated immediately demanded a retraction, notifying Mr. Gallagher there was "no truth whatever in that damaging statement." Mr. Gallagher acknowledges that he since has learned that Time Incorporated has no present plans to sell or suspend the magazine, and will so advise his readers in a future issue.

Readers of specialized newsletters say the publications often summarize useful information that otherwise would have to be gathered from many sources. "A hundred magazines and trade journals cross my desk," says a General Electric Company official concerned with heavy electrical equipment and utilities. Two newsletters in his field "are more prompt to distill the essence of what interests me most, and occasionally they report something important that hasn't appeared elsewhere. Sure, some of the stuff is gossip, but a man should know the gossip in his own field."

Many of the newsletters designed for broader readership capitalize on the widespread human craving to be part of a supposed inner circle. "I like to be in on things that ordinary newspaper readers don't know," says a Washington lawyer who pays $50 annually for an "inside dope sheet" about happenings in the capital.

One popular general interest newsletter caters to this attitude by calling itself the "Insider's Newsletter." Published by Cowles Magazines and Broadcasting, Incorporated, the $18-a-year weekly covers every conceivable subject. Items in the current issue range from a report that the United States is prepared, in event of a Berlin conflict, to conduct guerrilla warfare in East Germany by smuggling weapons through Berlin tunnels and by parachute drops, to advice for women who want a social register listing to go west to Chicago, Denver or San Francisco where there are fewer old families and lower social walls than in Boston, New York or Baltimore.

"Insider's" circulation is more than 100,000, roughly double a year ago.

The Kiplinger letter, "circulated privately to businessmen," protects its aura of exclusiveness by warning in each issue that other publications are forbidden to quote it. "Personal from Pearson," a Washington newsletter issued by the organization of newspaper columnist Drew Pearson, starts off each week's publication with the injunction: "Confidential—Not for Publication."

Like many newsletters, "Personal from Pearson" piques the interest of readers by printing rumors other types of publications might shy from. But it carefully labels such items as unverifiable reports; an example was a recent item suggesting that General Bernard Schriever, head of the Air Force's Systems Command, will be named the President's adviser on science and its role in warfare.

William Neel, who edits the Pearson letter, claims a high percentage of correct predictions. Example: There will be no steel strike (January 6 issue); the Justice Department will win anti-trust indictments in Hartford, Connecticut, against copper and brass companies (June 30 issue). But some forecasts do go awry, as one late June prediction that President Kennedy would send tax cut proposals to Congress during the summer.

"Newsette," the letter for women, is turned out by one of the oldest newsletter publishers, Whaley-Eaton Service of Washington. Since 1919 Whaley-Eaton has been issuing its "American Letter," a four-page weekly filled with capsule reports of political, economic and scientific developments. With the help of correspondents in London and Tokyo, Whaley-Eaton also publishes the "Foreign Letter," a compilation of news items from overseas.

New newsletters crop up constantly. Among those of recent origin are the "EEC Newsletter," which keeps readers abreast of Common Market trends, and the "Humor Exchange Newsletter," which provides comedians, columnists and Congressmen with joke ideas. Scheduled to appear next month is a $25-a-year biweekly "that links you with happenings in the world of love and sex."

One reason for the rapid growth of newsletters is that they are relatively inexpensive to produce. A newsletter publisher "can get from twice to 20 times the price from subscribers for a publication produced at least 20 times less expensively than a magazine," claims a man familiar with the field.

Some newsletters have proved highly profitable. Mr. Gallagher says he expects a "clear profit of $75,000" next year from the "Gallagher Report," which has a circulation of slightly over 10,000 and whose subscription price will jump from $18 to $24 in January. Industrial Research, Incorporated, of Beverly Shores, Indiana, last March launched a $75-a-year weekly letter called "Research Trendletter" and started making a profit with the first issue, according to Neil P. Ruzic, president. By way of contrast, three years and an investment of $550,-000 were needed before the firm's $7-a-year monthly magazine, *Industrial Research,* broke even.

The business has its pitfalls, however. "Probably in no other area of publishing are there as many failures as in newsletters," says Frederick G. Ruffner, president of Gale Research of Detroit. "I would say that 350 newsletters will start this year and 250 others will die. The turnover is tremendous."

Newsletters are especially vulnerable to circulation declines because they take in no advertising revenue. Attracting new subscribers and spurring old ones to renew can be costly, and many newsletters fail because of a lack of funds for adequate promotion.

A. KENT MACDOUGALL

November 11, 1962

TV in the Plains

AMARILLO, TEXAS—Most people in this part of the country
seem to dispute the proposition that television is a vast wasteland. Instead, they consider it a fertile field that's simply been planted to corn.
And here that's not necessarily so bad.

Of all the subjects introduced by a reporter sampling public opinion
in five Western states, none brought freer replies than the question of
television program quality. Clearly, this was something everybody knew
something about. And although few people indicated an overriding
interest in the current Federal Communications Commission hearings
in Washington, most of those interviewed expressed strong views on the
proper role of that agency and what they liked and did not like to see
on the home screen.

There is little regard in the West for the tastes of television critics
in the East. While viewers would like to see more serious drama and
more documentary-type news programs, they are fearful greater power
for the FCC would turn their TV sets into forced-culture vending
machines.

Speaking of television critics, bus driver Bill Dugan remarks:
"They'd like to give us Shakespeare and long-hair music. And I think
Shakespeare and long-hair music are overrated myself."

But if most people are wary of Government "censorship" of television, they are still far from satisfied with the programs now offered.
There is no antagonism toward cowboy shows, and in fact some viewers
would like to see more of them. "I never saw a Western I didn't enjoy,"
says a cowboy in Clayton, New Mexico. Private-eye programs, however, seem to be losing their appeal and almost everybody claims he's
stopped watching domestic stories featuring a dopey father, a saint of
a mother, and various bratty kids.

If TV critics living in big cities think the choice of viewing fare is
too limited, they should sample what's available in the West. In areas
where it is possible to receive only two or three channels clearly enough
to watch, the choice is restricted indeed. Moreover, local stations often
subscribe to the same news wire service so that announcers on all available channels frequently read identical news scripts. (They even fluff
the same words.)

The question of violence on TV brings an interesting and fairly general response. Some violence is enthusiastically endorsed while other kinds are deplored. Widely appreciated out here is the saloon brawl which, it is held, provides a therapeutic, vicarious release from inner tensions. Also highly respected is the Western gun fight and the fistic exchange on top of a stagecoach or at the edge of a cliff.

But knives, axes, garroting cords, blackjacks, brass knuckles, sledge hammers, submachine guns and poison gas are regarded as unfit for the living room. Homemade bombs are considered all right so long as they aren't overdone.

Most people say they are careful about what they let their own children watch. Several housewives claim TV viewing is restricted to definite times and definite programs. "If a story gets too bloody or dirty we switch it off," declares one woman.

One frequently heard criticism, from women, is that television shows supposedly designed for the whole family are often too sexy. Dance costumes come in for special raps. "Those girls don't care what they show," declares Mrs. Jane Thompson, a farmer's wife.

A woman who was shopping with Mrs. Thompson elaborated on this point: "It once was I could never get my two teen-age boys out of bed in the morning and off to school. Then they put on this exercise program with a pretty girl bending and twisting in a little nothing of a costume. Now the boys set their alarm so they won't miss her. It sounds funny but I don't think it is."

Most housewives say they're too busy to watch daytime television, but their clearly informed opinions on the subject suggest that they do now and then steal a moment to see what's on. Soap operas, a man is told, cannot be discussed intelligently in general terms. "It's like anything else. Some are very interesting and some are terrible," observes an Amarillo housewife. She adds, "And those game shows are ridiculous but sometimes they're pretty good."

The favorite programs seem to be "good" comedies and "good" movies. Examples most often given of the former type are the Jack Benny program and a domestic series called "My Three Sons."

Evan Peet, an insurance man, said he enjoyed both those programs because "they're corny but it's good corn, and there's nothing wrong with good corn."

Professional TV critics, of course, have not suggested that "good corn" be stripped from the home screen. Their argument has been that a more reasonable balance should be struck between that kind of entertainment and more serious fare. People in this area seem to agree with that, but they want to be sure the programs they now enjoy won't be axed to make way for a violin recital they may not like.

There is no support for Government regulation of TV programing, but several of those interviewed said they think the Washington hearings are a good thing because they will scare the industry into improving itself.

"No sense in letting the network big shots get too comfortable," says feed salesman Andrew Esty. "But I think the best thing the FCC is doing is trying to open up more channels. Once you do that you up the competition and it's good for everybody."

This sampling of opinion about television, of course, doesn't pretend to be representative. It was done on a spot-interview basis, usually when the person approached shied away from answering questions on larger topics.

Even more interesting than the views expressed about TV was the general enthusiasm for expressing them. Whereas the United Nations and the foreign trade controversies seem remote to some people here, television seems remote to none of them. It is as close as their own living room. It is a subject that is within everyone's competency.

"Sure television goes in for a lot of corny stuff," says bus driver Dugan, "but driving this thing around isn't corny at all. When I get home at night and turn on that little old set, a little TV corn don't bother me at all."

EDWIN A. ROBERTS, JR.

February 8, 1962

"Yes, but don't you find it reassuring to know that we're all in this rut together?"

The World of PR

Shortly after the Communists erected the wall that now divides Berlin, a U.S. manufacturer opened a new factory near the barrier. An enthusiastic public relations man prepared an elaborate announcement, with pictures.

"It seemed like a dream situation," he recalls. "The U.S. Government was appealing to Americans to prop up West Berlin's morale with bricks and mortar, and here we were doing our bit." But the story was never released; higher-ups overruled the PR man because they feared stockholders would protest the plant was in too vulnerable a position.

In another case, management of Carling Brewery Company of Natick, Massachusetts, wholeheartedly endorsed a one-year campaign dressed up by its public relations counseling firm, Boston's Newsome and Company, to build good will in the New England area. In the course of the campaign, Carling paid for the annual Connecticut River Shad Derby, rescued an ailing baesball league and helped fight highway "litterbugs" in Vermont. Carling credits the campaign with helping to lift its sales in the area by 14 per cent.

The instances illustrate the frustrations and opportunities in one of the fastest growing phases of corporate activity, public relations. Referred to by some executives as a nebulous but necessary function, public relations has as its purpose telling people—the public, employees, stockholders and others—what companies are doing and portraying the companies in the best possible light.

But PR, as it is usually called, is not without its critics. Some believe the corporate PR man as often tries to obscure the truth as to spread it, and in either event too frequently bungles the job. Some executives charge that PR practitioners, often ex-newspapermen with little or no previous background in business, sometimes don't really understand what their companies are up to.

Some corporate PR operatives have been accused at times of showing more interest in running up the price of a company's stock than in establishing an effective long-range program for keeping stockholders and investment analysts informed of a company's plans and performance.

If many corporate public relations programs are ineffectual, PR men say, it's partly the fault of executives who lay down the policies within which they must operate. Elmo Roper, head of the New York opinion-polling organization which long has tested the effectiveness of many corporations' public relations programs, declares that "in big companies maybe one-third and in little companies maybe one-tenth" of the chief executives know what PR is all about.

In most cases, PR men complain, their superiors either expect impossible things from them—like the president of a Midwestern company who almost fired a PR aide for "allowing" an adverse story already in a reporter's hands to be published—or give them too little support.

In any event, the PR field has been growing at an impressive rate. An almost infant activity at the end of World War II, PR is now costing corporations about $1 billion a year and is providing full-time employment for some 50,000 persons, according to Robert L. Barbour, president of P. R. Publishing Company of Meriden, New Hampshire. Some observers would double both these hard-to-measure figures.

Much of this activity is carried on by more than 1,000 outside public relations counseling firms, but more of it is concentrated within the rapidly growing PR departments of companies themselves.

Monroe J. Rathbone, president of Standard Oil Company (New Jersey), gives some indication of the lofty status which PR now enjoys: "We never do anything of importance without first considering in great detail the public relations aspects."

Despite the marked growth of PR activity, corporate PR men remain highly vulnerable to cost-cutting efforts, and every now and then a company will order a wholesale reduction in its PR staff. Last year the Jacob Ruppert brewery of New York eliminated its PR staff entirely. More recently Allied Chemical Corporation trimmed its headquarters PR staff to five persons from 13.

Even where PR departments are firmly entrenched, there has been some deep soul-searching recently. Nothing has given a greater jolt to PR men than U.S. Steel Corporation's attempt last spring to raise prices and the furor that followed, after which the company backed down. For one thing, PR men concede, it shows that a large PR budget, which Big Steel has had for years, is no guarantee that a company won't get into hot water with the Government and at least a portion of the general public.

Two other companies with large public relations staffs also have found themselves in embarrassing positions recently. Leading officials of Ford Motor Company and Sears, Roebuck and Company are members of the Committee for Economic Development, a private group of business leaders which undertakes studies of major economic problems. When the CED recently issued a controversial report calling for the removal of two million farmers from the nation's farms in the next five years because of overproduction, members of the National Farmers Organization reacted by staging angry demonstrations at some Sears stores and Ford showrooms.

The companies, in response, have insisted the CED report does not necessarily reflect their views, only the personal opinions of the individual executives who endorsed it.

There are a number of signs that the growing business outlays for PR have done little to improve the standing of business—especially big business—with the public.

Recently the American Institute of Public Opinion, better known as the Gallup Poll, asked adults which profession they would advise a young man to go into. The two categories of "businessman" and "banker" ranked seventh and ninth, respectively, out of nine possible choices, far below doctors, engineers and teachers. Another straw in the wind is a recent poll by Opinion Research Corporation which showed that today 39 per cent of the public favors stricter Government control of business, compared with only 29 per cent taking that position in 1953.

Few corporate executives, confronted with such findings, would argue that their PR outlays are misspent, however. On the contrary, most of them say that with companies operating more in the public eye and with broader stock ownership, it's more important than ever to have some sort of public relations department run by an astute director.

The hand of the corporate PR man is seen in a host of activities. When Koppers Company ran into opposition to a new wood treatment plant it planned to build in an Eastern community, PR men for the company decided to fly the town's fathers to a similar plant already in operation at Salem, Virginia. As a result of the trip, opposition in the Eastern town evaporated.

A year ago, when a citizen's committee was seeking funds for tractors to ransom Cuban prisoners captured by the Castro regime in the ill-fated Bay of Pigs invasion, International Harvester Company, after considering the public relations aspects, refused to have anything to do with the effort, or even to supply tractor prices to the committee.

ACF Industries' decision, in November, 1961, to close its plant in Berwick, Pennsylvania—the town's biggest factory, employing 2,000 workers—was softened somewhat by public relations considerations. Among other things, ACF arranged to sell the plant under liberal terms to the Berwick Industrial Development Association, a non-profit organization formed locally to lure new companies to the town.

Public relations is responsible for the Educators Conference held for the past 13 years by Du Pont Company, in which college professors are invited to see how a giant chemical company is run, and for the recent decision by Grumman Aircraft Engineering Corporation to donate land worth $720,000 to Oyster Bay, Long Island, for a park.

PR men frequently deal with problems of employee morale, too. As executives of American Cyanamid Company quietly planned a few years ago to move the company's headquarters office from Manhattan to a 192-acre site in Alpine, New Jersey, news of the pending change leaked out and was published in a New York area newspaper. Employees, who had known nothing about any intention to move until then, were stunned.

Cyanamid later withdrew its plans because many Alpine villagers opposed the necessary zoning changes. Months afterward, when the company bought a site in Wayne Township, New Jersey, a PR staff that had learned some lessons in the aborted Alpine affair prevailed on management to lose no time in informing employees. Within 24 hours after contracts were signed to purchase the land, illustrated brochures stressing the advantages of living in Wayne County and pamphlets detailing the company's plans for assisting moving employees were distributed.

One thing PR cannot do, public relations counselors say, is hush up adverse publicity such as "payola" scandals or last year's sentencing of officials of several electrical equipment manufacturers on price-fixing charges. Nevertheless, once a storm blows over, PR men move in to rebuild their companies' reputations by stressing the positive. The new 50,000-mile warranty on engine and transmission which Chrysler Corporation now offers on its new cars, some auto men contend, is more than a mere sales hook. It also reflects, they say, a desire to restore the company's reputation for integrity and sound engineering following conflict-of-interest scandals that rocked the company two years ago.

Public relations men have pulled their share of bloopers, some due to sheer incompetence and some due to intracompany pressures and other hazards beyond their control. Consider the Chicago press conference staged last February by Rival Packing Company, a division of Associated Products, Incorporated, of New York, to introduce a new dog food. A French poodle, brought onstage amid a great fanfare, sniffed at the food and then refused to eat it.

Last December Remington Rand Univac Division of Sperry Rand Corporation showed newsmen and security analysts a new type of computer using a thin-film memory, but held up the printing of the story for about a week. Word leaked out anyway, the price of the stock began to rise on the New York Stock Exchange and the Big Board invoked its rules to force the company to unveil the new computer several days sooner than it had planned.

Sometimes companies play down mergers or acquisitions in the naïve hope of their escaping the attention of the Justice Department's anti-trust division. Such was the motivation, according to PR men, of the president of one company who, overruling his public relations staff, allowed a story about an acquisition to be released only to local papers. It was a futile effort. The next day alert newspapers published elsewhere picked up the story and, even if they hadn't, PR men say, the Justice Department sooner or later would have found out.

Frequently, by not telling its side of a story, a company passes up opportunities to gain sympathetic publicity. One strike-bound transportation company, for example, refused to talk to reporters and expelled television cameramen from its headquarters building. Now and then, of course, there may be good reason to keep quiet. Another transportation company, discovering that termites had eaten away at the roof of a passenger terminal, parried newsmen's questions about work being done at the terminal until the damage was repaired. When an announcement finally was made, there was no mention of the fact the roof had become dangerously weakened before the trouble was spotted.

Corporate close-mouthedness often merely reflects the over-cautious-ness of company lawyers. But it may also be due to reticence on the part of top executives. Many of these are still reluctant to meet person-ally with newsmen in interviews or press conferences—a factor which, in the view of some public opinion authorities, goes far to explain some of the anti-business sentiment in the land. Says one corporate PR man: "Much of the value of a large public relations budget is nullified if the top man won't see the press."

Frederic G. Donner, who as chairman of General Motors Corpora-tion heads the world's largest manufacturing corporation, almost never grants press interviews and hasn't held a no-holds-barred press confer-ence since November, 1960. Others who almost never meet the press include Ralph W. Burger, chairman of the Great Atlantic and Pacific Tea Company, and Juan T. Trippe, president of Pan American World Airways.

Though the heads of corporate PR staffs are gaining increasing stature within their companies—many have been elevated to the vice presidential level in recent years—they often complain they still must clear their ideas with a battery of other executives, including over-cautious lawyers.

An instance of a company appearing to place little trust in its PR people: A reporter seeking to confirm the correct names of three Ba-hamian subsidiaries of Bethlehem Steel Corporation was asked to put his request in writing. Later when the reporter complained about a delay in getting an answer, a harassed PR man explained that a mem-ber of the board of directors had to authorize the giving out of such information—even though the names of the three subsidiaries were dis-played in public view in Bethlehem's building in Nassau.

The job of the PR man is further complicated by the fact that he must consider not one "public" but four—the company employees, the stockholders, the general public and the government. A glowing earn-ings statement, for example, may delight stockholders but may also whet a union's appetite for pay increases.

EDMUND K. FALTERMAYER

November 19, 1962

Hiding a Railroad Wreck

One of the first stories we covered as a budding reporter was a rail-road wreck. We had our troubles because the attitude of the road officials was that the less said the better, and preferably our paper shouldn't carry a word about it. They lost.

So ordinarily we would laugh off the outraged cries of some airline press agents at the "publicity" given the recent plane hijackings. The happenings did indeed get some notice in every paper we read, and the gist of the press agents' complaint is that this undermined public confidence in one of our vital industries and, moreover, encouraged others by example to try a bit of plane snatching. Also bad for business.

But unfortunately, nowadays, the press agent's protective instinct has also become a common reflex in Washington. Not so long ago, President Kennedy himself was extolling the merits of journalistic self-censorship and hinting that if we didn't do it ourselves the Government might do it for us. And since then cabinet officers, agency heads and other bright young men in the official family have been giving newspapermen more pointed private warnings.

All this usually couched in phrases about giving away secrets to the enemy, which is a thing nobody approves of. But when pressed, nobody names a bill of particulars against the newspapers for this crime. The specific complaints always relate to something else.

There was, for example, the Cuban affair. The "publicity" given to the abortive invasion of counter-revolutionaries, so we are told, did great injury to the prestige and dignity of the United States in the eyes of the world. You might suppose, from the indictment, that some news-paper reporter caused that bit of wreckage or that if the American newspapers hadn't mentioned it the world would have remained in ignorance of Washington's fiasco.

But this is not the only example. Washington reporters have been verbally spanked for publicizing disagreements within the Administration. Editors have heard that they are being "irresponsible" for criticizing policies of other governments that the State Department wants to be nice to. Press and radio have been privately criticized for giving too much advance publicity to space shots—except when, as in the case of astronauts, the event turned out well.

Now none of these complaints, we hasten to note, has turned into any kind of Administration policy. But when politicians begin to talk like press agents, and the praises of self-censorship begin to be sung, it's time to reflect on what is involved.

It's easy to retort that a wreck, whether on a railroad or on the beaches of Cuba, is no reporter's fault. But that misses the issue. The central question is, first of all, whether the American people should or should not know about the wreck that occurred on the beaches of Cuba. And then the question: who has the omniscience to decide what the people shall or shall not know?

We would hardly deny that the news of the Cuba fiasco was a bad blow to our prestige. But the injury was in the event, and it would no more be possible to smother the news of it than, years ago, to hide a train wreck in which 30 people were killed. And the very act of trying, whether by self-censorship or by Government censorship, would in fact increase the injury.

Indeed, it would turn the injury inward; for then it would not be just to our prestige abroad but to the very fundamental basis of our society, which rests upon the right of the people to judge those who run our railroads or our Government. And patently they cannot judge if they do not know what has happened and what is happening.

If the Secretary of Defense and the Chiefs of Staff have a disagreement it is not just a piece of gossip to titillate editors. It is an important thing for the American people to know; more important, they should know what the disagreement is about, and why. If there are critical things to be said of a foreign government, it is important that the people hear them, however annoying to the State Department.

Even the trivial is not unimportant. Public servants have been rightfully turned out of office when "invasions of privacy" disclosed they had peculiar friends. Serious faults in public programs have very often been corrected precisely by news that did our prestige in the world no good.

True, we would hardly deny either that sometimes things written in the press strike us as irresponsible. But we have known things we thought important to strike others as irresponsible. It is on this that all censorship founders, whether by Government or by some committee of editors. Among our colleagues there are many whom we admire and respect; none whom we think has that infinite wisdom to say, "This the people shall know. This they shall not know." And we may doubt if any of our colleagues would attribute to us such omniscience.

So we sympathize with those in Washington who do not like to see their mistakes, their arguments, their plans or their foibles noised about in the public forum. So too with our friends in the airline public relations offices who shudder at every headline about a hijacking.

But the news of that wreck we covered years ago forced a railroad to improve its safety devices. And ever since then we've never believed that the public was well served by hiding news because somebody thought it was bad.

VERMONT ROYSTER

August 15, 1962

———————◆◆◆———————

FREAK OF NATURE

The human intellect is odd—
Sometimes it seems akin to God.
It conquers interstellar space,
And to perpetuate the race,
Develops death-defying drugs,
But can't make worms or lightning bugs.

—MARGARET FISHBACK

Blurred "Backgrounders"

WASHINGTON—The President has returned from Palm Beach, Congress is back, legislative and budget battles loom, new foreign crises threaten. As capital activity increases, so will the use of the "background" news conference, a traditional but dubious technique that perhaps more than any other lends itself to Government "management" of news.

The background briefing or news conference is, simply stated, a session at which a Government official with something to say tells it to a group of newsmen on condition his identity be concealed. There are gradations of concealment. Sometimes the story can be attributed to the official's agency, reporting, for example, that "the White House believes" or "State Department officials are convinced." Sometimes the statements cannot be attributed even to the agency but must be rather vaguely pinned on "Administration sources" or "the Government." Sometimes the statements can't be attributed at all but must be said by the reporter on his own.

The perils of the practice increase, both from the point of view of the reporter and the reader, as the source of the story becomes more heavily cloaked. The more remote the attribution, the less clearly the reader is alerted to possible bias on the part of the source and the more likely the reporter is to be used to sell a partisan point of view or float some new official trial balloon.

One recent example will illustrate. Just a few days ago, lengthy news dispatches from Palm Beach purported to give, "on the highest authority," President Kennedy's private thinking on a wide range of foreign and domestic problems. The White House yesterday finally laid bare the quirk by which so many reporters simultaneously showed such laudable enterprise. The "highest authority," Press Secretary Salinger admitted, was Mr. Kennedy himself, holding a background briefing for reporters obliged to endure with him the rigors of the Palm Beach holiday season. The identification of the source of the reports was wrung from the White House after several British correspondents who weren't present identified Mr. Kennedy as the backgrounding official and quoted him directly on some matters.

Actually, the President said little he hadn't previously set forth in his television fireside chat last month and in his last two or three news conferences. But somehow, with his views portrayed as coming not from him but rather from "friends of the President" or "visitors who've talked to the President here," an extra mantle of authenticity was laid over them. These were no longer the views of a President guardedly talking to newsmen, knowing full well that every word would find its way into print even though not directly attributed to him. Rather, these became the President's most sincerely held convictions, laid bare honestly and fully to friends and aides in the privacy of his own home.

Now Mr. Kennedy may well believe—as reported from Palm Beach —that unemployment will exceed six per cent if the tax cut he wants is not enacted swiftly. But he also knows that this argument helps generate pressure on Congress to abide by his tax proposals and identification would alert the reader to this possible motivation. Similarly Mr. Kennedy surely believed House refusal to enlarge the Rules Committee would have been a bitter setback for him; whether he believed deep down that—again quoting the "highest authority" in Palm Beach—it would have meant a "completely barren" two years is somewhat more questionable, and identification again would help make the reader aware of the politics involved.

The recent security breakdown involving Mr. Kennedy has probably halted—at least for a while—the President's use of the technique. But it will certainly survive in other parts of the White House, the Administration, the capital generally.

The backgrounder is by no means a New Frontier innovation; it is a Washington institution that most authorities trace back at least to the Woodrow Wilson era. The original idea was to permit a Government official to talk freely to newsmen, without worry that some offhand remark would embarrass him, his agency, his party, the U.S. Government. It's still legitimately used for that purpose, particularly on foreign affairs and national security matters.

But the anonymity of the backgrounder has also been increasingly abused to test public reaction to new schemes and projected appointments, to mobilize opinion behind some Government project, to advance one agency's cause against another's, to persuade a foreign government of the sincerity with which the United States holds an official position.

Individual reporters, of course, constantly seek information on a "background" basis from Government officials. They want as complete a story as possible, and frequently in order to receive particular pieces of a story they have to promise not to quote the man they're talking to or even his agency.

But the individual reporter seeking background information on his own has a full opportunity to cross-examine the witness, to check the evidence with other sources later, to choose the information he regards reliable and accurate and throw away the self-serving propaganda. The background technique on this basis is a useful device for the official, the journalist and the public.

The formal background briefing or news conference, however, is quite another matter. The conscientious reporter usually feels he can't stay away because he may miss a top story. Once he attends, however, he is a prisoner of the system. He does not have the same opportunity to cross-check and pick and choose as when he gets background information on his own. Other reporters present will be rushing their stories into print. He must meet the competitive pressure.

If a particular argument advanced in the briefing seems misleading or self-serving, he can omit it from his story only at some risk. Other reporters will be declaring that the "U.S. Government believes General de Gaulle is ready to accept the Polaris missile offer." How come, his editors and readers may ask, he didn't get this vital piece of information—did he fall asleep halfway through the backgrounder?

The Army occasionally holds background briefings, the contents of which correspondents must state on their own without attribution. The briefing officer may argue that the war in South Vietnam is going great, or that the Army is not trying to undercut Air Force missions. Is the reader truly served, however, when this is presented as the reporter's own conclusion rather than the official Army viewpoint?

Reports from State Department briefings frequently must be kept free of any official U.S. tag; they turn up as the reporter's own views, or perhaps as the thoughts of "Western diplomats." The theory is that the Brazilian government should not know it was a top State Department man who told 45 reporters that Brazil was tottering on the brink of financial chaos, and that the Iranian government should not know that U.S. officials believe land reform in Iran is going frustratingly slow. But, of course, within an hour or two of the first dispatches over the news wires, the Brazilian ambassador or the Iranian ambassador or any other alert official in Washington knows exactly the source of the background news. Only the average newspaper reader and radio listener is kept in the dark that this is the official United States point of view.

It should not be all that difficult to come by better procedures. Government officials could quite easily re-examine their rules and confine the use of the backgrounder to legitimate attempts to inform the public—not to lead or mislead opinion. Many background briefings could certainly permit fuller identification of the source. Even a vague attribution to "U.S. officials" or "Administration spokesmen" is an amber caution signal far to be preferred to no warning at all, and identification of the specific agency would be even better.

When this cannot be negotiated, a reporter has a special obligation to weigh the material received. It may be necessary to report that the White House or the State Department or the U.S. Government is viewing a particular event as a great victory, but the reporter who has good reason to believe it isn't certain seems obliged to insert pertinent information to suggest the official view may be somewhat colored.

The very fact that the backgrounder is becoming a more widely practiced technique underlines the need for care both by the Government and the Fourth Estate.

ALAN L. OTTEN

January 1, 1963

Durable Plugs

"We don't see anything unethical or unfair about TV plugs," declares J. A. Wagner, vice president of Scholl's Manufacturing Company, a producer of products to soothe aching feet.

"We intend to continue using this kind of promotion," snaps a Western Union official. "We see no reason to change our policy as long as we get our money's worth."

"Plugs will continue," observes Edouard L. Cournand, president of Lanvin Parfum, Incorporated, which produces in the United States such French perfumes as Arpege and My Sin. "You can't take out of the vocabulary names like Tiffany, Rolls-Royce and Arpege."

These comments reflect the reaction of many of the businessmen who use television plugs; a plug involves display or mention of a product or service in a newspaper or magazine story, in a movie, or on a radio or television program sponsored by another company. So far, as the remarks suggest, the publicity that plugs have received in connection with the continuing TV investigations has done little to change the practice.

"There are just as many plugs as there ever were," says Herbert A. Carlborg, director for Columbia Broadcasting System, Incorporated. Stockton Helffrich, director of continuity acceptance at the National Broadcasting Company, echoes Mr. Carlborg's observation.

In Hollywood, where plug specialists strive to slip their products into movies as well as into filmed TV shows, a veteran observer says: "The plug is as prevalent today as it ever was."

In some cases, a manufacturer may have nothing to do with placing his plug in a program. In other cases, the program's producers may request permission to display or mention a manufacturer's product.

More often, however, the manufacturer takes the initiative by hiring a specialist to slip his products into TV shows. The specialist often uses part of his fee to send gifts to cooperative script writers, producers, prop men or others connected with programs.

The Federal Communications Commission is investigating the legal status of plugs and trying to determine its authority, if any, to deal with them. The House Commerce subcommittee which delved into rigged TV shows is planning to look into plugs next month, along with payola. Payola involves payments to disc jockeys to use certain records on their programs. In New York, where many television shows originate, District Attorney Frank Hogan is investigating both plugs and payola to try to determine whether any state law has been violated.

Although the networks say they've noticed little change so far in the number of plugs, they insist they've tightened editing of scripts over which they have control. The networks contend that they always have tried to limit plugs. They note that it's difficult to distinguish between the plug inserted by a paid specialist and the plug that is used by a comedian merely because it adds punch to a monologue.

In addition, the networks argue that they have no direct control over the specific content of many of their programs. These are the shows that are produced by independent contractors.

Somewhat surprisingly, the networks say they've had little pressure from sponsors to cut down on plugs. It's perhaps noteworthy that some of the bigger buyers of television time also are among the principal beneficiaries of plugs on the programs. Some sponsors say they strive to prevent plugs on their programs but have taken no new steps in this direction. In some cases, sponsors probably prefer to retain a particular entertainer, with plugs, rather than to lose him by forcing the issue. An entertainer, similarly, may prefer to keep a certain writer, with plugs, rather than lose him.

The networks' efforts to cut back on plugs are opposed by a group of businessmen who value such promotion highly.

"We attach considerable importance to this kind of publicity, and we pay many thousands of dollars a year to our agency to get it in newspapers, radio and television," says a spokesman for Remington Rand Electric Shaver division of Sperry Rand Corporation. The company's New York publicity agency, Brown and Rowland, Incorporated, explains it gives $20 shavers to writers and producers of TV shows that mention Remington, but never hands out cash.

"Plugs get you recognition," says an oil company executive. "It's like plastering your name on a billboard."

Mr. Cournand of Lanvin outlines the lengths to which his company goes to get plugs. "We hire writers to give us a supply of jokes about Lanvin perfumes," he says. "I have a young lady who knows a lot of television writers. She calls them up and says, 'I have a good joke on Lanvin.' Of course, if they use it, we send them some perfume."

Lanvin's West Coast plug specialist stays in close touch with writers and others involved in preparation of TV shows. When he hears of "any jokes where a perfume product has to be mentioned," continues Mr. Cournand, "he sees to it that it's Lanvin rather than some other brand that gets mentioned. Whenever the writers do a good job for him, they get a little present, like whisky or something. On the Coast, liquor seems to be the currency of exchange."

The plug has a long history. "Television plugs are just an extension of a practice that has been around since the early days of movies," says NBC's Mr. Helffrich. Comedians such as Fred Allen and Will Rogers on early radio mentioned products as a part of their brand of topical humor, he says.

In movies, auto makers work hard to get their cars used in as many scenes as possible. Bourbon distillers have been able to get stars to sidle up to movie bars and ask for "bourbon and water," rather than "Scotch and water." In a reverse twist, one plug specialist devotes his time to keeping trucks out of movie accidents.

Newspaper gossip columnists are a favorite plugster target. A Broadway publicist explains, "Columnists are really editors of copy supplied by guys like me. For every three items of legitimate dirt I give them, they use one of my client items."

Television plug men go about their business with organized diligence. They circulate lists of products they'd like plugged to script writers, producers, prop men—anyone who might be able to plant a plug in a show.

Dick Fishell and Associates, of Beverly Hills, one of the biggest specialists, circulates a list that includes some 93 company or product names. He carefully instructs writers on the front cover of the four-page list to "please be sure to clear text of all plants in advance so that we can make arrangements" for monitoring the program. He also tells them, "We have 24-hour service on the above telephone numbers and can be reached any time."

On one of his recent lists are such names as A. C. Gilbert Toys, Diners' Club, Lanvin, Luchow's Restaurant in New York, Sands Hotel in Las Vegas, Western Union, and a number of Schenley Industries, Incorporated, liquors.

Perry Lafferty, young, articulate independent producer of "The Big Party" on CBS, says: "For years writers have been leaning back in their chairs and running down these lists of companies trying to figure out how to work them into a script. Sometimes their mentions are funny and sometimes not so funny."

He says the reward is a case of the writer's favorite liquor, a gift certificate or cash if he wants it. The cash was "something in the neighborhood of $70" in cases he knows about.

"There's almost no one in this business who hasn't participated some way in plugging," he adds. "It's not that they need the money. It's more like a child who is stuffed with cookies but still slips a couple more from the jar when his mother isn't looking."

Plug specialists generally charge clients about $300 to $350 for each mention, but the worth of a plug varies with the popularity of the show and the "length of the exposure," says a West Coast observer. A major auto maker not long ago paid about $75,000 to one Los Angeles plug man to get the writer of a TV comedy series to feature its auto in one episode in an auto showroom and in three subsequent episodes involving a tour of the United States.

The plug specialists and his clients try to make it easy for cooperative show people. For example, stock film footage covering a variety of situations is made available to producers for splicing into sequences. Pan American World Airways happily provides celluloid scenes of overseas air travel, while American Express Company stands prepared to provide any of a variety of earthbound foreign shots.

Plug specialists maintain warehouses full of client props, from gasoline pumps to office machines, to rush to a studio set at any hour.

General Electric Company's housewares division lends such items as vacuum cleaners, irons or toasters for settings. Burroughs Corporation and Remington Rand in the business machines field lend typewriters, adding machines and computers. From the producers' point of view, the machines lend authenticity to office scenes, and, incidentally, reduce the cost of outfitting sets.

"Prop men have to get this stuff from someone, and it might as well be us as a competitor," says a Burroughs spokesman. However, he adds hastily that the company sees little practical value in the plugs because it makes no products that attract the general consumer.

A farm equipment manufacturer also doubts "the positive value" of a plug to him, yet he hires a plug man to get his product used "because it prevents them (TV and movie producers) from showing someone else's machinery."

A. C. Gilbert Company retains plug man Fishell to see that its electric trains make as many Christmas scenes as possible. Gilbert Vice President Harvey Rath points with pride to the fact that, both this year and last, the Lennon sisters have sung Christmas songs on the Lawrence Welk Show while an American Flyer train has chugged around in the background. He concedes that Mr. Fishell has said that at times it is necessary to provide something like a case of liquor to put a deal across.

The spokesman for New York's William Esty advertising agency says most sponsors don't object to this sort of plug. "If it adds something to the program, then it's all right. If there's an office scene we don't expect them to cover up the manufacturer's name on the typewriter." The Esty spokesman, however, stresses that the agency is firmly opposed to verbal plugs "which dilute the time you have legitimately bought for your client."

The persistence of the plug men and their allies on the staffs of some shows is seen in an effort to place a plug for a well-known perfume. In the first rough film footage of a show, NBC editors caught a plug and ordered it out. It was still in the second version of the film, and the exasperated network ordered it out again. But on the finished film, it was still there.

"We finally stopped it by blurping the sound (cutting it off) just as the actor was making the plug," says Mr. Helffrich.

The networks spike other potential plugs more easily. CBS caught this line written for Martha Raye in a "Big Party" script: "Play me some sick music. I've got Blue Shield." Editor Carlborg explains: "We don't know if it was planted, but we aren't taking any chances."

At NBC, Mr. Helffrich says it is network policy to slash out a plug if there is a known payoff involved. However, if there is no known payoff, as he says is the case most times, "I try to consider whether it is worthwhile leaving in for the contribution it makes to the show."

He asks, "Is it wrong to spoof about all the different flavors of ice cream Howard Johnson's claims it has? Or take Bob Hope. The other night he came on right after the NBC peacock that flashes on the screen to identify a color show and said, 'You may think that's a peacock, but it's really a turkey with its feathers washed in Clairol.' We could have insisted he say 'washed in hair dye,' but it wouldn't have been as funny."

EVERETT G. MARTIN AND MITCHELL GORDON

December 15, 1959

Executive Reading

CHICAGO—Flipping through a heap of magazines on his desk, tall, bespectacled L. D. McDowell bends down to count a few more in his wastebasket. "I must be getting nearly 80 magazines here every month," he says, with a surprised air.

The figure is all the more surprising because Mr. McDowell is not a librarian or engaged in literary pursuits but is chief works engineer of American Steel Foundries, a maker of railroad car parts.

The magazines Mr. McDowell receives are all "trade" publications, aimed not at entertaining him but informing him about his business— and, through their advertising columns, selling things to his company. His reading experience is becoming increasingly common as a swelling flood of trade magazines of all sorts pours across the desks of business and professional men.

The roster of trade "books," as they are often called, rose to 2,178 as of last year-end from 1,772 a decade earlier, according to a count by *Industrial Marketing,* a trade magazine published by Advertising Publications, Incorporated, Chicago. Publishers think growth has been as robust this year as in 1959, when the list swelled by 70 publications. New publications already are being planned for 1961, including *Family Physician,* by the American Academy of General Practice, Kansas City; *Marine Products,* by the Chilton Company of Philadelphia, for boat supply dealers; and an as-yet-unnamed entry in the drugstore field, by Fairchild Publications, Incorporated, New York.

There's at least one trade magazine now for almost every conceivable business or occupation, ranging from *Variety* for theatrical folks to *Casket and Sunnyside* for funeral directors. Macaroni makers have the *Macaroni Journal,* and missile men have *Missiles and Rockets.* People in the metal fabricating field alone have some 60 trade books to scan, including Fairchild's *Metalworking News,* launched last month.

Little known outside their own fields, many trade magazines count a circulation of only a few thousand copies, although some have grown to relatively fat circulations, like Hoard's *Dairyman,* with 327,000 paid subscribers. Many are sent free to readers the editors think will be interested, relying solely on advertising for revenue, but the publishers of Platt's *Oilgram News* asks a princely $210 a year from oil men receiving their daily service.

Altogether, trade magazines now reach more than 43 million subscribers, double the number 10 years ago. Their advertising revenues will total an estimated $550 million this year, up from $225 million in 1950. With the growth of the trade magazines, the battle for ad revenue has become increasingly bitter. It seems unlikely that all the new magazines will survive. For the present, however, the factors underlying the growth of the field are strong.

Increasing specialization in the American economy is a key reason for the growth of trade magazines. "Engineers and factory superintendents once read the same magazines," says Norman D. Buehling, president of Fensholt Advertising Company, a Chicago agency specializing in trade magazine advertising. But now alongside such broad-range old timers as McGraw-Hill Publishing Company's *Factory*, dating from 1891, are narrower-scope ones such as *Power Transmission Design* and *Control Engineering*. Supplementing the "vertical" publications like *Steel*, which cover a whole industry, are "horizontal" ones focusing on a job function regardless of the industry, such as *Industrial Purchasing Agent*.

The rise of new occupational specialties accounts for some of the new magazines. "We found men with titles like procurement engineer appearing in our fields, and learned they were a whole new class," says Edward S. Safford, chairman of Rogers Publishing Company, Englewood, Colorado, publishers of *Design News* and *Electrical Design News*. The new jobs arose because neither design engineers nor purchasing departments could keep abreast of the multiplying number of suppliers. "Today there are about 85 sources for transistors, while six years ago there were only five," Mr. Safford says. So a year ago he created *Electrical/Electronic Procurement*, which now goes to about 15,000 technical procurement men each month.

The rapid expansion of certain fields has spawned a great many trade magazines, too. Many publishers have been attracted to electronics, for instance, a field in which manufacturers' sales have jumped to an estimated $10 billion this year from $6.2 billion in 1955. They have established at least 20 new trade journals in the same span, bringing the electronics total to 44, according to one compilation. Among the newest: *Electronic Preview, Industrial Electronics* and *Industrial Electronic Maintenance*. And the new space industry has given rise to such publications as *Space Age News, Astronautics* and *Missile Design and Development*.

The publishing empires that have grown up in the trade field themselves provide much of the impetus for expansion. They find new trade journals the most logical outlet for the profits they have accumulated from older ones, especially since they can often spread some duties on a new magazine among existing staff members. And it is the big publishers that are often in the best position to afford the two or three years of red ink that usually come until a new book attracts enough advertising to stand on its own feet.

RICHARD F. JANSSEN

November 15, 1960

Dilemma of the Airwaves

If it were possible for an unlimited number of radio or television stations to broadcast without getting in each other's way, there would be no excuse for any sort of agency, Federal or otherwise, to decide who may broadcast and who may not.

There isn't, for example, any Federal Publications Commission charged with issuing or denying licenses to anybody who wants to start a newspaper or magazine or publish a book. Anyone who wants to can go into the publishing business. And he can publish just about anything he wants to, from fine poetry to the trashiest sort of junk.

The broadcasting business is different only because a radio or a TV station has to broadcast, or "publish," on a band of frequencies called a channel. The airwaves will accommodate only a certain number of non-overlapping channels in a given area, else all broadcasting turns into an unintelligible jumble. And at present the number is so limited that only a few people have the privilege of broadcasting.

That being the case, somebody has to apportion the available space. That somebody is the Federal Communications Commission. Its job is to grant to one man, and to deny to another, a share in a commodity in short supply which has substantial commercial value to him who possesses it.

This power of a political agency to dole out a valuable privilege, however necessary that power may be, immediately raises some difficult questions. Some of them may be unanswerable. But none of them will be answered by pretending they are simple or by epithets tossed back and forth between the television industry and the officials of the FCC.

How, for example, is the FCC to decide between one applicant and another? It begs the question to talk of financial requirements or proposed program standards, for while inadequacy here may quickly eliminate some candidates, it is no help when there are two or more eminently qualified seekers for the prize. There are times when the most honorable and intelligent commission must be wholly at a loss for any sensible grounds of choice.

How much supervision should the FCC exercise, for example, in regulating advertising? It would be dubious, and in any event futile, to argue that it should exercise none. Wherever the public grants an exclusive license—be it for bus service, electric power or broadcasting

—its companion must be enough public regulation to set at least minimum standards. This is the price paid for the lack of regulation by a free market into which any competitor may enter.

An even more complex part of the question concerns freedom of speech on the airwaves. If a man wants to print a publication devoted exclusively to advocating one set of ideas, the public's protection lies in the fact that anyone else is free to use the same medium to correct imbalances or rebut opinions. This freedom to publish is the rock on which freedom of the press rests, and without which it cannot exist.

It is because this "freedom to publish" does not exist on the airwaves that we have rules about "equal time" and all the rest. It cannot be otherwise; the public could not tolerate the granting of an exclusive license in such an important area and let it be an absolute license.

All this poses a terrible dilemma. For neither is it in the public interest to have our radio and television programs chosen to suit a Washington official's idea of what they ought to be.

Personally we share Commissioner Minow's lament that radio often sounds like a "clamorous casbah of pitchment" and that TV is too much of a "vast wasteland." But there's no law that forces us to listen to radio or watch TV, and if some people like soap-plugging operas and the clamor of disc jockeys, it is none of our business—nor of Mr. Minow's.

Moreover, there must always exist a real danger that political regulation will slide into political censorship or direction. It is not inconceivable that someday a Washington Administration, under the guise of regulating time for public affairs programs, should use this medium to shape the ideas presented to the people. The pressure need not even be overt—the power to license is also the power to revoke licenses, and it would not be easy for any broadcaster to stand up to an angry Government.

For the moment, the only answer to this dilemma is restraint by the broadcasters in the use of their prized licenses and restraint by the Government authorities in the application of their regulations to the industry. And finally, a vigilance by the public to see that the one does not abuse privilege and the other does not abuse authority.

But there is only one way, ultimately, out of this dilemma. And that is by progress in technology which will permit the multiplication of radio and TV channels to the point where, if they are not unlimited, they will be at least so numerous as for all practical purposes to permit those who will to enter the broadcasting business. There is much that can be done now even in the present state of radio science.

It is to this end that the FCC ought to work. It is to this end that every broadcaster who values his freedom must work. All arguments about overcrowding the industry and squeezing profits have no place here. It is not the business of the FCC to issue guarantees against bankruptcy, and those broadcasters opposing the expansion of the channels cannot ask at one and the same time both protection and freedom.

For the simple truth of the matter is that Government dependence and true freedom are incompatible. The man who must get permission to write a book, produce a play or print a newspaper can speak his mind only within the tolerance of the authorities. Only when the broadcasting industry, out of its laboratories, puts an end to this dependence can the public ever listen to airwaves that are truly free.

VERMONT ROYSTER

May 10, 1962

Mangled Words

MIAMI—Amid the recriminations and questions still obscuring last week's abortive Cuban invasion, there's at least one clear point: In Cold War skirmishing of any kind, words are a key weapon—and in the past week the words were as badly handled as the landing itself.

It was mishandling of words that reinforced Castro's grandiose claims to a major military victory, that helped back the United States into a position where anything it said would meet with disbelief and that enabled Premier Khrushchev to make a bluff he knew would not be called.

Part of the blame for all of this, to be sure, lies with the American press. Some correspondents here have reached a long way for fresh angles or tried to keep the invasion yarn going by solemnly relating rumors that simply couldn't have any basis in fact. These failings, however, merely magnified other far more fundamental shortcomings, inept handling of information by the anti-Castro Cuban exiles here and the failure of U.S. officials in Washington to damp down a story they knew was running wild.

Military operations naturally lend themselves to rumor and confusion. But the exiles managed to compound what would have been near-chaos at best, partly by letting some of their "official" spokesmen approach the invasion story as if it were a campaign introducing a new brand of soap flakes.

The voice of the Cuban Revolutionary Council, which was nominally running the invasion, was a public relations outfit in New York which admitted quite freely that its information filtered in through a mysterious Cuban holed up in a hotel room in New York, or Miami, or on a ship at sea—it all depended on whom you talked to.

In the PR office, run by a genial, harassed man named Lem Jones, there was a low-pressure but marked effort to discourage reporters from going to Florida on the grounds that "this is where all the news will be given out." That may have been the intention, but the exiles and Mr. Jones both should have known it wouldn't work; even small wars tend to flow off the organization chart.

Here in Miami the invasion had no voice. It had a babble. The babble was loudest at the drab, two-story brick house that served as headquarters for the Democratic Revolutionary Front, the extremely tenuous amalgamation of a half-dozen anti-Castro organizations. All

day and most of the night, crowds of Cubans milled around the Front
building. There were some officials about, but it was impossible to
shout more than half a dozen words into anyone's ear before two
other people started shouting something totally different into the same
ear. This situation changed though, by midweek; realization that the
landing had failed reduced the babble but still failed to produce any
more information.

The Revolutionary Council now insists the landings never were
intended as a full-scale invasion, but, rightly or wrongly, nobody
could have come away from the hectic Front headquarters with that
impression early last week.

More serious to U.S. prestige was Washington's failure to realize,
when things started to come unstuck in the south Cuban swamps, that
Castro's triumph was being falsely inflated. The Central Intelligence
Agency has badly misjudged Cuban affairs for many months, but it
presumably knew, at least roughly, how many invaders went ashore.
There weren't anywhere near the 5,000 figure that was being bandied
around even in Washington. The U.S. Government obviously couldn't
call a press conference to announce that the Cuban attacking force
was really rather small. But some quick, quiet passing of the word
would have helped keep news stories from the United States in perspective and moderated the apparent scale of Castro's victory.

There was nothing anybody this side of the Florida straits could
do about what Fidel claimed, but a little more candor in Washington
would have made it harder for him to quote American news stories
as "proof" of the size of the force he had thrown back into the sea.

Setting straight the fact that Cuba wasn't under full-scale attack
also would have helped show up Khrushchev's promise of help for
what it really was—a low-cost, little-risk bluff. As things stand now,
a good many people throughout the world are going to think the
Kremlin threat did thwart major U.S. intervention in Cuba.

The question of American involvement in the landing naturally
was a ticklish one, but there never was any real chance the initial
complete denials of U.S. participation would stand up. Too many
people knew too much about the training, arming and financing of
anti-Castro Cubans that's been going on for many months. There are
times when belief can be better served by not making denials.

Ironically much of the complaining here about the CIA role in
the landing is being done by the Cuban exiles who were being aided.
Some of this stems from frustration, from a growing feeling, at least
among the Cubans, that it was the United States which bungled the
invasion effort. It may be ungracious, but seeking a scapegoat is a
very human reaction. The key point, however, is that as far as anyone
can tell here, little or no thought was given in Washington about what

to do or say if the invasion effort went awry. This also disturbed some exile leaders who are beginning to argue that their present position would be better if more thought had been given to alternatives and less stress put on enthusiasm.

Admittedly, there's no perfect way the words could have been handled in the past week. But with Cuba so much in the headlines the anti-Castro exile leaders and, much more especially, the U.S. Government should have realized that a words deluge would begin when the first invaders moved over the beach, manufacturing a host of problems.

By mismanaging information, both Cubans and Americans have done themselves a disservice, and not the smallest one of the past week in which many were contrived.

JAMES N. WALLACE

April 25, 1961

News Gap

CLEVELAND—Radio and television stations here and in New York have been bravely trying to fill the news gap created by strikes against newspapers in both cities. The results have been mixed, and occasionally explosive.

In Cleveland, for instance, a TV station stirred up a hot controversy over civil rights when it rolled its cameras inside a police cell block to interview a 75-year-old physician charged with manslaughter.

"You have been charged with first degree manslaughter," declared the television reporter. "How do you plead?"

"Not guilty," replied the doctor, who is specifically charged with responsibility in the deaths of two women patients, both within a month.

This extraordinary interview occurred prior to the defendant's arraignment and even before a grand jury had heard all the facts in the case. Moreover, in other scenes on another channel, the doctor is shown being interrogated by police detectives.

The TV stations involved say the accused man freely consented to appear, but his attorney denies this. His attorney also claims police denied him a visit with his client even while opening jail doors to camera crews.

One result of this reportorial zeal has been to foment the wrath of the Cuyahoga County Bar Association along with that of a large number of viewers.

The committee of lawyers named to investigate the incident scored the coverage as "an abridgment of civil liberties," "a shameful blot on the administration of justice," and "a degrading and barbaric spectacle reminiscent of witch-burning."

Aside from the handling of news in the doctor's case, feeling about the way broadcasters are trying to compensate for the absence of newspapers is decidedly mixed.

In Washington, a Federal Communications Commission official says he believes stations in Cleveland and New York "generally are doing a good job" in filling the gap. Particularly commendable, he adds, is TV-radio coverage of the newspaper strikes themselves.

But Cleveland publishers and striking unionists think otherwise. "They're missing a lot of news about the strike, and they're playing it out of proportion," declares an official of the striking Cleveland

Newspaper Guild. "One newscaster hardly ever mentions the strike any more."

Publishers are more outspoken. They point to the temporary employment of Guild members by the broadcasting media to bolster its news staff. One station has 18 Guildsmen on the payroll. This, according to the publishers, tends to give a Guild bias to the strike news.

Says a spokesman for one newspaper, "They (TV stations) take any rumor that happens to float around and put it on the air without even checking whether it's true."

Cleveland broadcasters admit that despite beefed-up staffs and more air time for news, they continue to suffer such handicaps as constant repetition, "deadlines every 20 minutes," and problems in controlling what is aired.

"We'd have a celebration if the newspaper strike were settled today," says one telecaster. "Newspapers had almost become a crutch. We've had to add five men to the news staff."

Part of the problem lies in the limitations of the medium itself. "A certain amount of exaggeration is built in," says Pat Trese, news director of station KYW–TV. A TV station, for example, does not have a newspaper's option of playing minor stories with small headlines and on inside pages.

Radio and TV newsmen run into peculiar and frustrating situations during a newspaper blackout. A Federal judge who headed up a citizens' committee formed to find ways to end the newspaper strike bluntly refused to talk to them despite their protests that they were the only spokesmen for the public at the moment. "You aren't speaking for the public," the judge retorted, "I am."

Meanwhile, broadcasters in New York have been trying to keep their audience informed with extra and inevitably repetitious news programs. Chiefly deprived are probably the subway riders who depend on tabloids for their daily diet of murder and sex. Television can't handle sensational items with the enthusiasm of Gotham's livelier dailies.

Several stations have hired newspaper columnists to read their reports over the air. To listeners accustomed to stentorian news announcers, the sometimes sing-song, often nasalized deliveries are a little shattering.

Nevertheless, the New York broadcasters are offering more news in more detail than they usually do. But it's still clear, both in New York and Cleveland, that electronic journalism just can't do the full job of newspapers—even for a little while.

DAVID C. SMITH

January 15, 1963

Farewell la Femme

Helen Woodward's *The Lady Persuaders* is about the birth, pro-liferation and (in some instances) the decay of women's magazines. A rather dull subject, you might say, for the masculine reader.

Well, it could have been—but Mrs. Woodward, an inveterate defender of men, is of the irreverent Menckenian breed. It is her considered opinion, which she expresses in sparkling prose, that the women's magazines went entirely too far a generation ago in encourag-ing Mom and the children to play "amusing" tricks on "poor, silly Daddy." Though he had his uses, particularly on payday, Daddy was "a kind of Dagwood Bumstead, likable, lovable, but also foolish, irre-sponsible, and in need of feminine management."

"Never underestimate the power of a woman." So ran the successful slogan of one the greatest of the women's magazines. But the male sex, according to Mrs. Woodward, did not listen to the warning of Mr. Edward Bok of the *Ladies' Home Journal,* and in a period of masculine heedlessness the women's magazines managed to saddle American life with a virtual matriarchate.

Things eventually went so far, says Mrs. Woodward, that the women themselves "became frightened" and are now rebelling against the power that has been thrust upon them. In line with the newest trend, the women's magazines are now trying to restore some dignity to "silly Daddy," at least to the extent of bringing him back to a "shar-ing relationship" with the rest of the family. "Togetherness" is the new theme. Mrs. Woodward hates the word—and she does not think it will save the women's magazines. Only new ideas, she says, will do that.

Mrs. Woodward thinks the women's magazines had a worthy beginning. When Sara Josepha Hale, a small, beautiful and determined widow, when to Philadelphia from Boston to take over the editorship of *Godey's Lady's Book* before the Civil War, women had a most subordinate status in society. In those days of the patriarchate, a woman—or, rather, a lady—lost control of both her pocketbook and her person the day she was married. In terms of legal rights, she was "classed with a minor, a lunatic or an idiot."

Mrs. Hale changed all that by 40 years of "sweet and gentle" but completely "unrelenting" command. She coaxed, she wheedled, she soft-soaped—but she had her way. Under her "feather-duster prose,"

she was "clear and she was a fighter." She never campaigned for
women's suffrage, but she did get across the idea that women were
entitled to as many rights as men.

Coming closer to the present, Mrs. Woodward is not a detractor of
Edward Bok, who took over the *Ladies' Home Journal* in 1889 and
made it a force in the land. Bok admired women (if they were
like his mother and grandmother), and he fought for worthy causes.
He fought the patent medicine advertisers, he tried to get "germ-laden
plush" out of the Pullman cars, he campaigned against billboard
advertising and dirty cities, and more than anyone else he "brought
the bathroom into the house."

It was after the Bok era that the "decline and fall" of the women's
magazines took on impetus. Mrs. Woodward blames the editors, but
the fact is that society itself was changing. When women achieved
leisure and independence, they were confronted with a problem: either
to seek education or to seek power. Mrs. Woodward thinks they
elected to strive for power over the male. And this, she thinks, was a
turn which the women's magazine editors should have fought. Instead,
they encouraged it—or so Mrs. Woodward suggests in many a delightfully barbed sentence.

But there were other things that accounted for the decline in the
quality of the women's magazines. When women were predominantly
homemakers, there was a need for "trade magazines" for the professional housewife. But today, when the tin can and the deep freeze
are ubiquitous, the need for expert guidance through a maze of
kitchen mysteries is obviously less compelling. Taking on some of the
attributes and prerogatives of men, women have less reason for magazines of their own. And it follows, in Mrs. Woodward's analysis, that
the editors of women's magazines have to scratch for subject matter.

The current trend in women's magazines, as Mrs. Woodward says,
is toward specialization. We have *Mademoiselle,* we have *Seventeen,*
we have *Parents' Magazine.* Some of the older magazines in the
women's field have disappeared; others have come to resemble general
magazines. Mrs. Woodward does not weep for the change. Among
her friends, women who are "cool-headed" professionals in business,
"hardly any ever reads a so-called women's magazine." They read
what men read—and that's that.

JOHN CHAMBERLAIN

December 29, 1960

DIPLOMAT

The carpenter we're looking for is one who can keep a straight face while repairing a customer's do-it-yourself project.

------◆■◆------

Letter to an Author

Dear William Saroyan:

We are in receipt of your autobiography, *Here Comes, There Goes, You Know Who, William Saroyan,* and beg to acknowledge it with thanks for a lot of fun. We can't say that we really know who and what you are after reading it, but who cares? We don't know who and what a hummingbird is either, but we do know it can dart about in bright sunlight, making a pretty picture.

Everything about you seems to be swathed in paradox. You had a terrible time as a boy, losing your father and being shunted off for a while to an orphan asylum so that your mother could take a job to keep herself alive. But you had a wonderful time as a boy, too, finding beauty and humanity in the Irish cook at the orphanage.

You hated your teachers in a Fresno, California, school, but you did learn how to put the English language together, so they couldn't have been too bad. And you had to work long hours as a boy selling papers, but it takes all kinds to buy papers, so you learned about people by standing on that street corner, rain or shine.

Now, in your sixth decade, you are part of American literature. They read you in the schools you hated. Whatever can be said for you or against you (you have vitality, you lack form), you have it made as a creative artist, just as Jack London and Frank Norris, your brother Californians, also had it made before you. So you can't quarrel about not being appreciated.

In pleasing yourself (even when you write for money, it turns out that you cannot fake), you have turned a pretty penny. Most of it you have gambled away, but that's all right, too. For, as you say, it's only money, and the fact that you have lost it has kept you sitting at that desk, writing, writing, writing. And so the books have piled up, filled with warm and wonderful creatures who would go well in a play by George Kaufman if you hadn't got to them first.

Ordinarily, we would feel very sympathetic with your plight vis-à-vis the Internal Revenue Service. A writer can live for years in a garret, then strike it rich—and because a bestseller which has been decades in the making earns a lot of money in a single year, Uncle Sam or Uncle Deadbeat or whatever you want to call him grabs the surplus that should have been distributed over the years.

Since you missed up on the 1959 payments because you gambled away the money you made in one big year as a moving picture scenarist, you are probably now in permanent hock, like Joe Louis or Sugar Ray Robinson or any other public performer who didn't have it checked off at the time it came in. If your autobiography is a bestseller, it will get you off the 1959 hook. But it will put you on another hook for 1962.

It's like being a rat on a treadmill, this making lots of dough all of a sudden. But it's good for your readers—for you will just have to go on writing, writing, writing. "Snow money," you call it, "it just melts away." But the words will remain.

They're magic words, Saroyan. When you describe those Armenian meals your mother used to cook, it takes us far away from the land of hamburgers and hot dogs. When you tell about eating hothouse grapes in wartime London, at heaven-knows-how-many bucks for a single bunch, we can taste those grapes as we have never tasted anything else. When you describe your sensations as a boy when the school principal whipped you, we ache and ache. And when you talk about your feelings as a parent, we love all children.

The only thing we can't understand, Saroyan, is some of your prejudices against people who have never done you any harm. For example, you attack Bernard Baruch—"old Baruch," you call him—most spitefully for having made money and kept it. In behalf of all the hobos in the world, you have warned him against taking up good space on park benches.

Hell's bells, Saroyan, "old Baruch" is just as much an artist as you are, only it's in a different field. If he hadn't backed a cheap method of getting copper out of low-grade ore, your own life would have been more difficult. You once worked for the Postal Telegraph Company, which probably wouldn't even have hired you if copper wire had been more expensive.

Every time you pick up a telephone and make a call to your publisher to hurry that advance, you owe something to "old man Baruch." Besides which, in running the War Industries Board in World War I, he helped beat the Turks, who had driven your family out of Armenia. You ought to love him for that.

So live and let live, Saroyan. Writers aren't the only people in the world. They just think that they are, sometimes.

JOHN CHAMBERLAIN

January 30, 1962

POLITICAL LABELS—
READ WELL BEFORE USING

What Is a "Liberal"?

WASHINGTON—Describing just what constitutes a political "liberal," never an easy chore, is becoming downright impossible these days. And this predicament reflects the deep and sometimes hidden rifts within the liberal movement and the Democratic Party.

To most professional party chieftains, officeholders and labor leaders, the aims of liberalism have changed little since the days when Franklin D. Roosevelt was fighting the depression. They are those issues tied directly to the pocketbook and indirectly to the voting booth—medical care for the aged, construction of low cost housing, Federal spending to combat unemployment.

But to the intellectuals, to idealistic volunteer party workers and to a scattering of practicing politicians who comprise a smaller but highly vocal segment of the liberal movement, liberalism should look beyond mere bread and butter. These liberals want to concentrate on world disarmament, international rather than national solutions to world problems, an honorable and negotiated accommodation with the Soviet Union and Communist China, and encouragement for the underdeveloped nations of Asia, Africa and Latin America whether they're pro-Western or not. To this brand of liberals, civil rights and civil liberties are the most pressing domestic issues but do not challenge international issues in importance.

To be sure, a doctrinal dispute of this nature does not signal a violent rupture within the liberal camp. It's even less spectacular within a Democratic Party that has withstood a century of more basic disagreements between its Northern and Southern wings. Nevertheless, the spectacle of dual-headed liberalism is turning into an increasingly nagging headache for Democratic leaders.

An extreme manifestation of this headache can be found in the case of Senator Thomas J. Dodd, a Connecticut Democrat who preaches a militant nationalism and has been unrestrained in his condemnation of State Department policy, past and present, in Cuba, Berlin, the Congo and elsewhere. As a favorite of the right-wing anti-Communist movement, Mr. Dodd is seen by many liberals as a prime enemy.

But this feeling is not shared by a good many other self-professed liberals in Congress. They view Senator Dodd as a sure vote in favor of almost all social welfare measures and a consistent supporter of the Kennedy Administration's domestic program (he won an 80 per cent positive rating from the liberal Americans for Democratic Action on the basis of key Senate votes last year, though he is anathema to ADA leaders). Far from suffering ostracism at the hands of his Democratic colleagues in the Senate, Senator Dodd was quite a chum of Lyndon B. Johnson in the days when the Vice President was Senate Majority Leader.

A contrast to Senator Dodd can be found in Senator J. W. Fulbright of Arkansas, a segregationist and quite often a conservative on economic issues. Senator Fulbright endeared himself to liberal intellectuals a decade ago by attacking Senator McCarthy and again last year by denouncing the right-wing anti-Communists. "If liberalism means more than just voting for the minimum wage bill (opposed by Senator Fulbright), and I think it does," contends a nationally known liberal leader, "then Bill Fulbright's a liberal." Yet, the Arkansan's ADA report card gives him only a 60 per cent liberal rating.

The Dodd-Fulbright contrast is extreme but by no means isolated. Numerous bread-and-butter liberals in Congress detest international liberalism quite as much as Senator Dodd but are less outspoken about it. While unconditionally opposing admission of Communist China to the United Nations and demanding that the Berlin wall be torn down by the West, Senator Paul Douglas of Illinois maintains universally accepted liberal credentials partly because he avoids open debate of foreign policy questions with his fellow liberals. Even so, one ADA leader attributes Senator Douglas' militancy in foreign affairs to his heroic World War II exploits as a combat Marine and regards it as a "blind spot" in the Illinoisan's public philosophy.

Moreover, the present Janus-like image of liberalism cannot be explained away as eccentricities of individual lawmakers. Consider the contrast in outlook between two unofficial auxiliaries of the Democratic Party, the AFL–CIO and the ADA. The labor federation, delighted by passage of a batch of bread-and-butter bills, applauded last year's record of Congress. But the ADA, demonstrating its primary focus on world affairs, grumbled that passage of bills creating the

Peace Corps and the U.S. disarmament agency were the only real bright spots in an otherwise humdrum session.

True, the ADA, a limited membership organization with neither manpower nor financial resources, cannot be equated with the AFL–CIO, which supplies so many frontline troops for the Democratic Party. But the ADA is symbolic of an important segment of the party: the voluntary party workers who play influential and sometimes dominant roles in Democratic affairs outside the big cities and the South.

Thus, the two heads of liberalism show themselves frequently in state politics and most vividly within California's feuding Democratic Party. The California Democratic Council, which represents the state's thousands of crusading volunteer workers, is a constant irritant to the party professionals because of its demands for a more liberal foreign policy. The pros, who would rather stick to such tried-and-true vote-getting issues as more Government help for the aged, fear the council will publicly recommend UN admission for Red China and thereby damage Governor Brown's hopes for re-election this year.

Although President Kennedy has managed to keep himself and his Administration above this doctrinal split, he has evoked some grumbling from both liberal camps. The bread-and-butter liberals would prefer greater Administration attention to unemployment and other easily understandable political issues. The internationalist liberals have been unhappy about the President's emphasis on an arms buildup and—in their opinion—de-emphasis of disarmament efforts, his call for fallout shelter construction, and the downgrading of such a liberal favorite as Chester Bowles in the State Department.

Basically, the emergence of two brands of liberalism is attributable to a lack of mutual causality between domestic and international liberalism. That is, there is no philosophical connection between medical care for the aged and world disarmament. Nor is it philosophically inconsistent for an opponent of tighter Federal regulation and Government spending to advocate an international rather than a national approach to world problems.

Assuming that bread-and-butter liberalism still has political appeal and that militant nationalism could attract votes in these troubled times, a combination of the two might present a device to be used by Republicans in prying union members from their allegiance to the Democratic Party. Certainly, this political formula was used brilliantly in past generations by Theodore Roosevelt in the United States and Joseph Chamberlain in England.

But this is no more than political daydreaming. The very Republicans who most ardently champion a bellicose nationalism are die-hard domestic conservatives who would blanch at the thought of making common cause with organized labor and its domestic program. Rather, the political repercussions of two-headed liberalism will be less cataclysmic than a frontal assault upon the foundations of the Democratic Party.

And one of these repercussions is suggested by this comment from Joseph Rauh, a crusading internationalist liberal and perennial national officer of the ADA: "This is one time that I'm not sure that the program we're advocating today will be the program of the politicians generally tomorrow."

Despised though they may be by the professional politicians, the ADA-style liberals have set the doctrinal course of the Democratic Party in recent years. If this now is to end, it is indeed a significant development.

ROBERT D. NOVAK

January 12, 1960

Conservatives' Creed

Conservatism, like liberalism, changes with changing times and varies in emphasis from country to country.

Just now, American conservatives are engaged in a lively discussion as to whether the views of Mr. Robert Welch, founder and leader of the much-publicized John Birch Society, are compatible with authentic conservatism. A recent issue of *National Review,* a fortnightly devoted to the exposition of conservative philosophy, subjects the views of Mr. Welch to analysis on the basis of his own published writings, mostly in a personal organ called *American Opinion.*

According to Mr. Welch, America is in a very bad way indeed, because many of its leading citizens are Communists, many of its most trusted agencies of governing have been taken over by Communists and movements which, on the surface, are directed against communism are really masterminded by mysterious Kremlin plotters to serve the Communist cause. So, in Mr. Welch's sight, former President Eisenhower and his brother Milton are Communists. The CIA is "on the Communist side." So is the State Department.

The revolts in Poland and Hungary in 1956 were generally interpreted as the first big cracks in the structure of Soviet imperialism. But Mr. Welch knows better. "Both revolts," he writes, "were deliberately precipitated by the Kremlin for its own purpose."

NATO is regarded in the West as an alliance, if an imperfect one, of free peoples against communism. It is denounced as an imperialist conspiracy in the Soviet press. But Mr. Welch knows better. To him, NATO, which has the backing of almost all conservatives on both sides of the Atlantic, is "probably the biggest—and certainly the most expensive—hoax in all human history." And so on, and so on. Everyone is out of step but Mr. Welch, who might even, before long, be suspecting himself as an agent of the world Communist conspiracy.

It seems evident that all this has very little to do with serious conservative thinking, or indeed thinking of any kind. More serious is the debate that periodically breaks out as to where the taproots of conservatism are to be found, what are its abiding principles. For there is an unmistakable difference between what might be called the old-fashioned conservatism of Great Britain and Europe and the ideas that appeal to most American conservatives today.

Old-fashioned conservatism was closely linked with such institutions as monarchy, aristocracy, an established church. It conceived of society as clearly divided into classes, each with its special duties and functions, and with admission to the ranks of the upper classes pretty jealously restricted. In this old-fashioned conservatism there was a sense of *noblesse oblige,* of the king devoting his life to the service of his people, of the country squire looking after his tenants in distress.

But the coming of industrialism and its ultimate consequence, the affluent society, accompanied also in Europe by tremendous social and economic upheavals in the wake of war and revolution, have made this kind of conservatism as extinct as the traditional dodo. It never had real roots in America, which started its national existence without monarchy, aristocracy or established church.

Conservatism, which started as a vindication of a status society, has now taken over many traits of 19th–century liberalism, while liberalism, at least in America, is often a pleasing synonym for at least a mild version of socialism. And it is by no means illogical for the American conservative to take up what most self-styled liberals have abandoned, the principles of 19th–century liberalism. It was by these principles—limited government, individual opportunity, self-help rather than state help, respect for the rights of property—that America lived before the coming of the New Deal.

Incidentally, all these principles find abundant support in the writings of the greatest British conservative thinker, Edmund Burke, who, as Professor Hayek likes to remind us, did not consider himself a Conservative, in the party sense, but rather a Whig, or old-fashioned liberal, especially in his economic views.

While the emphasis of conservatism may shift from country to country and from one era to another, there are certain traits that mark the conservative in all ages. While no reasonable conservative denies the need for change and reform in a vital society, he will oppose change that is made only for change's sake. He will take his stand with Lord Falkland, the middle-of-the-road man in England's struggle between King and Parliament, who said: "If it is not necessary to change, it is necessary not to change."

The conservative places more trust in the inherited experience of the race than in the operations of a doctrinaire individual intellect, however brilliant. He sees society, in Burke's fine phrase, as a compact between the dead, the living and those who are yet unborn. Because he takes a less optimistic view of human nature than the liberal or the revolutionary, he is more faithful to the conception of an elaborate system of checks and balances as a safeguard against hasty and arbitrary intrusion by government on the rights of the individual. Our greatest theoretical conservative was our second President, John Adams, who wrote:

> To expect self-denial from men, when they have a majority in their favor and consequently power to gratify themselves, is to disbelieve all history and universal experience; it is to disbelieve Revelation and the Word of God, which informs us the heart is deceitful in all things and desperately wicked.

If this theology may seem a little harsh, it may be recalled that Rousseau's excessive faith in the natural goodness of man and the belief of French intellectuals of the 18th century that a new order could be installed by doctrinaire reason alone ended in ghastly disillusionment on the guillotine.

Conservatism at all times and in all countries has stood for patriotism, religion, the integrity of the family and respect for private property as four pillars of a sound and healthy society. Add to this the instinct for guarding against excesses of an individual dictator or of a mob-minded majority, and one has a creed on which most authentic conservatives would agree. A good expression of this creed is the United States Constitution, a profoundly conservative document.

WILLIAM HENRY CHAMBERLIN

February 23, 1962

Conservatism—Real and Unreal

It is a familiar phenomenon that any movement will generate its own extremists or attract them to it. And, the world being as it is, the extremists sometimes get more publicity than the real representatives of the movement.

The "liberals," as the word is currently used in American politics, have long had this problem. And now the "conservatives," enjoying a boom in the country if not in Washington, are having a taste of being linked to extremists.

So perhaps it may be useful to take a brief look at what does constitute the main stream of contemporary conservative thought. It is, of course, no single, rigid body of doctrine; as Professor David McCord Wright notes in *Modern Age* Magazine, it is "a spectrum of thought, not a single beam." In other times some who would today be called conservatives were called liberals, and today some of conservative view find the conservative label unsatisfactory. The label is only a convenience; what matters is the thinking.

In any case, conservatism is—and this the liberals rejoice in overlooking—a highly intellectual movement. Both historically and at present it embraces, under whatever label, some of the world's most brilliant minds in the field of economics and politics. Locke, Burke, Mill in the past; von Mises, Hayek and a host of others today. Many articulate conservatives teach at universities, and in recent years there has been a new surge of conservative opinion among college students as well.

Most conservatives would agree on certain fundamental principles, whatever their other differences. They start from a philosophy of man which puts the stress on his individuality and diversity, and from this it follows that his fullest development will be in conditions of maximum economic and political freedom.

How is it, then, that conservatives are sometimes viewed as reactionaries hankering for an unattainable past? Partly, no doubt, because of the extremists. As for the main stream of conservatism, this view is a misapprehension.

Conservatives do indeed value order in a society, and only a foolish society would not; devising institutions that combine order with maximum individual liberty is one of man's more complex intellectual undertakings.They do value the teachings of the past, as it would not be very intelligent to ignore them. While they do not oppose change, they do oppose reckless or thoughtless political and economic tinkering.

That is the exact opposite of a reactionary view. After all, what conservatives today want to conserve is the most revolutionary body of political thought on record—the doctrine of freedom as expressed in the writings of this nation's architects.

It must be said that history provides much support for the conservative view. The great threat to man's freedom has always been the power of the State. There is a danger in the constant encroachments of the central government; how can there not be a danger? Order preserved by a reasonable degree of government is one thing; but constantly growing State power can only be at the expense of the individual.

So there is nothing negative about opposing that trend and urging a Jeffersonian limited government. That is only another way of saying that the fullest prospering of the individual and the community depends on staving off all-powerful government.

For our part, it matters little whether or not we are called conservative. What we are, however, trying to say is that the approach to life which is usually called conservative is an intellectually respectable movement firmly grounded in common sense and man's experience.

It has nothing in common with authoritarian secret societies or with strident, indiscriminate accusations of Communism, although conservatives are the strongest foes of Communism. Yet individuals and groups like the John Birch Society are being publicized as conservatives and exaggerated out of all proportion to their significance. If some of these people sound a little silly when they go around appealing for the impeachment of the Chief Justice, it is no less silly to regard them as some kind of threat to the nation.

The groundswell of genuine conservative thinking in America is a healthy thing, particularly at this time. It will be a pity if a few extremists, abetted by exaggerated comment, succeed in distorting its meaning.

JOSEPH E. EVANS

August 14, 1961

"The radical right caught on and the radical left caught on—but I can't seem to get any support for my radical middle-of-the-roadism."

The Confused Debate

Many of us can appreciate former President Eisenhower's impatience with such "shopworn and meaningless terms" as "liberal" and "conservative." It's almost impossible to use these words any more without elaborate qualification.

"Liberal" has a nice sound and an honorable history in the sense of support for individual freedom against the aggrandizement of the State. Yet today's liberals advocate that the central Government be given much greater power to plan and control the lives of individuals.

What does that advocacy entitle them to be called? Leftists? Reactionaries? However appropriate these might be, it is unlikely that the so-called liberals themselves would accept the designations.

"Conservative," for its part, is such a headache that at least one distinguished thinker of what is nowadays called the conservative persuasion refuses to wear that label. And the word has suffered unwarranted injury in the recent exaggerated hoopla over "right-wing extremists," who have little in common with most self-styled conservatives.

Since the typical contemporary conservative champions the individual against the regimentation of the State, he might properly be called a liberal. But that would only compound confusion. The same is true of "new liberal." "Libertarian," which some essay, has a somewhat artificial sound. So it goes.

Finding suitable substitutes for "liberal" and "conservative," then, is no easy matter. Even more difficult, it seems, is finding the people and the programs that could restore clarity to the political debate in this country. For the semantic confusions reflect philosophical confusions within the contending political camps.

Of the two groups, the present-day liberals appear to have a clearer conception of where they want to go. True, there is confusion enough; they range over a political spectrum of their own, from the extreme liberal who argues for something akin to socialism or communism to the Republican brand of "me-too" liberal.

But in essence they are joined in the belief in the centralization of Government; they argue that practically all problems, the great and the small, the national and the local, are best solved on a Federal basis. If this seems inescapably to lead to a form of collectivism, many of them do not mind, since they would be the drivers of the collective machine.

Now this approach, stripped of its various rationalizations, is plain enough. It automatically suggests what its political competition should be. Opponents of collectivism must, in President Eisenhower's words, devote themselves "to the protection of every man's personal, political and economic freedom"; they must demonstrate their faith in the citizen's capacity "to carry the nation further and faster along the road of true progress than can any planned economy of paternalistic bureaucracy."

It is not particularly difficult to translate these generalities into a program of concrete political action that would be positive and forceful rather than negative and defensive. A program of freedom would envisage many appealing things, such as tax reduction, which hold out the promise of greater material abundance and a fuller life for all.

Yet where is such a program? The opposition party, the GOP as such, does not espouse it; only some individual members of it do so.

And it can hardly be a coincidence that the Republican Party has fallen on evil days. Thanks in part to Republican confusion and lethargy, the drift toward centralization and collectivism goes on almost unchecked, and indeed with scant discussion of the basic issues.

It would be a service to clarity if our political lexicon contained better words than conservative and liberal, or if these words could be given more precise definitions. But the real need is for men who, whatever they call themselves, are willing to work for the expansion of freedom instead of apathetically condoning its contraction.

JOSEPH E. EVANS

February 8, 1962

Campus Conservatives

The resurgence of conservatism on college campuses around the country has sparked extensive theorizing by politicians and educators about the movement's motivations.

Some people would like to ascribe the agitation to youthful frustration with the problems of the cold war. Others see it as an intellectual reflex action to the nation's protracted leftward drift. But while conservative students certainly have been stirred by the world impasse and the burgeoning welfare state, there is evidence that they are making their stand on higher ground.

The young conservative is apt to sum up his views with an ideological credo similar to this one delivered by Jim Henrick, a 19-year-old junior from Champaign, Illinois, who is vice president of the University of Illinois Student Senate:

"Even if it means the material well-being of other people or myself may suffer because of it, I believe in individual liberty. I believe the individual, not the Government, should be responsible for himself."

If spoken by a professional politician, these words might seem trite and hollow, but coming from the mouth of an undergraduate conservative, they somehow have the ring of freshness and genuine conviction. For the student right-winger is essentially a theorist and an idealist. He prefers rambling through the generalities of non-Marxian dialectics to discussing the dreary specifics of Federal budget balancing or the tax structure.

Student conservatives interviewed at an Ivy League university, a

Midwestern state university and a privately endowed Southern university (Yale, the University of Illinois and Tulane) are at their best in propounding the doctrines of libertarianism. Deadly serious and virtually humorless, their faith in the individual and suspicion of Government are unbounded. Regarding himself as a crusader against statism, the campus conservative rarely admits to a desire for accumulation of vast personal wealth.

Since the student right-winger uses this ideological base to form his stands on individual issues, he never finds himself in the position of the industrialist who opposes Federal regulation but welcomes Federal subsidies. But this search for ideological consistency often leads to radicalism—a term the campus conservative does not necessarily find offensive.

Take the case of Bill Johnson, 19, Glastonbury, Connecticut, a Yale sophomore (and outstanding half-mile prospect on the track team) who is president of the local chapter of the right-wing Young Americans for Freedom. Sharply disapproving of what he considers Republican temporizing with social security and Federal minimum wage, he advocates outright repeal of both laws.

Not content with the doctrines of states' rights or local home rule, some students carry their distrust of government to the point of anarchy. Haywood Hillyer, a 24-year-old Tulane law student from New Orleans, urges abolition of public schools on the ground that education is not a proper function of any level of government.

For the same reason, 20-year-old Prentice Smith of Houma, Louisiana, a Tulane junior, opposes state regulation of the oil and gas industry, though conceding an end to production controls would bring chaos.

To be sure, the campus conservative is not concerned exclusively with domestic matters. He readily concedes that survival against Communism is the central issue of our time. And there is a consensus among the collegiate right favoring more aggressive cold war steps: Marine expeditions to liberate Cuba and stem the Red tide in Southeast Asia, destruction of the Communist-built wall dividing Berlin, vigorous support of the separatist, anti-Communist Katanga regime in the Congo.

But campus conservatives generally must be led into a foreign policy discussion. They prefer ideological discussions that give them a better chance to flex their intellectual muscles. For the liberals' description of the young conservative as a loutish anti-intellectual is calumny. He is very much a product of the academy, delighting in intellectualism that sometimes verges on intellectual snobbery.

This snobbery is a part of the strange relationship between the campus conservative and Senator Goldwater. Although the newer student disciples of conservatism may revere the Arizona Senator as an unerring leader, the more sophisticated frankly regard him as a convenient mouthpiece for their views, as the only practicing politician who even approaches their ideal.

Some are clearly disturbed by the facts that Mr. Goldwater is neither a college graduate nor personally writes his own material. A few look to Senator John Tower of Texas, a one-time college professor, as a more intellectual conservative chieftain.

Actually, no mere politician who must live in the real world of elective office could be the saint of the campus conservative movement. That role is firmly held by William Buckley, 36-year-old conservative polemicist and editor of the *National Review,* chief publication of the intellectual right. Occupying only a peripheral role in the greater world of politics, Mr. Buckley and his magazine are prophet and holy writ for the campus conservative.

But aside from their adoration of Mr. Buckley, the student conservatives do not even faintly fit the picture of slavish imitation of their elders often painted by liberals. Their attitude toward the American businessman, for example, ranges from head-shaking sympathy to contempt.

Arguing that the businessman is inexcusably apathetic toward politics, Richard Cowan, a 21-year-old Fort Worth, Texas, senior who heads Yale's conservative Calliopean Society, asserts: "Businessmen remind me of sheep being led to slaughter. They've got it coming to them, and they're going to get it."

Similarly, student conservatives are by no means admirers of the numerous adult right-wing groups that have sprouted during recent years. Tulane's Haywood Hillyer is a member of the John Birch Society (he claims he exerts a moderating influence on his fellow Birchers), but this is exceptional.

More typically, the campus conservative scorns the rather plodding, unsophisticated leadership of the adult groups. Here again, there seems an element of intellectual snobbery—exemplified by the Tulane conservatives' condescending attitude toward Kent Courtney of New Orleans, an extreme right-wing leader who once charged that Senator Goldwater was tainted with left-wing tendencies.

Nor do the students share the belief of many adult right-wingers that Communists in positions of authority at the State Department and Central Intelligence Agency are responsible for the deterioration of the U.S. position internationally.

Criticizing the John Birchers, Yale's Richard Cowan contends: "They're generally seeking the right goals, but they are naïve and limited in taking such an inward view of things. They see Communism as an internal rather than an external force."

A group of student conservative leaders at the University of Illinois who generally agree that the Kennedy Administration is soft toward

Communism were asked whether Communist infiltration caused this. The answer was a unanimous "no."

Again contrary to liberal contentions, the young conservative movement is no monolith. "Put 100 young conservatives in a room, and you'll get 100 opinions," says Bob Schuchman of New York, a 23-year-old Yale law student and a national leader of the Young Americans for Freedom. This may be something of an exaggeration, but the campus right-wingers do rejoice in doctrinal clashes and can dispute an esoteric point with all the relish of a medieval scholastic.

Student conservatives also tangle among themselves on more substantial issues, such as international trade policy; purist libertarians argue the virtues of free trade over protectionism.

Even more heated debate is generated by the race question, a burning topic on the college campus. Aside from some predictable segregationist sentiment at Tulane, the conservatives interviewed are remarkably solid in their opposition to enforced separation of the races; they split over the question of whether the Federal Government should break down the racial barriers.

Again, the student conservatives split over whether a political conservative must also be a religious conservative. Like many right-wing students, Cass Apple, 21, of Verona, New Jersey, an Illinois senior, is attracted to novelist Ayn Rand's philosophy of studied selfishness that excoriates collectivism. But he stops short at Miss Rand's atheism.

On the other hand, Unitarians and other liberal religionists are fairly common in conservative ranks at Yale. Bill Johnson, the Young Americans for Freedom leader, left the Catholic Church during his high school days and now considers himself a Unitarian. And at Illinois, 20-year-old Jim Noland, a junior from Toulon, Illinois, flatly denies that belief in God is an essential component of conservatism.

This then is the campus conservative: Doctrinaire, contentious, unconquerably idealistic. But for all of the uniqueness of an articulate right wing on the college campus after decades of silence, these are characteristics common to youth generally rather than to conservatism alone. Thus, if some of today's campus conservatives some day wind up in the halls of Congress as they hope, it's a safe bet that the rigidly ideological tone of their conservatism will be somewhat softened by then.

ROBERT D. NOVAK

November 30, 1961

Campus Liberals

Because student conservatives were in hibernation for so long, their recent awakening has made news—so much news that one might think the student liberals had evacuated the forums. But this is hardly the case.

While one would think they'd have less and less to complain about as the Federal Government has expanded in size and power, the campus liberals aren't satisfied by a long shot. But they have undergone some changes since the days when they could exercise their lungs in unison about the "social injustice" they professed to see everywhere.

Today the Bomb figures importantly in their polemics, and as they have concerned themselves more and more with the great international questions, their once concerted voice has broken up into many voices urging a variety of answers.

Dennis Weeks, an 18-year-old University of Illinois sophomore from De Kalb, Illinois, is a pacifist who believes the very existence of a U.S. nuclear arsenal poses the threat of an accidental atomic holocaust.

Don Bierman, a 21-year-old Tulane University senior from Miami, Florida, enthusiastically endorses President Kennedy's arms buildup, resumption of underground nuclear testing and shows of force in Berlin as exercises in "international power politics."

A wide divergence of opinion here on an overriding issue of our time. Yet, each of these young men, both leaders in student politics, considers himself a liberal.

Student liberal leaders interviewed at Yale, the University of Illinois and Tulane (representing an Ivy League school, a huge Midwestern state university and a Southern university) eagerly poured out views covering a large chunk of the political spectrum. For the sake of convenience, however, they can be divided into two groups: the radicals and the moderates.

The left-wing radical of the campus is probably a socialist, usually a pacifist and not in any permanent way attached to the Democratic Party. Communists and fellow travelers are rare though some student radicals are exceedingly gentle in their assessments of Castro's Cuba and even Russia.

The campus radical is well read and probably an exceptional student; he may quite possibly be a graduate student performing some teaching chores on the side. But this bookishness does not keep him from spending weary hours on the picket line demonstrating against nuclear weapons or racial segregation.

He is invariably a rigid doctrinaire and committed emotionally to those doctrines. If he resembles the radicals who dominated campus political life between the stock market crash of 1929 and World War II, it is no coincidence; he is their legitimate successor.

The moderate liberal adheres more closely to the current political positions of his liberal elders. He is an advocate of the welfare state but stops short of outright socialism. He contends international arms control is the only hope of the world but opposes the unilateral disarmament schemes of the pacifist.

If he belongs to any political organization, it probably will be the Young Democrats rather than the Student Peace Union or the NAACP. Consequently, the moderate is more likely to be ringing doorbells for some mayoralty candidate than carrying picket signs for world peace. Generally, he is less serious in his devotion to political causes than the campus radical and far less familiar with the issues involved.

Obviously, this two-part division of the campus left is artificial. Innumerable shades of opinion abound. And the moderate student liberal may be a moderate only in reference to the campus political spectrum.

Far from echoing the approval of the Kennedy foreign policy voiced by Tulane's Don Bierman, he may stand well to the left of the President and berate him for overly aggressive stands against Moscow.

"I think Kennedy ought to do more to explain to the American people that we're not the top dog any more, not the strongest country in the world," declares Carey Winget of Clayton, Illinois, a 20-year-old junior who is active in the Young Democrats Club at the University of Illinois. "We just can't muscle our way around any more."

Internal disputes between factions ranging from the Communists to the New Dealers also characterized the vigorous campus left-wing movement of a generation ago. But today's disagreements among campus liberals are accompanied by disorganization, inactivity and a certain impression of listlessness. Why?

"Liberalism is the prevailing political philosophy now, and we don't have to make as much noise to prove our point," contends Lance Leibman, 20, of Frankfort, Kentucky, a senior who is editor of the *Yale Daily News*.

This answer, however, seems a bit too pat. More convincing are the theories by other campus liberals that they have been paralyzed this year with disillusionment about President Kennedy. Although his previous appeal to the student left-winger was minimal, Mr. Kennedy stirred campus liberals of all varieties during his campaign for the

Presidency. The disillusionment began as early as last December with the new President's first nominations, particularly his choice of ex-businessman Luther Hodges as Secretary of Commerce.

The break between Mr. Kennedy and the campus left was completed with the ill-fated invasion of Cuba April 17, not because the expedition failed but because it was attempted at all.

"I parted company with Kennedy on April 17," snaps Joe Tuchinsky, 24, of Philadelphia, a pacifist who is working on his doctorate in English at Illinois.

More moderate student liberals may not be quite as sweeping in their rejection of the President. But it is difficult to find a campus endorsement of Mr. Kennedy much more enthusiastic than this one from 20-year-old Ken Harding of Washington, D.C., a Yale senior and a leader in the Young Democrats Club: "I suppose Kennedy is doing a pretty good job, but I wouldn't call myself gung ho about him. I never have been."

Nor are campus liberals particularly entranced by any other practicing liberal politician. Adlai Stevenson, who would have been the Democratic nominee for President last year if liberal students had their way, no longer is the darling of the collegiate left.

Most significant is the lack of one emotion-charged issue that could unite the collegiate left-wingers as did the Spanish Civil War during the 1930s. True, the student liberals close ranks in their devotion to the cause of civil rights, and many regard it as the most critical issue of the day.

But the race question somehow falls short of cementing the campus left, possibly because it is not really an exclusively left-wing cause. A few members of the Yale Young Republicans Club belong to the campus NAACP chapter, and many college civil-rights advocates steer clear of all other political issues.

Moreover, the bread-and-butter issues which so stirred the prewar campus leftists and still preoccupy practicing liberal politicians bring yawns from contemporary student liberals. The Kennedy Administration's victory in winning passage of the fattest housing bill ever goes practically unnoticed on the campus.

The most that is heard about approval of the first significant broadening of the minimum wage law in 23 years is occasional camplaint that low-wage laundry workers were excluded from coverage. Even the avowed student socialist seldom denounces capitalism, preferring to condemn the evils of war and racial segregation.

This apathy toward economic causes sometimes changes to animosity when it comes to organized labor. "The power of the labor unions is far too great," argues Dean Gotteherer, 20, of Miami, Florida, a junior who is president of the Tulane Young Democrats and tends toward leftist stands on foreign policy matters. "Before you know it, they'll have the economy right in the palm of their hand."

Whatever vigor and purposefulness is shown by campus liberals is found generally on the extreme left. The student radicals claim the frustration and feeling of defeat prevalent in their ranks no longer than two years ago now is fading away. The success of Southern "sit-in" demonstrations and the "freedom" rides have encouraged them to apply such tactics to pacifist as well as civil rights causes.

But though the frustration has abated, the sense of isolation from contemporary American life remains. Leaders of the Tulane liberal club, most of them avowed socialists, plan no future career in politics —not because politics repels but because they see no place in it for anyone of their philosophical persuasion. And even the more moderate left-wingers who are neither socialists nor pacifists sometimes feel themselves to be outside the acceptable bounds of practical politics.

Such a liberal is Richard Portes, 20, of Glencoe, Illinois, a personable and articulate Yale senior who is about to win his bachelor's degree with a double major in philosophy and mathematics after only three years. He once seriously considered trying for public elective office some day. But after spending last summer as a student intern in the office of a liberal Democratic Congressman and observing the compromises a liberal must make to survive politically, he now shies away from a political career.

This isolation is the true dilemma of the campus liberal. The most dedicated, able and promising of the student leftists seem irrevocably wedded to radical concepts that bar them from elective office and genuinely effective public service. To gain a hold on the reins of power, either they or the nation at large must revise its views. And, the student radicals wistfully assert, neither change is likely.

ROBERT D. NOVAK

December 1, 1961

Handy Glossary for Conventions

WASHINGTON—This month the nation will again be treated to its great quadrennial spectacular—the national political conventions. To enjoy the show to the full, every American should have a working knowledge of the words, traditions and institutions he'll be reading about in his papers and hearing about on radio and television during those feverish weeks. As a public service, we offer this abridged lexicon that has long guided politicians.

Convention Hall: A large building normally used for cattle auctions, horse shows, and ice hockey, and smelling of all three.

The Party of the People, the Party of Peace and Prosperity, the Party for All Americans: Our party.

The Party of Drift, the Party of Special Interests, the Party of Corruption, Depression and War: Their party.

Active candidate: A politician who wants the nomination, is fighting hard for it, and admits it.

Inactive candidate: One who wants the nomination and is fighting hard for it, but maintains he would take the job only to save the country from the worst possible fate—nomination of any of the other candidates.

Keynoter: The party leader who looks best on television with his mouth open and his arms upraised.

Platform: A compilation of lofty platitudes, outrageous charges and hedged promises unparalleled in the history of the written word—or, rather, since the last convention.

Platform Committee: A group of creative writers who let themselves go, secure in the knowledge their work will be filed away and forgotten immediately after the campaign.

Convention Chairman: A party wheelhorse with an arm strong enough to shatter a gavel, a voice loud enough to shout down anyone in the hall, and an astigmatism that can conveniently overlook any delegate demanding the floor at the wrong time or for the wrong purpose.

Open Convention: A convention made notable by the fact that the party bosses have been able to rule out only eight of the leading ten contenders, rather than nine of the ten.

Frontrunner: The candidate who leads the pack—as attested by the cluster of knives in his back.

Dark Horse: A candidate with so little chance of success that nobody can take the time to be vigorously against him—and therein lies his strength.

Bandwagon: A badly creaking conveyance each candidate tries to convince the delegates they'd better get aboard before it's too late for them to share in the credit for nominating him. When a candidate announces his bandwagon is rolling, it means he has been pledged 14 more delegates, giving him a total of 62 of the 761 he needs.

Delegate: The flower of the home-state political machine. He has paid in advance for this hour in the sun by 20 years of doorbell ringing, escorting old ladies to the polls and doing all the other little chores that keep a political machine in running order.

Alternate Delegate: His presence doubles the number of party faithful getting a free trip to the convention and also prevents the delegation from being too deeply decimated by hangovers and other convention hazards.

Nominating Speech: A description of the candidate in terms so glowing that he is clearly too good for the job, if not for this world.

Demonstration: A wild parade, complete with banners, cheerleaders and a cast of paid marchers, carefully staged to prove that support for candidate Jones is massive and hysterically enthusiastic.

Spontaneous Demonstration: A demonstration.

Passing: An evasive maneuver on the roll call conducted when a state can't decide which candidate is most likely to be nominated and therefore wants to skip voting until things clear up a little.

Nomination: An inevitable consequence when the maneuvering, trading and hatchet-wielding have finally brought the convention to the point where one more than half the delegates have decided that the man they really preferred has been stopped dead.

Nomination by Acclamation: The ritual of burying the hatchet, arranged for the benefit of press and television cameras. Frequently, as the campaign progresses, the candidate later finds his former rivals have actually buried the hatchet in his back.

Running Mate: The man who is most different from the nominee in age, place of residence, political orientation and, possibly, religion. This qualifies him to run for the vice presidency. It's only a matter of time before a difference in sex will also be considered highly desirable, too.

The Next President of the United States: Our nominee, of course.

ALAN L. OTTEN

July 7, 1960

RED CHECKMATE . . .
PAWNS AND GAMBITS

Pawns and Gambits in a Long Game

The Russians are famed as chess players, and chess is a game in which every move opens up such infinite possibilities that no man can foresee them all.

Today there are some people who think the Russians merely blundered when they got so deeply involved in Cuba. Others think it was all part of a devious strategy, and even now these people look for the "catch" in the Soviet's sudden turnabout. But it is just as likely that their whole Cuban adventure was, at one and the same time, simpler and more subtle.

Like a skilled player boldly attacking with a pawn, the Russians probably considered two possibilities. If the United States was in fact too spineless to respond to the Cuban threat, they would gain a forward position in the Western Hemisphere. If we did respond, the response might well be ineffective (remember the Bay of Pigs?) or so divide Western councils that it would still offer opportunities to the Communists—to swap the base in Cuba, say, for the Western base in Turkey.

They were wrong on both counts. But the wise chess player does not commit himself irrevocably to the defense of a pawn when to do so becomes dangerous. He sacrifices the pawn, withdraws and takes a fresh, cold look at his position everywhere. To a chess player there need be nothing mysterious about Mr. Khrushchev's sacrifice of his Cuban pawn.

This move too opens up infinite possibilities. And if no man—neither Mr. Khrushchev nor Mr. Kennedy—can foresee them all, it is still wise to consider as many of them as possible. Against a good chess player speculation is never an idle exercise.

The most obvious possibility is that Mr. Khrushchev will counter his setback in Cuba with a thrust somewhere else.

If the Russians do actually retreat in Cuba, it is because they are realists. This is a place in which we can muster more strength than the Soviet Union. Short of a nuclear war—which the Russians want no more than we—what could Mr. Khrushchev do about our blockade once the President made it perfectly clear that he would not waver?

There are other places in the world, however, where the Communist strength in non-nuclear forces is equal or even a little superior to our own. We are handicapped in Laos by the same things—distance, for one—that handicap the Russians in Cuba. So no one ought to be surprised if one result of Cuba is trouble somewhere else, such as Berlin.

But this does not exhaust the possibilities. For a number of reasons, it is equally possible that our firm stand over Cuba, with its clear indication that we will not draw back from the consequences, even of war, may have brought about a greater alteration of the world situation than we yet know.

For another mark of a good chess player is that he can recognize the weaknesses in his own position before they are apparent to the bystanders or sometimes to his opponent. And the whole history of the Cuban affair points to some very real weaknesses in the Soviet position.

First of all, if it were true that the Soviets had the military superiority they so often claim, there would have been little necessity for the Cuban adventure to begin with and no reason for them to back down so completely at the first calling of their bluff. At the very least, if they were so sure of themselves they could have kept the crisis going while they pushed harder for a "deal" which would give them a quid for the quo.

The on-again-off-again history of the proposal about Turkey suggests the possibility of another weakness, a division in the Kremlin councils. From the outside anyway, it looks as though the Kremlin was the scene of a major political struggle during the past few days, with reason winning out over recklessness.

The "reason" here may be something that has struck every recent visitor to the Soviet Union. Soviet agriculture, by the Kremlin's admission, is skirting the edge of disaster. Soviet industry is stretched wire taut. In the Soviet Union proper as well as in the satellite countries there is dangerous unrest, as witnessed by the recent worker riots in Soviet territory. You cannot dismiss the possibility that the Soviet Union is simply in no condition to meet any great trial, such as a war, and that the more sensible Soviet authorities know it well.

Nor can anyone dismiss the problem that China poses for the Soviets. At this very moment the Chinese are erupting in India, and everywhere they are showing signs of acting on their own and creating a conflict-of-interest with Soviet foreign policy. If the men in the Kremlin are not uneasy about the threat to their safety from Chinese adventuring, they certainly ought to be.

How much of all this entered into Mr. Khrushchev's calculations on Cuba—and in what proportions—is impossible to tell. But it is not necessary to measure these things precisely. For the point of considering all the possibilities is not to choose one over the others; it would be foolhardy to suppose that our apparent success in Cuba means that trouble will not erupt elsewhere. The point is simply to avoid the opposite mistake of overlooking changes that might be further to our advantage.

At least we have taught both ourselves and the Russians that we can play this long-drawn-out game. And if we will just keep that in mind in the future, we don't have to lose.

VERMONT ROYSTER

October 30, 1962

Playing with Matches

It is always embarrassing for a nation to be caught red-handed in the act of gathering information. It is even more embarrassing when a nation is forced by circumstances to admit it.

The gathering of information has always been an accepted business among nations. It even has two names. Those who are in the act of doing it call it intelligence work; those upon whom it is being practiced call it spying. It is dangerous work, and largely thankless. No country will ever acknowledge a spy when he is caught if it can help itself.

That, of course, explains the first nonsense issued by the State Department that the unarmed U-2—a highly specialized craft capable of flying 10 miles high—was on a weather flight for the National Aeronautics and Space Administration. From first reports, this country doubtless thought the pilot was killed. But since the Russians claim to have captured him, the United States now admits that we do engage in intelligence reconnaissance near the borders of Russia, as a safeguard against surprise attack. But we say no flight over Russia was "authorized" by Washington.

Mr. Khrushchev, we may be sure, will get all the mileage he can out of this event. It should be noted that he has already used it to boast of the speed with which Soviet internal defense operates: he himself ordered the plane shot down after it penetrated Soviet territory. And he ordered it shot down, he claims, with a new missile in one shot.

But it is not likely that the worldly Mr. Khrushchev is really as upset about all this as he makes out. Delighted in the way it turned out, yes. Disturbed, no. The head of as far-flung an espionage system as Russia's would think us fools if we weren't doing this sort of thing to keep an eye on the Soviet and to ferret out Mr. Khrushchev's intentions wherever possible.

All the same, it seems to us that some questions ought to be raised about the judgment used in gathering intelligence.

Sending a cloak-and-dagger operative into Russia to pick up papers is one thing. Sending an unidentified plane far into Russia is quite another. A cloak-and-dagger operative could hardly start retaliatory missiles on their way. A plane, even unarmed, might.

We do not know what the United States would have done if an unidentified plane had flown across our borders, declined to answer and refused to land. But we think we know what should have been done.

So while we are as mindful as anyone of the need for intelligence about what goes on inside Russia, it still seems to us that somebody is playing with matches. There may be reasons having to do with national defense that require us to do that. But when you start striking sparks around a tinderbox you run a grave risk of starting a fire.

WILLIAM H. FITZPATRICK

May 9, 1960

"We can't give them an ultimatum. They just gave us an ultimatum."

Summitry Through the Ages

Though summitry is sometimes regarded as a rather novel diplomatic procedure these days, it is probably the oldest. And the troubled record of "heads of state" meetings is a far from certain augury of success for the one Messrs. Eisenhower, Macmillan, de Gaulle and Khrushchev are scheduled to hold in Paris.

What seems to have happened is that the summit technique, for all its antiquity, has fallen into disfavor at times as other diplomatic usages developed, and is now once again being revived in a big way. History, at any rate, abounds with summitry, or at least the summit approach. In 1271 B.C. a treaty of peace and alliance was concluded between Ramses II of Egypt and the Hittites, for one example; in the 14th century A.D. dynastic alliances were constantly redrawing the map of Europe.

In more modern times, one of the most useful international conferences, in terms of creating a long-lasting peace, was the Congress of Vienna in 1814 and 1815; it can be called a semi-summit because one of the four principal participating nations was represented by its ruler, Czar Alexander I of Russia. The other three, Austria, Prussia and Britain, sent foreign or principal ministers, for this was a period in which organized diplomacy through elaborate foreign ministries and complex protocol was getting into high gear.

Incidentally, Britain's Lord Castlereagh was fearful of Russian expansion at that time, whereas today Britain seems the most anxious of the Western powers to make accommodations with the Soviet Union at the summit.

Held to dispose of defeated Napoleon's empire, the Congress of Vienna had plenty of rough going and it certainly didn't pay much attention to the feelings of the people in the empire being disposed of. Yet it made a workable peace for a long time; the century from 1814 to 1914 was not free of European war, but compared to our own times it was halcyon.

The same, alas, cannot be said of the summit which followed the war that shattered that relatively quiet period. Delegates of more than 30 countries came to the Conference of Paris in 1919–20, but it was dominated by U.S. President Woodrow Wilson, British Prime Minister David Lloyd George and French Premier Georges Clemenceau. All three have been described as contemptuous of conventional diplomacy.

The Paris Conference, designed to clean up the debris of World War I, was an unwieldy wrangle from the start; at one fracture Mr. Wilson was on the point of abandoning the whole thing. It attempted not only to make peace with Germany but to deal with—and rearrange —all the problems of Europe, as well as acting as midwife to the a-borning and abortive League of Nations.

Perhaps the Treaty of Versailles, which came out of the Paris Conference, was the best that could be had in the circumstances (one could make that argument about many agreements). But quite apart from anything else, its terms were excessively severe on the Germans, arousing their immediate and fierce opposition, while paradoxically incapable of holding back a Germany determined to break the terms. It opened a door through which in time walked Hitler and World War II.

The Congress of Vienna and the Conference of Paris were both held to make peace after major wars, which is what the summit meeting starting a week from Monday is also—still—trying to do 15 years after the end of World War II. And out of the Paris Conference came, in the inter-war years, a whole raft of meetings which were concerned with peace and with a specific issue in the foreground of the forthcoming Paris conference. That is the issue of disarmament.

From 1920 to 1932 disarmament sessions of various sizes and sorts were held, with little result. Principles such as limitation on arms spending and limitations on periods of service were agreed to, but so heavily hedged with reservations as to be all but meaningless. In 1921 a special five-power naval disarmament treaty was signed at Washington.

Finally in early 1932 the disarmament conference proper got under way, attended by representatives of 59 nations. A limited agreement was reached providing, among other things, that air attack against civilian populations should be totally banned. The splendid spirit in which this was lived up to was shown in World War II. As a matter of fact, Germany, as well as the Soviet Union, voted against the agreement. In 1933 Germany pulled out of both the disarmament conference and the League of Nations.

The conference never came to a formal end but by 1934 its futility was sufficiently evident. While the statesmen talked about disarmament, Germany was busily rearming with Soviet connivance.

The outstanding lesson of these efforts between the wars would seem to be that arms do not cause wars; people do. If statesmen intend to start war they will see to it that they have the arms, and telling them they can't have them won't prevent them if they are determined and skillful at evasion. That is just as true of nuclear weapons as of any other kind. Indeed, nothing could very well be more pertinent to the imminent Big Four summit session than this sad tale of the disarmament work that so resoundingly failed to prevent World War II.

During that war we got back to full-fledged summitry. Of the various meetings, the one between Roosevelt, Churchill and Stalin at Yalta in February, 1945, was notable. These "allies" confirmed the division of Germany into occupation zones; in this and other ways the conference prepared the Communization of Central and Eastern Europe. The division of Germany, of course, is still used by the Soviets to plague the West, and is one of the issues at the forthcoming meeting in Paris, though no one expects it to be solved there.

Yalta also gave Stalin valuable concessions in the Far East, in return for the promise of his brief, token and needless entry into the war against Japan; in the opinion of some, Yalta made possible the Communist victory in China. But it is not necessary to get into these debates in order to see another vivid lesson for Paris: Yalta proves that the Soviets will use any conference or any negotiation not to promote real peace but to serve Soviet interests, one of the chief of which is the destruction of the West. Since the allies today are something less than perfectly united, the Soviets will have plenty of opportunity for mischief-making at Paris.

An ironic footnote to Yalta is the agreement there that Germany was entitled to only a minimum level of subsistence and that "we are determined to . . . eliminate or control all German industry that could be used for military production."

These interesting theories were spelled out a little more at Potsdam; that conference, attended by Truman, Churchill (at first; then Attlee) and Stalin in the summer of 1945, reached certain agreements about the German economy and the reparations to be extracted from the defeated nation.

After Potsdam, summitry fell into desuetude for quite a while. One reason was that Potsdam itself created the council of foreign ministers, which was supposed to meet from time to time and specifically to hammer out peace treaties; the heads of state seemed to be turning diplomacy back to the diplomats. More importantly, Stalin launched the cold war and then the Korean War and seemed at times bent on World War III, and so there wasn't much point in further meetings with a madman.

Fortunately for the world, Stalin died. Thereafter the new Red look was slowly born. The Korean and Indo-Chinese Wars ended, the Soviets agreed to leave Austria. By the time Khrushchev seemed to have largely consolidated his power, the Western nations (reluctantly in the case of the United States) were willing to meet him. Thus the most recent summit conference, in Geneva in July, 1955, was arranged.

On that occasion President Eisenhower met with Prime Minister Eden of Britain, Premier Faure of France, and Premier Bulganin and Party Boss Khrushchev of Russia. No concrete settlements were achieved, but it was agreed that the unification of Germany by means of free elections should be carried out. The foreign ministers met in the fall to find Molotov ("the abominable no-man") rejecting that agreement and, indeed, absolutely adamant on every important issue. Thus the Geneva conference saw the materialization of one of the dangers inherent in summitry—the creation of false hopes.

A good many people doubt that the new Paris get-together will be any improvement—if it actually is held after Khrushchev's recent tirades. Certainly the checkered history of summitry suggests it is a somewhat questionable diplomatic procedure.

JOSEPH E. EVANS

May 6, 1960

Red Gyrations

Weeks after the event, Khrushchev's decision to remove the corpse of Josef Stalin from public view continues to fire speculation about the bizarre gyrations of Communist high policy.

In the West, where nations do not as a rule stuff their dead leaders and mount them like beasts in a hunter's trophy room, Stalin's latest disgrace has provoked some serious thought about the stability of a regime that would indulge in such side-show antics. Moreover, the macabre body-snatching has set off a wave of anti-Stalin moves throughout the Soviet sphere—the full meaning of which, in terms of the cold war, is still a question mark.

Towns, streets, and factories which once were named for the tyrant, are being rechristened.

Stalin-Allee, the chief spot of life and color in drab East Berlin has been renamed Karl Marx-Allee and the new industrial town of Stalin-stadt has been transformed into Eisenstadt. In the Paris suburb of Ivry, where the Communists are strong, the name of Stalin has been erased from one of the town's thoroughfares.

Russian specialists in America and abroad have been pondering the question of why Khrushchev has embarked on a course that is not without political and psychological risk. Stalin had impressed his iron heel very deeply on Soviet public consciousness and associated himself with every military success and industrial achievement.

The older generation of the present Soviet rulers is deeply committed to the Stalin myth. Khrushchev himself is on record as having delivered a speech, on January 30, 1937, after a group of alleged Trotskyists had been sentenced to death:

> These miserable wretches raised their treacherous hands against Comrade Stalin. When they raised their hands against Stalin they raised their hands against us all, against the working class, against the toilers. . . . Stalin, our hope. . . . Stalin, the beacon light of progressive humanity. . . . Stalin, our banner. . . . Stalin, our will. . . . Stalin . . . our victory.

Three considerations seem to have decided Khrushchev to carry to the end the process of discrediting Stalin which he left half finished after his first critical speech at the Twentieth Party Congress early in 1956, a speech never published in Russia.

First, there was the hope that, by a thorough repudiation of Stalin, he could give the Soviet younger generation some assurance that the fearful days of arbitrary Stalinite terror and lawlessness would not return.

Second, a frontal attack on Stalin's memory served two purposes of internal politics. It was an assertion of Khrushchev's own power and prestige. And it was a warning to any sympathizers with the memory and methods of the dead dictator who may remain in the Soviet bureaucracy.

Third, to denounce Stalin in root-and-branch fashion was an indirect way of attacking Peking, where Stalin's name is still held in honor. The whole atmosphere of the recent Party Congress was charged with animosity between Moscow and Red China.

Obviously Khrushchev believed that a thorough denigration of Stalin would pay political dividends. It remains to be seen whether his calculation is correct. For all the hypnotic effect of his awesome power, Stalin was not an object of much genuine love. His terror struck too widely; there was scarcely a family in the Soviet Union that did not know of a member, or at least a friend or acquaintance, who had been arrested or sent to a concentration camp.

Khrushchev may also feel that the rising generation in the Soviet Union, better educated and more sophisticated, cannot be effectively governed by Stalin's method of crude Asiatic despotism.

But it may be easier to win popular acceptance of the view that Stalin was a monstrous tyrant than to prevent at least some Soviet citizens from drawing conclusions unfavorable to the whole system of Red dictatorship.

Unrest in Poland and revolt in Hungary were direct responses to Khrushchev's half demolition of the Stalin myth in 1956. Further seismic disturbances, even in the Soviet Union itself, conceivably could follow its total demolition in 1961.

At any rate, the Russian people have been given plenty to think about, and that in itself is always bad news to the Communist czars. For all their indoctrination and re-indoctrination, the people of the Soviet Union must still be capable of some rational thought.

And a rational mind just cannot accept indefinitely a system that is based on irrational action.

WILLIAM HENRY CHAMBERLIN

December 28, 1961

The Way of the Self-Righteous

Up until now it has been possible to say to the world that what came out of the Kremlin was deceitful and untrustworthy but that people could depend on what they were told by the Government of the United States.

Now the world may not be so sure that this country is any different from any other in righteousness. And that, we fear, may turn out to be the saddest injury we have suffered from the incident of the American reconnaissance plane brought down over Russian territory. Like the clergyman caught in nocturnal activities, we will no longer be able to be so self-righteous.

It is true enough that intelligence work—or spying, if you prefer that word—is an accepted business among nations. And we doubt if the world will be shocked, or even surprised, to find that the United States tries to find out as much as it can about the capabilities and intentions of Soviet Russia. Indeed, if the circumstances of our intelligence probing were somewhat different, both the American people and our friends abroad might be reassured to know that intelligence work is no monopoly of the Russians.

But this particular incident is doubly unfortunate. In the first place, it is going to be very hard to persuade people that sending a Government plane deep into the territory of another country to photograph its terrain is not what the diplomats would call "provocative." We need only imagine what the reaction of Americans would be if we caught a

Russian airplane over Chicago or a Russian submarine in New York harbor.

In the second place, it is going to be hard to convince people here-after that explanations from Washington can be taken at their face value.

For the first reaction of Washington to Mr. Khrushchev's announce-ment about the U-2 was to dismiss it as pre-summit ranting. Then we were told that there was after all a "weather plane" that had been miss-ing for several days near the Turkish border, and that maybe the trigger-happy Russians had shot down this innocent pilot. Only when it became impossible to maintain this cock-and-bull story was it ad-mitted that "someone" had deliberately sent a plane into Russia on an intelligence mission.

So we have been caught not only in a rather provocative act but also in dissembling. The one can be explained as a piece of bad judgment. The explanation for the other will come harder.

No one will argue, we suppose, that this country has done anything different from what the Russians do all the time. Being provocative is habitual with them; deceit is part of their normal way. Therefore, the argument that we have done no more than what others do all the time is quite accurate.

The difficulty is that we have told others and ourselves we are different. The image we have created before the world is that "we don't do what the Russians do." We don't engage in international provocation. We do tell honestly what is going on.

And now the sad part is that this image, which has been one of the strengths of America, is now sullied by our own self-righteous zeal that led us to believe that anything we choose to do is right.

Vermont Royster

May 11, 1960

A Lesson from the U-2

Since just about everybody is drawing lessons from the U-2 affair these days, we would like to offer one. That is that in the affairs of nations, as in the affairs of men, "pushing things too far" is a treacherous business.

That was the mistake of Mr. Khrushchev. At Paris he lost all that he might have gained from the uneasiness the incident aroused among our allies by trying to make out Russia as Innocent Nell and the United States as a wicked ogre. The President's political critics at home have also not been content with scolding the Adimination for ineptness, which might have scored them some political points; they have pushed on to blame just about everything that's happened abroad on the handling of the U-2.

Only last week, for example, Senator Fulbright spoiled some otherwise thoughtful comments on the affair with the contention that the "essential point" is that "the U-2 is the reason" Mr. Khrushchev wrecked the Summit. This is such patent nonsense that nobody is apt to swallow it.

The real mistake the Administration made in that business, it seems to us, was in the untenable way it tried to justify what it did. And properly recognized, that mistake can offer a valuable lesson for the United States in the future.

The big mistake lay not in spying on Russia or necessarily even in sending planes flying over the country to do so, although that is a dangerous procedure. Nor even in the dissembling about it, although that would better have been avoided. Nor, when put to it, frankly saying, "Yes, we have been spying."

For it is profoundly true that the necessities of this world make espionage imperative and it is splitting hairs to say one method is "right" and another "wrong." Furthermore, every nation in the world recognizes this imperative; whatever their statesmen say publicly, privately they understand and, rather than being incensed at the U-2, would marvel at its success.

So far, so good. The basic trouble was that the State Department, taking this as a premise, then pushed on to declare that not only were "overflights" dictated by necessity but that we claimed the privilege of making them as a matter of right. And not in the past only, but also in the future.

This may seem like a subtle distinction, but it was a mistake because it put the United States in an untenable position, a thing proved by the fact that we were forced to abandon it.

Here Senator Fullbright's analogy is apt. If a starving man steals, his justification lies in the imperative of survival; few of us would hesitate to act on it. But his justification must be that alone; it cannot be converted into a claim that burglary is in itself right. For that becomes a kind of moral juggling that the world will not accept.

Recognizing that distinction, however subtle, will let us keep the whole business of the U-2, and spying in general, in a proper perspective. And if we remember it, it will stand us in good stead in the future.

For it may well happen that the realities of the world may someday require us to act again in a way contrary to all that we stand for or preach to others. For example, we do not believe in forcible interference with the internal affairs of other nations. Yet conceivably events in a neighboring country might so endanger us that we will do what we do not believe in.

If such a necessity arises, let us act on it. But we can learn one lesson from the U-2. Our justification for the act is our safety; that, and nothing more. Even then people may debate the necessity for the deed, or its timing, or the adroitness of what is done. But these are quarrels of judgment only, and we will not be put in the untenable position of claiming the privilege to do what we would excoriate in others.

Because we are civilized, it is difficult for us to live by the laws of a jungle. Yet if we must, then we will do better to understand and to say frankly that in the affairs of nations, as in the affairs of men, there are some deeds to be done simply because survival is the first imperative.

VERMONT ROYSTER

July 5, 1960

Rosy Red Dreams

Nikita Khrushchev announced to the Communist convention in Moscow that by 1980 the Soviet Union will have surpassed the United States in production and will have achieved for the Russian citizenry a standard of living of unprecedented altitude.

There is, of course, one area in which Soviet production has long outstripped the United States. That is the area of promises—promises which the Communists have been turning out on an assembly-line basis since before the Romanoffs were displaced.

It is part of the Kremlin way to support its optimistic predictions with other optimistic predictions, a not very persuasive debating technique perhaps, but apparently adequate for keeping hope alive in the breast of the Soviet people.

Thus, Khrushchev says his country's industry will grow by 500 per cent by 1980, with agricultural production zooming by more than 300 per cent. This would indeed be quite an achievement, but Kremlin predictions have in the past been wrong with a remarkable consistency.

This promise of "overtaking and outstripping America," first voiced by Stalin some 30 years ago, is the nearest thing to a positive definition of what communism, in the Soviet view, really is. The founding fathers of Soviet society, Marx and Lenin, have been chary with detailed blueprints of what the new order which should follow capitalism would be like.

The Soviet Communist Party Program, issued last August and holding up the "Communism in 1980" perspective, offers this explanation:

Communism is a classless social system with one form of public ownership of the means of production and full social equality of all members of society; under it the all-around development of people will be accompanied by the growth of productive forces through continuous progress in science and technology; all sources of public wealth will gush forth abundantly, and the great principle, "From each according to his abilities, to each according to his needs" will be implemented.

From Plato to the fantastic Frenchman Fourier, who wanted to organize human beings into "phalansteries," or communal colonies, in which, among other things, marriage would be abolished and prosperity would be assured through harmonious common labor, there have been vivid utopian schemes for societies organized along collectivist lines. One of the most attractive is Sir Thomas More's "Utopia," a word which, significantly, means "Nowhere."

But Lenin, the great practical revolutionary who actually succeeded in making a vast Eurasian empire a proving ground for Marx's theories, was no spinner of fantasies, no maker of Utopias. One of his most important theories was that the overthrow of capitalism must be followed by the so-called dictatorship of the proletariat (in practice this proved to mean the dictatorship of the Communist party) which would last for an indefinite period until the time was ripe for the transition from the intermediate stage of socialism to the final stage of communism.

Then, by some process which Lenin never outlined very clearly, the necessity for dictatorship and even for the existence of the state would disappear and complete freedom would prevail in the final communist stage of society.

And he insisted that members of the Communist party, as a guaranty of sincerity, should be limited to a skilled worker's pay, no matter how high their positions in the government.

But Stalin scrapped this egalitarianism, and the Communist party member for the last three decades has enjoyed the salary and the standard of living that go with his job.

And, although the system of state ownership of factories and mines, land and natural resources rules out big fortunes earned through private enterprise, there are tremendous variations in salaries and in standards of living, with a privileged elite of high party and state officials, industrial managers, scientists and writers, living on a scale unimaginable to the great majority of workers, peasants and government employees.

Is Khrushchev's promise of "communism" by 1980 a reality or a mirage?

There is no reason to doubt that Russia, barring some catastrophic war, can and will make big gains in industrial and mineral output. Agriculture, however, is a much more doubtful prospect. It has proved much easier to create a normal incentive system in industrial enterprises, where there is a tremendous spread in compensation between the manager and the unskilled laborer, than to compensate the peasant for the loss of his old sense of personal ownership of his land.

Agriculture has lagged badly in all Communist-ruled countries and, when Khrushchev talks of trebling and quadrupling farm output by 1980, it may be recalled that three years ago he promised that Russians would soon be eating as much meat as Americans. He was wrong.

One of the jokers in Khrushchev's vision of 1980 is that he takes no account of the fact that the United States and Western Europe are just as committed to economic growth and development as is the Soviet Union.

As for work becoming a joyful necessity of life, the columns of Soviet newspapers are full of indignant stories about Soviet citizens who do their best to avoid honest toil and earn a fast ruble by supplying goods and services which are not taken care of under the ponderous system of state planning and control.

All in all, it seems very doubtful whether the tremendous transformation of human nature which would be necessary before a communist system could work freely, voluntarily and naturally will have taken place by 1980, or by any other fixed date. Nor is it likely that Americans and West Europeans will then be eagerly taking out Soviet citizenship as a way to a better future.

But, if Khrushchev's latest predictions prove only another mirage, he has one satisfaction. He will, in all probability, not be around to answer the questions of disappointed Soviet citizens in 1980.

WILLIAM HENRY CHAMBERLIN

November 3, 1961

"*I may not defend to the death your right to say it, but I agree with what you say.*"

Relentless Flower

The Kremlin several years ago assigned family gardens to city folk who wanted to raise fresh fruits and vegetables. Unfortunately, from the Communist viewpoint, many of these weekend farmers took to selling their produce to other Russians to make a little pocket money.

When word of this practice hit Moscow, party officials cried treason, jumped up and down on their hats, and reminded citizens that the goal was to overtake the United States, not the A & P. Free trade in fruits and vegetables promptly stopped, or so the Soviet press reported, and today people no longer "spoil their conscience by selling in the market."

Perhaps. But this is just one more case when these enterprising Russians have had a small taste of capitalism—and a small taste is often enough. While a commodity exchange is not likely to appear in Moscow any time soon, we suspect that more than one comrade occasionally still fills his pockets with onions for a little back-alley bartering.

Even in the Communist wasteland, capitalism is proving a relentless flower. The commissars can bring down their hoe on its bloom, but its roots are beyond their reach.

EDWIN A. ROBERTS, JR.

August 1, 1960

Pedestrian Moscow

We read with interest that Moscow's pedestrians are ignoring traffic lights, "Walk" and "Don't Walk" signs with reckless abandon. Indeed, so many citizens are getting run over that a major educational campaign is being planned to persuade them that it pays to observe the signals.

We suppose what makes playing roulette with the lights such a popular game among Muscovites is that the choice between "Walk" and "Don't Walk" is one of the few free ones they have. But our guess is that the pedestrian problem will be solved rapidly as soon as the Moscow authorities tumble to the fact that their citizens are actually emulating decadent capitalistic Americans.

Cowl Rider

December 15, 1961

"*At last I have some savings to invest, and just my luck—there's no stock exchange.*"

TAXING THE IMAGINATION

Thoughts for April 15

It has long been a truism that high taxes make people disdain the law. That has been notoriously the case in France, for example; it is becoming increasingly the case in the United States.

Thus a survey recently conducted by this newspaper showed that two out of five American taxpayers interviewed admitted cheating on their returns. It was not that they used every legal provision to their advantage, but that they deliberately shortchanged the Government.

Though such a poll naturally doesn't pretend to be statistically precise for the whole nation, it is at least indicative of the mood of quite a few people. Others, who wouldn't think of cheating, pay their taxes with annoyance, anger or disgust.

For the Government to create such a mood is bad enough; what is worse is that the thing doesn't end there. Excessive taxation breeds, in many people, a disrespect for the Government as a whole. Moreover, much of what the Government does with tax money invites both disrespect for Government and the corrosion of individual morality.

Consider the farm program, for one instance. People with a tradition of self-reliance become inured to accepting Federal handouts. Some of them, oppressed by controls, become lawbreakers. Meantime the entire spectacle hardly enhances the dignity of Government. Because Congress refuses to face today's farm facts, the program resembles something dreamed up in a madhouse. And yet a good hunk of the tax dollar goes to pay for this folly.

Similarly, few healthy veterans can possibly believe that they are entitled to innumerable Federal benefits, but they keep on taking them because they are available—why not get what the others are getting? For its part, Congress, skittish of imagined political hot water, refuses to reform and reduce the veterans program. Again, for the public at large, the impression is created of the Government handling tax money in a silly fashion.

The more the Government gets into matters of private concern the more these twin effects show up—the undermining of individual independence and the placing of Government in an unattractive or ridiculous light.

And the outlook for the future is not auspicious. There are too many in Congress who want to expand Government much further, apparently without limit. They are looking at human existence through the wrong end of the telescope, for Government is not and cannot be the generator of wealth, as our own history abundantly proves. On the contrary, every expansion of Government, paid for through higher taxes or more inflation, is a powerful depressant on the true sources of wealth. Existing taxes are already far too high for sound economic growth.

To put it another way, just suppose that we had sound money and confidence that the Government was going to keep it sound; that we had a Government constantly cutting spending, gradually paying off the debt and reducing taxes. The effect would be electric; the economic goals proclaimed by the statists would seem piddling by comparison to what a free people would accomplish. This is the lesson of our history, and it seems incredible that so many people can manage to misread it.

We all know, or ought to, that this Government was founded in reaction to excesses of Government. It was meant to be limited, for the very good reason that the people who founded it understood that in the freest possible play of individual initiative was not only the best guard against tyranny but also the surest route to material abundance. And so long as the Government remained limited it was not the target of the widespread disrespect of the people.

Now in these reflections on April 15 it is certainly not our purpose to condone those who cheat on their taxes. What we are saying is that it is an inevitable reaction to exorbitant taxation—a tax revolt in fact—and a part of the general malady of Big Government.

After all, Government can hardly expect anything but disrespect when it permits excessive taxation and inflation to cheat the people of their present livelihood and future hopes.

JOSEPH E. EVANS

April 15, 1959

"*Does a poor devil by the name of Harry Masters work here?*"

The Withholding Craze

Once the principle of the progressive income tax is accepted, it is, we suppose, fairly idle to complain about the withholding system. Withholding is merely a collecting procedure and hence seems to raise no question of principle.

And yet, with the withholding craze spreading (New York State, for example, recently adopted it), it may not be out of place to note a few of the effects of this tax-taking method.

The latest target of Federal withholding is stockholders' dividends. A plan to require corporations to withhold Federal tax on these payments now appears to have a good chance of Congressional passage, perhaps this year.

It sounds like a peculiarly clumsy and inaccurate application of withholding. The burden on both companies and the Internal Revenue Service will be greatly increased. Error on the side of either too much or too little withholding is assured in practically every case—in the latter circumstance requiring numerous refunds, thus adding to the bureaucracy and cost of tax-collecting.

But the question of withholding taxes on dividends also serves to divert attention from the more basic question in this connection. That is whether it is proper for the Government to tax dividends twice—first as corporate profits and second as income to the stockholder. (Present law provides only a partial remission for the stockholder-taxpayer.)

And that is one of the vices of withholding in general—it tends to withhold attention from the taxes themselves. You may know perfectly well that your stated salary is not your real one and feel unhappy about the difference withheld. But every taxpayer also knows that it is a smaller shock to have the weekly paycheck show less than the ostensible salary than to have to pony up scores, hundreds or thousands of dollars all at once.

The intent of withholding is not, of course, to ease the burden on the taxpayer; it is to try to squeeze every possible drop for Government. Yet the effect on the taxpayer, no matter how much he may grumble when he adds everything up, is to dull his senses to the violence being done his pocketbook. In this process of distorting what a man really makes, Government panders to confusion on monetary matters.

By the same narcotic token, the withholding system makes it easier for Government, state or Federal, to raise taxes, as some states have been doing. As for the Federal Government, it's true it has not raised income tax rates for quite a long time, but that is not the same as saying that Federal taxes have not gone up.

If you have had a raise in a decade, your taxes have gone up; it is the essence of the progressive system to penalize you precisely for your ability to make more money. The general prosperity of individuals and firms—the result of their own initiative—has boosted Washington's take by something like $15 billion in the past five years, with no increase in rates.

These things too the taxpayer may know in his mind, but withholding makes the punishment for enterprise seem less grievous.

For these reasons we are not so unrealistic as to suppose the withholding addiction will be tempered any time soon; it is too convenient for Government and, in its unfortunate way, for taxpayers. In any case, to attack withholding is to attack only the surface of the evils; what must in time be modified is the progressive system itself.

That kind of fundamental reform, though, is not likely until the people tear away the veil of withholding that helps hide the Government extravagance that now thrives on the people's thrift.

JOSEPH E. EVANS

March 7, 1960

ON WRAPPING A PACKAGE

If the paper were stronger
And the string longer,
It would be grand.
But what's desired most
And required most
And in greatest demand
Is another hand.

—RICHARD ARMOUR

———◆———

The Just and the Unjust

We guess we don't run in the right social circles.

For years we have been reading those books about wild living in the suburbs and wondering somewhat plaintively why the excitement seems to pass us by. In years of suburban living the wildest shock to the even tenor of our domesticity was the day the dog drank up the cocktails and bit the mayor. It was weeks before we were forgiven.

For almost as long, we've been reading about all this notorious high living on the expense account, boats and all that, and groaning over what we seem to have missed. After a quarter century in that den of iniquity, Wall Street, no one has tempted our journalistic virtue with even so much as a night at a hunting lodge, much less a seagoing voyage. Where, indeed, are all those expense-account yachts?

True, we aren't without sin, as defined in the new dogma of the Internal Revenue Service. We suffer business luncheons dreadfully often and when we turn in the voucher we don't deduct the $1.25 we would have spent anyway for the Blue Plate special. A man is entitled to some recompense for punishment in line of duty.

When business takes us to Peoria or Dubuque, as it does all too often, we take an apéritif before dinner, choose the steak over the chicken-à-la-king and sometimes splurge on the movies, charging the lot to the stockholders. If it weren't for their business we wouldn't be there at all, and frankly we have better steaks at home.

Moreover, the children being more or less at the age of discretion, we have lately taken our wife along on some trips. We haven't persuaded the curmudgeonly auditor to okay her expenses, but not long ago we drove to Washington on legitimate business (if talking to a Senator is legitimate) and our wife rode along in the car. Even that baleful auditor didn't ask us to reimburse the company for the equivalent price of her bus ticket.

Give or take a few details, this is not unlike the situation of thousands of businessmen in a country where men at work are ceaselessly traveling to and fro. The door-to-door salesman and the flying corporate executive are brothers under the skin; they are working also when they pass the time of day with the lady at the door or the business acquaintance across the luncheon table. Sometimes the smartest business is not to talk "business" at all but to be friendly, interested; to listen and to learn. Only ignorant and petty minds could imagine that the "free" lunch is all beer and skittles.

But now it turns out that all this is under the suspicion of undermining the public morality and the solvency of the U.S. Treasury. In any event the Government is going to treat all the people as crooks until proven otherwise.

This suspicion of malefaction flows from every word of the new regulations on record-keeping, pedantic in language and picayune in detail, drawn up by the Internal Revenue Service.

Hereafter you must account to the Government not only for your yacht but the beer you buy a business acquaintance. The documents for any "entertainment," no matter how trivial, must include the amount, date, place by name and address, type (martini or ham sandwich?), explanation of the "benefit" to be returned for this bounty, the name of the recipient and sufficient documentation to explain your extravagance to the satisfaction of any revenue agent who subsequently examines your tax report.

And if perchance on a trip you spend more than $25 in any day you must itemize everything else too—the day you left home, day you got back, every telephone call, meal, cup of coffee, taxicab and bus fare. If you want your books to balance, you'd better even keep track of the postage stamps for the letters to the home office.

The sheer absurdity of this avalanche of paper work is only the beginning. The metaphysicians of Mr. Mortimer Caplin's bureaucracy have now gone off to mull such esoteric questions as: What, precisely, constitutes a "business meal"? What is the allowable difference in cost between a lunch for a life insurance prospect ($5,000 policy) and the prospect for an electric dynamo ($5,000,000 sale)? Can you also buy lunch for the prospect's wife, or do you suggest she go eat in the drugstore? What if your own wife is along too—do you leave her back in the hotel room to munch a hamburger and watch television?

As ridiculous as these questions sound, they are precisely the sort of thing that must now be decided upon at the highest levels, and Mr. Caplin confesses—quite understandably, we think—that it will be some weeks before we can expect any official enlightenment. It has never been easy to decide how many angels can dance on the head of a pin.

Yet it is neither the absurdity of the paper work nor the ridiculousness of the metaphysics that is the true evil.

Here is a situation in which the Government is, no doubt about it, confronted with a problem. Some people do hide yachts in expense accounts, just as some do hide misbehavior in the suburbs, and the Government has the power to deal with the real tax cheaters. But the vast majority of the people everywhere lead quiet, placid and upright lives, and the vast majority of those whose taxes support the Government give an honest accounting of their affairs.

Yet here we use the majesty of the law to treat every taxpayer as a potential cheater because pinhead minds can think of no other way; the integrity of all must be insulted, and the conduct of their affairs made insufferable, because of the sins of the few.

Now, completely apart from this question of expense accounts, this is a philosophy of government which is evil in itself. We once had an example of this when, to stop a few people from drinking too much. we adopted prohibition which treated all men as potential alcoholics. Surely the results have not left our memory.

The results of this noble experiment can also be foreseen. These new rules will give trouble only to honest men. The real "operator"—the man who is really out to cheat on his taxes—can drive a truck through them.

The smart lawyers are already figuring out the perfectly legal loopholes; beyond that, those with larceny in their hearts will not be disturbed because they will show records, receipts and paper accounts by the carload. As sure as the sun rises tomorrow, today's rules will have to be followed tomorrow by new rules upon new rules "tightening" the rules.

And while all this is going on, the honest man—the man who takes a business trip to do an honest job for his company and with no desire to cheat either his company or his country—that man will see himself not merely laden with burdensome paper work but with the fear that everything he does is under suspicion.

Because he honestly tries to keep honest records, all the records will be there and he can be called up a year later, two years later, and find that what he did in good faith is adjudged wrong by some petty bureaucrat imbued with the idea that any expense account must conceal some wickedness. The smart operator will have his lawyers; the little taxpayer will be helpless against the insolence of office.

We submit that to order the public affairs in this manner is an affront to the public morality, just as it would be for the state to require of every citizen a detailed accounting of his home-coming-and-going because some men cheat. That government governs ill which can find no other way to deal with malefactors than to maltreat all of its citizens, the just and the unjust alike.

VERMONT ROYSTER

January 8, 1963

TRADE
WINDS

The Road Downhill

Let us suppose that when foreign cars first began to make inroads in the American market, the Government had promptly slapped on prohibitive duties or quotas or otherwise excluded the imports.

Certain results would follow. The American consumer would be denied the opportunity to choose between, say, a Volkswagen and a Ford—and in many cases that would be denying the choice between a lower-priced and a higher-priced product. Equally important, the major American companies would feel little or no spur to do anything new or different, such as bringing out small cars. The economy as a whole would suffer from stultification.

As it actually turned out, the imports have come in and the American firms, under competitive heat, have brought out their compact cars. The American consumer today has a choice among scores of different cars in a wide range of prices. The consumer has benefited, the American companies have benefited, the economy has benefited from innovation and vigorous competition—quite apart from the benefits to the foreign economies in whose health we are supposed to be vitally interested.

Such is the essence of free, or relatively free, international trade. The point is worth making because today a new surge of protectionist sentiment is building up in this country. As just one of numerous signs, the annual meeting of the American Cotton Manufacturers Institute was dominated by demands for more stringent tariffs and quotas against textile and clothing imports.

And the protectionist upsurge is perfectly understandable. A number of American industries, from textiles to autos, are feeling the heat of increasing foreign competition, and the instinct is to turn to Government restrictions for help.

One reason for the rising competition is that some of the nations we have helped revive with public funds—Germany and Japan are notable examples—have introduced a lot of modern, cost-cutting equipment; they are much better able to compete against U.S. technology than they were a few years ago. Another reason is that in many places in the world labor costs, despite increases, are still well below those in this country.

These circumstances are not in dispute. But surely it is unrealistic to look at only the foreign side of the coin. What has been done here has caused many of the competitive difficulties of some American firms.

A very clear thing that has been happening here is a serious postwar inflation that has boosted the price of almost everything. Some of our foreign competitors have learned to master or sharply restrain inflation. To the extent that the American people have permitted the Government to practice inflation, we are all to blame for the competitive troubles. Inflation, it should be remembered, is not something that just happens or has to happen; it is something chosen by politicians through reckless Federal spending and heavy budget deficits.

Thanks in part to this excess of paper money, it has been possible for labor unions to win raises far beyond anything justified by a reasonable definition of productivity gains. A further explanation of the one-way wage elevator is the monopoly power of unions which enables them to dictate their terms to employers.

Still another factor, as a U.N. economist has just reminded us, is that the U.S. Government props the prices of many basic commodities. This simultaneously makes them more difficult to sell abroad and makes them more expensive for American manufacturers trying to compete against foreigners in the U.S. market.

Such explanations may sound like cold comfort to the firms actually experiencing competitive troubles. Yet it is completely defeatist to contend that this supposedly intelligent nation is incapable of dealing with the real causes of the troubles. The Government can stop inflation dead in its tracks; Congress can restrain the untrammeled power of union leaders; Congress can undo the mess that indiscriminate subsidies have made.

If instead of tackling the real causes, we compound them with more protectionism, we will gain nothing. Not even the protected industries will gain except in a temporary illusory sense, for the expansion of the economy as a whole cannot come about through high-priced rigidity, inefficiency and consumer restriction.

Competition has been the path to this nation's economic pre-eminence; should we ever turn decisively from it, we will be on a road that leads straight downhill.

JOSEPH E. EVANS

April 19, 1960

The Trouble with Walls

Those who resist a policy of freer trade have a number of seemingly persuasive arguments on their side. For one, it is beyond dispute that lower wage rates prevail elsewhere in the world, and this puts some American manufacturers at a competitive price disadvantage.

But today's protectionists fail to answer the central question: What happens if the United States raises instead of lowers its walls against imports? What, for one important instance, of Japan?

No one needs to be told that Japanese imports are all over the place; the United States is that nation's biggest trading partner. Far less frequent, however, is it noted that Japan is this country's second biggest trading partner and that our exports to Japan exceed our imports.

According to a report by Johns Hopkins Professor Warren Hunsberger, prepared for the Boggs subcommittee on foreign economic policy, Japan hopes to more than double its exports to the United States—to an annual $3 billion—by 1970. The other side of that coin, it would seem plain, is that if Japan can do so, the United States can correspondingly increase its exports to Japan.

Indeed, Mr. Hunsberger says the United States, with a growing national product, could absorb that rise of Japanese imports without significant "damage." The import increase has already been great since World War II, and yet the United States "industrial sectors actually affected have been, for the most part, very small, and the actual injury apparently very limited."

Such statements naturally will not soothe those industrial sectors that have been affected. Still, the questions facing them and all other Americans will not go away. If we want to shut off or drastically reduce Japanese imports, are we prepared to take the risk of Japan's going down the political drain? Or, looking across the Atlantic, is it preferable to have a thriving trade with our allies in the burgeoning European Common Market, or a trade war with them?

What would the United States be doing to itself if a new protectionism comes to prevail? American exports are on the order of $20 billion a year; that represents a lot of production and millions of American working people, and almost everyone says exports must be expanded. But we can export only if we are willing to import. Protectionism inevitably reduces exports, which means unemployment, lower national income and a worsening of our already serious international payments deficit.

Nor is the question solely one of international politics and dollars and cents. At its heart is competition—and all the innovations, the national economic growth and the advantages for the consumer that flow from vigorous competition. It would be pretty hard for anyone to contend today that the influx of small foreign cars in recent years has been a bad thing, since it stimulated American manufacturers to offer a profusion of cars of all sizes. Such competitive stimulation constantly occurs in conditions of comparative economic freedom.

We do not for a moment deny that some businesses have difficulties because of foreign competition. It is the recognition of this that prompts a number of advocates of freer trade to suggest limited Federal assistance to such companies to help them turn to other lines or more efficient methods. Whatever may be said in favor of that approach, it is not a real answer; we have more than enough subsidies as it is, and no company has an automatic right to succeed.

The real answer lies elsewhere. In part it is to make sure that wage increases are held within reasonable bounds. Even more important, it is for the Government to pursue sound fiscal and monetary policies and so prevent the inflation in which a wage-price spiral would flourish. That is the best help the Government could give to companies facing foreign competition and to everyone else.

We deceive ourselves if we think there is true protection in protectionism, for it is the way of defeatism and decline. If we try to hide behind that wall, we had best realize it is ourselves we are sealing in.

JOSEPH E. EVANS

November 30, 1961

U.S. Trade Solution

WASHINGTON—A sharp question calls for a straight answer. It's about time now for those arguing about future American trade policy to pause and really listen to the question.

That question is raised by that muscular adolescent, the European Common Market, and it sounds like this: "We foreigners are soon going to throw out into world markets the greatest flood of low-cost manufactures ever seen in history; what are you Yankees going to do about it?"

The straight answer, and it does seem pretty obvious, would be this: "All right; America is going to whip its costs into line with the best you can do. Then see if you can lick us." But oddly enough, any remarks along this line have scarcely risen above a murmur.

The loud talk is about tariff tinkering; some plump for protection and the rest for freer trade. Presumably, roughly half this advice is correct—yet it's a bit like choosing the moment when the kitchen is on fire to argue with your wife about whether the front lawn needs sprinkling. You might be right, but are you pertinent?

When the plainly visible elements of the foreign cost-cutting challenge do intrude on the eye, the trade disputants' suggested cures run to symptom-treating and faith-healing. It is soberly suggested that U.S. companies be banned from building more factories abroad, as if that would halt the overseas surge to mass production. Or a touching optimism is expressed that workers in Europe (despite their long tradition of genuine discipline) will soon be grabbing as high pay as those in America (where it's considered acceptably "non-inflationary" to award auto workers their biggest boost ever).

This is to reduce economics to escapism. It could lead to eventual devaluation of the dollar. Any enduringly successful answer, it would seem, must come from searching examination and rigorous reform of the U.S. economy, with the plain straight objective of cutting production costs. Like all major surgery it cannot stop short of the sufficient.

But isn't the American economy already an efficient organism, the wonder of the world?

The truth of the matter is that it is nothing of the sort, viewed in the whole. The hope of the future, the prospect for progress, is to be found not in admiring its many efficiencies but in recognizing its myriad inefficiencies. Strip these away, then America can compete and thrive.

The first task is to look for them. Our vision of even admitted economic flaws is preoccupied with a need for "growth," for smoothing the business cycle, for full employment. These are desirable, yet so far removed from cost analysis that they impair realistic peering at the economy. Perhaps the point requires illustration:

If the United States were to decide to produce half the bananas it eats, it could assuredly do so by subsidizing enough hothouses and propping prices for the fruit. The thousands of tons of glass and steel and the millions of bananas would all boost the magical figures of gross national product to accomplish "growth"; clever timing of construction could relieve unemployment.

Or, if it be imagined instead that this segment of the economy were an existing legacy from an earlier generation, then all these national yearnings could still be served by, say, accelerated tax depreciation to spur modernization and expansion of banana facilities.

It would remain an absurdity, nevertheless. And for the reason that it would be a high-cost burden upon the entire economy. Furthermore, its absurdity would be invisible to most if it were fact instead of fiction; anyone proposing to cut the banana business out of the economy would be abused as lacking both common sense and patriotism.

The actual absurdities, the high-cost inefficiencies of the national economy, deserve to be sought out boldly. We've considered hypothetical bananas. How about sure-enough sugar?

Is this genuine instance of high-cost domestic production less questionable? Is it not even more dubious, since the United States pays out far more than the world price not only for all its own sugar production but for all the foreign sugar it consumes? Why should our economy absorb and accept this inflation of cost?

How about the bulk of our agriculture—is it not even more fantastically warped into inefficiency? In its major commodities the United States could confront the Common Market and the world with an incomparable advantage of low cost and low price—for what other nation can match our huge farm belts, their soil and climate, their mechanization and men highly trained in crop technology?

Yet Republicans and Democrats have long agreed to cancel the advantage. Much of the best land is forced out of the production, for which it is best suited, to sustain poor acreage. The most skilled farmer must limit his output to aid the least efficient. Prices are pushed so high that inferior foreign agriculture expands and sells at lower cost; imports are restrained only by protectionism, and subsidized U.S. production requires further subsidy to be sold abroad.

Industrial costs are every bit as vulnerable to scrutiny. Consider the nation's expenditure for its energy requirements. Taxpayers' subsidies sponsor a little atomic power, a lot of hydroelectric power. Efficient low-cost oil wells are sharply restrained in output; low-cost petroleum imports are curbed; the Government attacks sales of efficient gas fuel to industrial consumers. In short, energy costs are propped with the deliberate aim of keeping marginal coal mines and oilfields in production.

As a rough rule of thumb, perhaps any U.S. industry presently in need of subsidies, tariffs or quota protection might be considered a candidate for abandonment or ruthless reform, if the rest of industry is to be saved from future need for protection. Encouraging cheap imports can be part of calculated national cost-cutting, because by reducing raw materials expenditures and cost-of-living wage pressures it can aid the efficient sectors of the American economy to survive and expand.

Of course, since a search for cost-cutting opportunities can respect no boundaries of economic interest, geographic section nor political party, no group is likely to give it wholehearted acclaim.

Suppose, for instance, it does become apparent that agriculture must be whipped into lean fighting condition, to help sustain the economy instead of draining it. This drive for low costs and low prices would certainly require the best farmers cultivating the best crops on the best land merged into units of the best size. This process would comb out millions of less fertile acres, thousands of less efficient farmers, and discard such fetishes as "preservation of the family farm" and "gains in total farm income."

Conservatives and liberals could even agree on the objective yet be in utter disagreement. Is the objective best achieved by yanking off all governmental controls and letting farmers adjust to a free market? Or would such a revolution call for the most energetic governmental planning and controls?

As the high-cost sectors of industry are spotlighted, the nation may similarly reach a consensus for action—yet debate whether the solution is to be achieved through more or less Government. It will be vital to make sensible decisions, without long delay.

Beyond agriculture the nation will have to reappraise many continuing Government policies, which are the environment for all industry, to see how accurately they aim at low costs. As a sample, consider anti–trust enforcement: Should it be tightened or relaxed?

In one respect, it is arguable that businessmen should be clapped in prison if discovered in price conspiracy to protect their own inefficiencies and increase their customers' costs. But along another front, it is conceivable that corporate mergers should actually be encouraged wherever they really cut production costs. Competition is an essential incentive for cost-cutting, but competition includes not just the number of competing U.S. producers but foreign competitors as well.

Government economists fret about "price leadership" by the biggest firms in various industries, yet privately they suspect that General Motors might cut auto prices except for the fear this might drive a couple of higher-cost competitors to the wall and the trust-busters would charge G.M. with monopoly.

Perhaps the U.S. auto industry would soon throw cheaper cars into domestic and world markets if this threat were removed, by redefining competition to include not just American automakers but Volkswagen, Renault, British Motors, Fiat, Volvo and a host of others. Such a shift in anti–trust policy might similarly provide cheaper steel, cheaper tires, cheaper paint—and all automakers could gain further low-cost strength in the world trade struggle.

Tax reform is also urgent business. Every executive knows his own corporation indulges in economic nonsense for tax reasons, and the Treasury knows the balance between entire industries suffers costly distortion from uneven burdens of taxation. An endless quarrel goes on between those who would reduce basic rates to diminish the pressure for odd escapes and those who would sew up the loopholes. Perhaps it is time for some of both.

Anyway, no major reform should proceed without examining its relationship to tax technicalities of the Common Market. Europe collects much of its taxes through various sales levies, which its manufactured exports escape. In contrast, American reliance on corporate income taxes weighs heavily on our factories' exports. Should not this element of high cost be eliminated, if necessary by revamping the whole manner of collecting revenue?

American taxes have been examined for their role in the business cycle, social reform, and economic "growth." Now may be the time to total them up as an element of production cost, to see how they compare with tax costs of production abroad. This could be used to buttress liberal arguments for more Federal spending—and conservative arguments that lavish welfare programs burden not merely the U.S. taxpayer but production costs and prices.

National labor policy is obviously in flux, but has any real prospect as yet appeared that it will contribute to getting U.S. costs in shape to compete? Automation, by nature a solution, is converted into a "problem," to be studied by national committees whose idea of progress is to phrase and limit its potential for slashing labor costs.

Featherbedding is a national joke, but what national policy attacks its most flagrant follies? As for "wage restraint," Government men congratulate themselves on a doctrine which even if followed encourages pay hikes and fringes to absorb all industrial productivity gains; how does this leave room for American price-cutting, or for reinvestment in new cost-cutting plants and machines?

If the fat should be cut out of U.S. labor costs, how? Should it be accomplished by labor "statesmanship," by laws breaking the monopoly power of the unions, or by Government dictation of wages and working conditions?

Clearly, every question will be open to debate, and some decisions cannot be made on economic grounds alone. If, for example, a true military necessity for shipping subsidies, oil quotas or textile tariffs exists, it should be heeded—but only after the same sort of harsh strategic review that has killed off the cavalry, the battleship and the Snark missile. Requirements of the economic contest with non-Communist lands will not always jibe neatly with requirements of the anti-Communist struggle. Yet there will be an affinity.

The prospect of trade wars between Europe and the United States, no less than the cold war itself, imperatively poses its question. The foreign threat of low costs demands that America respond by cutting its own costs. This can be done only by making hard decisions that will not wait.

The Old World has come to life to challenge American primacy. And the Communists are in the wings.

HENRY GEMMILL

December 8, 1961

*"In short, Ned, I tried to sell them our way
of life and they sold me theirs."*

Protectionism's Power

WASHINGTON—The legions of protectionism, seemingly out-gunned and outmanned by the diverse forces favoring free trade, are not about to sound retreat. Indeed, they seem more robust than at any time in a generation as another foreign trade debate looms in Congress.

Why? The secret of protectionism's power can be found within a seldom-recognized American phenomenon: This country remains even today far less centralized in its life than any other great power. The men of wealth, power and influence in their New York and Washington offices cannot automatically make their wishes felt across the continent. To a great degree, nameless men in crossroad hamlets can frustrate the designs of the mighty.

The apparently invincible array of powerful national organizations supporting freer trade thus is reduced to a façade in the light of political realities. "You just can't think of this issue in terms of a broad national campaign," contends a free-trade lobbyist who has grappled with the protectionists in many a Congressional war. "You have to consider each Congressional district separately. Protectionist pressure in each district has to be balanced by pressure from us. Sometimes we can't do it."

True, the protectionists are fighting a defensive war; there is no possibility of returning to the national trade policy of the bygone days when William McKinley's motto of "Prosperity, Patriotism and Protection" stirred the nation. But it has been a successful rear-guard action. The postwar decade saw the passage of protectionist devices to dull the impact of tariff cuts, and protectionists now threaten President Kennedy's bid for greatly expanded tariff-cutting power to cope with the European Common Market.

The appearances and realities of the opposing forces' comparative strength in the foreign trade fight can be seen by glancing at the list of witnesses that testified last month before a Senate-House subcommittee on trade problems. The long parade of free-trade advocates cut across ideological, party and social lines—Kennedy Administration and former Eisenhower Administration officials, Republicans and Democrats, respected economists, spokesmen for the U.S. Chamber of Commerce, the AFL-CIO, and the American Farm Bureau Federation. And, cheering them on in a remarkably unanimous chorus were the nation's most powerful newspapers and political commentators.

Opposing this impressive coalition on the witness stand was a lonely apostle of protectionism: O. R. Strackbein, a professional lobbyist with a penchant for long and repetitive oral statements. But allied with Mr. Strackbein was an unseen army, many of them members of organizations officially on record in favor of freer trade.

Whatever the U.S. Chamber may say nationally, member industries which claim injury from foreign imports—textiles, glass, plywood, minerals, pottery, footwear and many more—will demand tariff protection from their Congressmen. No matter what the staff economists of the AFL-CIO may argue, the member unions representing these same industries side with employers in opposing tariff cuts.

And disregarding the positions of their national party leaders, Republican and Democratic lawmakers alike tend to be more receptive to the pressures and conditions of their local districts—particularly in an election year.

The interplay between local and national pressures places many a Congressman in an uncomfortable crossfire of conflicting loyalties. Take the case of Senator Lee Metcalf of Montana, who might be expected to be fighting for the Kennedy trade program as a Democratic Party regular, a loyal Administration backer and a promising young liberal leader. But Senator Metcalf is at the same time a political representative of the Western mining country, a traditional stronghold of protectionism.

"How can I go to the miner or the lumber worker or the sheep farmer and say, 'We're going to put you out of business for the national interest,' " Senator Metcalf declares. "I can't, and I don't think I should." In the end, he may be more moved by national considerations and wind up supporting the Kennedy program, at least in modified form. But other lawmakers from areas similar to Mr. Metcalf's are totally preoccupied by parochial factors and probably will not.

There are, of course, powerful economic interests that benefit from expanded foreign trade, great industries with far more potential political muscle than the protectionists. But their voice on the local level seems muted when compared with the raucous cries of the protectionists. Conceding that a majority of businessmen in his state probably favor freer trade, an Eastern Republican Senator adds quickly that the minority protectionist sentiment "is concentrated, as though it came through a magnifying glass. It burns like hell."

This burning sensation felt by Congressmen is nothing less than the threat of an election defeat. A protectionist industry in one district may employ just a few hundred workers, but the Congressman is told frankly that he will lose those few hundred votes in future elections unless he performs correctly on the floor of the House. The warning has substance; fully indoctrinated by employers and union leaders, employees of some plants are given free time away from the work bench in order to write protectionist letters to their Congressmen.

Consider the pressures on lawmakers from Connecticut, for example. The import-conscious rubber footwear and brass industries in the Naugatuck Valley emit a constant call for high tariffs. But the state's export-conscious aircraft industry barely raises its voice in arguing for expanded trade. It would be no surprise, then, if Connecticut Congressmen feel they have much to lose and little to gain politically by supporting the Kennedy trade program.

The contrast between the aggressiveness of the local protectionists and listlessness of local free-traders is really not surprising. To the protectionists, this issue is a matter of economic life and death, threatening the destruction of industries and loss of jobs. The arguments advanced by free-traders carry less emotional appeal inherently.

Thus, businessmen who otherwise are apathetic about developments in faraway Washington spring to life when they consider their very existence endangered. Montana's dominant copper industry takes a tolerant attitude toward Senator Metcalf's liberal record on labor and social welfare measures. But if he should begin to support legislation that would open the dikes for a flow of foreign copper into the United States, the copper men might designate him for political liquidation.

Moreover, national organizations favoring freer trade often find it difficult to mobilize their local affiliates even if the local leaders aren't active protectionists. "It's easy enough to explain soybean legislation to a soybean farmer or wheat legislation to a wheat farmer," asserts Herbert H. Harris II of the American Farm Bureau Federation. "But it's a damn tough job to explain how the trade bill is important to him."

This pattern of local pressures does not seem likely to change any time soon. Mr. Kennedy's proposal for a variety of Federal subsidies to aid employers and workers injured by foreign imports may win the votes of a few wavering Congressmen. But it won't perform successfully the more important mission of extinguishing the protectionist fires back home.

"These industries don't want to get handouts or be helped into another line of business," maintains a prominent Republican Congressman. "They want to stay in business at the same stand."

Some pessimistic free-traders believe Congress will not authorize genuinely significant tariff reductions until the protectionist din is drowned out at the local level by an even more bellicose advocacy of expanded trade. And they feel that such a grass-roots backing cannot be built until the need for foreign trade becomes less academic and—

like protectionism—is a matter of economic life or death, of survival of industries, or retention of jobs.

In other words, these pessimists believe, nothing approaching Mr. Kennedy's trade program can be passed until enough industries have suffered from the exclusion of their products from Europe because of the failure to negotiate effectively with the Common Market. And by the time that happens, the country's trade problems may be far more complicated than they are today.

ROBERT D. NOVAK

January 24, 1962

"He said, 'If you care to step outside and repeat that, I'll punch you in the nose.'"

Protectionism's Past

Congress this month will open a new round in the battle over tariffs, a battle that has divided Americans since the beginning of the Republic.

President Kennedy will begin the round by requesting broad, new power to reduce tariffs. A number of the arguments, pro and con, will have a familiar ring. Like free-traders of the past, Mr. Kennedy will contend that we must offer tariff concessions to foreign nations to assure a continuing market for American exports in such countries; the President's prime worry is Europe's fast-growing Common Market.

Proponents of protectionism will be contending this year, as they have for more than a century, that American workers must be shielded from the products of lower-paid workers abroad. And representatives of some industries will be claiming, as other industries have in the past, that their operations are essential to the nation's security and must be shielded from foreign competition.

In most ways, however, this year's dispute points up the fact that the prime element of America's tariff history is change. Mr. Kennedy isn't the first President to push for freer trade, but his proposal is more sweeping than most of his predecessors would have dared to advance. Among the major advocates of protectionism this year are the textile makers of the South; the South of a century ago was the center of free-trade sentiment.

In the past, politicians also have often switched sides on the tariff question. An argument used by free-traders may turn up years later in the arsenal of the protectionists. Political parties seldom have been able to form a united front on tariffs, any more than they will this year. Even the ostensible purpose of tariffs has undergone a major change.

When Congress first tackled tariffs in 1789, the prime consideration was revenue. In 1789–1791, the total receipts of the U.S. Treasury were $4.4 million, of which all but $19,000 came from customs duties. Tariffs continued to be of major revenue importance for many years; in 1859, just before the Civil War, they accounted for more than 90 per cent of total Federal revenue. The percentage has fallen sharply since then; it's now about 1 per cent of the total.

This is not to say that, in the early years of the nation, there were no proponents of protectionism for its own sake. On the contrary, they were many and powerful. With the aid of the need-for-revenue argument, they often were able to shape tariff measures to achieve their specific tariff goals. Among the early protectionists was Alexander Hamilton, the first Secretary of the Treasury. Although Mr. Hamilton leaned toward paying bounties to industries that were to be protected, revenue considerations undoubtedly led him to endorse tariffs.

Tariff policy in the early days of America was complicated by more than the need for revenue; it became thoroughly enmeshed in the young nation's belligerent attitude toward much of the rest of the world. In 1789 James Madison had supported the principle of free trade, and in 1787 Thomas Jefferson had spoken glowingly of the virtues of a simple agricultural state, with no industries clamoring for tariff protection. But in 1793, when many Americans were sympathizing with revolutionary France in its troubles with England, Mr. Jefferson proposed strong protectionist measures directed against England, and Mr. Madison brought forth resolutions based on his recommendations.

The early backers of protectionism relied heavily on the "infant industry" argument. They contended that many industries, if they were shielded from import competition for a few years, would be able to develop and operate profitably in the United States. Once the young industries were established, the argument ran, they no longer would need protection.

This view, however, won little backing from the public. The economy still was chiefly agricultural, so people were more interested in maintaining a flow of cheap imports from abroad than in building up domestic industries. The opponents of new protectionist moves, interestingly enough, tried to buttress their case by arguing that wages were higher in the United States than in Europe. With this wage disparity, they contended, it would be at least impractical for the United States to attempt to build up industries that would compete with those of Europe. Before many years went by, of course, the high-wage argument was being used by the proponents of protection.

America's youthful industries got their first real protection from war rather than from tariffs; the War of 1812 was accompanied by an almost complete cut-off of imports. U.S. industries thrived mightily as a result and, just as predictably, were battered by import competition when the war ended. The plea for tariff protection was immediate, and customs duties began to move upward, though slowly at first.

In the 1820s, protectionist sentiment ran strong in such states as New York, New Jersey, Ohio and Kentucky. These were largely agricultural states. While the farmers wanted protection for their own wool, flax, hemp, wheat and corn, they were at least equally interested in developing a domestic market for their products and thus advocated protection for manufactured goods as well. Much of New England, on the other hand, was solidly for free trade, because the businessmen of the area were largely merchants, importers and ship owners, who would be hurt by any diminution of foreign trade. And the cotton-growing South also argued for free trade.

The division of the nation made things difficult for politicians. Andrew Jackson, though an avowed protectionist, was hesitant about stressing his views for fear of alienating his supporters in the South. In the election of 1828, when Mr. Jackson first won the White House, his supporters actually were firmly united on only one point: their determination to win.

America's tariff history frequently has been influenced by general business trends. Protectionists often have contended that recessions have been caused at least partly by earlier moves toward freer trade; free-traders have contended the reverse. The result usually has been determined by the sheer political power of the two sides, rather than by the power of their arguments.

The economic decline of the late 1830s stemmed chiefly from the country's banking and currency troubles, but protectionists were quick to blame the lowering of tariffs that began in 1833. Fortunately for their case, the Government also was in need of revenue, so tariffs were pushed up again in 1842. Business began to improve, for reasons that had little or nothing to do with higher tariffs, and in 1846 customs duties were lowered again.

The Civil War brought two developments that eased the protectionists' task: The South's free-trade views ceased to be a political factor, and Washington's revenue needs expanded enormously. After the war, with the South still impotent politically, the protectionists were able to keep tariffs at high levels for many years.

Later on, tariff rates generally fluctuated with business activity, rising in recessions and falling during prosperity. Increasing emphasis was placed on protection for agricultural products, as the farmers began more and more to flex their political muscle. The Smoot-Hawley tariff act of 1930, originally designed to aid agricultural goods, actually achieved the highest general tariff levels on record. The act was not generally popular either in the United States or abroad, and with the coming of the depression helped to set the stage for the trade agreements program.

The Reciprocal Trade Act was passed in 1934, and has been extended periodically since then. The latest extension of the act expires this year, and it is with this that Congress must deal. Under the act, the President is empowered to negotiate treaties with other nations, lowering—or raising—duties on a reciprocal basis.

Mr. Kennedy contends that the terms of the legislation as it now exists are too restrictive for dealing effectively with the Common Market; protectionists claim the President's powers already are too broad. Many arguments will be advanced on both sides in the weeks to come. Whatever the result this year, it may pay the losers to be patient. History indicates that both the arguments and their advocates are subject to change.

LINDLEY H. CLARK, JR.

January 5, 1962

THIS TENUOUS MIRACLE . . .

The Spreading Rot

"I have long been convinced," wrote Lord Macaulay more than a hundred years ago, "that institutions purely democratic must, sooner or later, destroy liberty, or civilization, or both." He had in mind specifically American democracy, which he was sure would go under in our century if not in his own.

Macaulay is neither the first nor will he be the last to indulge in head-shaking about democracy as a political system. There is a good deal of head-shaking going on in this country right now. For our part, though we are congenitally skeptical of either predictions or pat historical analogies, we must confess we too sometimes wonder.

Several circumstances have thus far combined to confound Macaulay's prophecy. The most obvious is that this country has never been a pure democracy, as the fact that it is a Republic plainly announces. Popular but representative government, with the ingenious checks and balances of our own system, is a powerful deterrent to mob rule and ruin, just as it was meant to be.

Moreover, American capitalism functioning in political liberty has worked a miracle Macaulay did not foresee. It has brought an unprecedented degree of material well-being to the people generally. And not only material; it has produced a highly literate, intelligent and civilized electorate—something never even attempted in the democracies of antiquity.

Yet, despite such bulwarks, disturbing echoes of Macaulay's forebodings can be heard plainly enough today—not least in the Congress of the United States.

What is one to make, for instance, of the proposed additional pension

for veterans of World War I? This subsidy would total $11 billion over
the years and benefit chiefly the veteran who doesn't need it. It is so
cynical a grab that it is opposed by all the major veterans organizations,
by the chairman of the House Veterans Committee and by almost all
Congressmen in their hearts. But the fear of offending veterans is so
great in Congress that it may quite possibly be enacted.

This in microcosm is what has been happening on a vastly expanded
scale. Big and little groups of people have concluded that the Federal
Government is, after all, a free lunch; that the Treasury of all the
people can be plundered, seemingly without end, for the presumed
enrichment of this or that interest. And the thises and thats are multiplying like rabbits. Almost nobody any more goes without a subsidy.

Now, the undeniable degeneration of America's political and economic institutions is not, in our view, primarily the fault of the public
at large. Plenty of local governments are corrupt, but in their own communities people continue to behave responsibly, building their hospitals
and churches and schools and, even more important, raising their educational sights for the sake of their children.

The trouble is that it becomes increasingly difficult to act responsibly
as the Federal Government encroaches more and more on all local
governments, communities and individuals. We personally have talked
with many farmers who would like to see the whole Federal subsidy-
control apparatus scrapped, but as long as other farmers are taking
their handouts they will take theirs too.

Strictly speaking, that is not a very admirable moral attitude, but it
is understandably human in circumstances that seem beyond the individual's control. And so the rot spreads through the land until almost
everybody figures, Who can stop Washington? And if it insists on pouring it out, why not get in on the gravy?

For it is the Federal Government that not only makes it possible for
the rot to spread but actively and, these days, increasingly encourages
it. Whether it is the White House demanding that the people submit
to compulsion for yet another handout, or the Congress passing yet
another boondoggle, there is only one word for it. The word is demagogy.

And when demagogy finally combines with a general willingness to
be bought, things may get beyond the power of even our powerful
political and economic institutions to check. The danger today arises
not from those democratic institutions but from their perversion.

The people and their institutions are resilient and capable of with-
standing much abuse; as we say, they have until now defied Macaulay's words of doom, and we hope they will go right on doing so.
But that is no reason for anyone, from Washington to the last subsi-

dized farm and business and household, to be complacent about his warning:

". . . when a society has entered on this downward progress, either civilization or liberty must perish. Either some Caesar or Napoleon will seize the reins of government with a strong hand; or your Republic will be as fearfully plundered and laid waste by barbarians in the Twentieth Century as the Roman Empire was in the Fifth;—with this difference, that the Huns and Vandals who ravaged the Roman Empire came from without, and that your Huns and Vandals will have been engendered within your own country . . ."

JOSEPH E. EVANS

July 24, 1962

"Some day, son, all these unplanted acres will be yours."

The Moral Issue in Mississippi

While statesmen were issuing statements and soldiers were marching to and fro, the mob before the gates of the University of Mississippi was singing a song.

Its title was "Never, No Never." And the lyrics made no pretense that the mob, in resisting a Federal court order admitting a Negro to the school, was pleading time and patience before overturning customs generations old. To the Negro people, and to the whole country, the song chanted one word over and over—never.

Governor Barnett, in all his legal maneuverings, has taken the same position as the battle song of the mob. Even as he yielded officially to the inevitable, he told the people of Mississippi that they should "never" accept a black skin in the halls of their university.

So now two men are dead, a score or more are in the hospital and no man knows what will be the end of mob violence.

We are no less conscious than others that many questions have been involved in the recent events in Mississippi, including a grave Constitutional issue. But it seems to us that nothing has put quite so starkly the central moral question as this word "never." It exposes clearly what is fundamentally wrong with Governor Barnett and the mob which he incites.

The Constitutional question of state and Federal responsibilities is one on which moral men may differ, even though the outcome of that struggle was from the beginning foreordained. President Kennedy, like President Eisenhower before him, did the only thing he could do, assert the supremacy of Federal authority against that of any state if the two are forced into collision.

The question of speed or slowness in changing old ways is also one upon which moral men may differ. Honest men must admit to themselves that there is some truth in the cry that immediate, wholesale integration, South or North, would do an injury to society because it would level down and not up. In any event, it is not so simple as many outside the South suppose to change a social order by a court order.

But the mob did not make these the issues in Mississippi. The mob, led by the governor of the state, tried to say that never shall there be any change.

This is indefensible. For what it says to the Negro people of Mississippi is that it no longer matters what they do with their lives. No matter what effort they make to lift themselves by character and intelligence, the State of Mississippi will not accord them the dignity of manhood. It would strip from them even the patient hope of time.

So it strips from all who utter it not only the support of reason but of morality. It leaves empty all the arguments about States' Rights, about the Constitutional division of powers, about the wisdom of leaving the people of a community free to work out in their own way their age-old problems.

These are weighty questions of long ancestry in our political history; wise men have stood upon both sides. But there is another doctrine of equally deep roots in our tradition. It is that men must come into court with clean hands, and it is an immutable doctrine when men come before the bar of public opinion.

For the most part, this has been the way of the South. Some states have yielded slowly on their custom of absolute segregation of the two races; doubtless all of them have been reluctant to meet changes of unknown consequence. Yet throughout the South, from Virginia to Texas, men of good will have nonetheless accepted the necessity of change because in their hearts they knew it was right; they debated only about how and when. It has been the pace, not the direction, that has divided them.

This being the case, people all over the country—including the men of good will among the Negro people—have offered patient understanding. Neither courts nor Presidents have tried to replace evolution with revolution. But there can be neither patience nor understanding when a mob arises to say to other men that their future is only hopelessness.

For any man to say this to another man is immoral. For an institution of government to elevate it to a policy of state is something that good men cannot tolerate. And the true lesson of Mississippi, whatever the Constitutional lawyers may say, is that they will not.

VERMONT ROYSTER

October 2, 1962

Science and Secrecy

Sixteen of the seventeen U.S. scientists who have won a Nobel Prize agree that Government secrecy about science does more harm than good. Their view was sought by Senator Hennings, chairman of the Constitutional Rights subcommittee, who is investigating complaints that scientific development is hindered by undue secrecy.

Walter H. Brattain, Nobel prize winner for physics in 1956, put the scientific community's plaint rather well. It just does not make sense, he said, to classify fundamental scientific information. "Most restrictions in the name of national security turn out to be foolish. A few restrictions well considered in special areas make a lot of sense. However, the tendency always is to allow such activities to expand."

The tendency to expand secrecy is the crux of the matter, we think. And a misunderstanding or ignorance of science is one of the basic causes of science secrecy's growth. An instance was reported by Senator Humphrey in testimony before a House Government Information subcommittee, which is also looking into the spread of secrecy throughout our Government.

The example cited by Senator Humphrey had to do with classification by the Central Intelligence Agency of part of the testimony of Dr. Hans Bethe, appearing before the Senate Subcommittee on Disarmament, Control and Reduction of Armaments. When asked why Dr. Bethe's discussion of earthquakes in the U.S.S.R. and China in relation to nuclear explosions had been deleted, the CIA official indicated he did not agree with the scientist's conclusions. "When challenged further on the point," the Senator said, "the CIA representative agreed to let the scientist's conclusions stand."

We don't know whether Dr. Bethe's testimony had or had not an important bearing on the Senator's approach to nuclear tests, but we do know that scientists will become increasingly loath to take part in Government if this sort of "when in doubt, stamp" attitude on the part of Government classifiers persists.

There are, unquestionably, certain areas in which national security requires Government secrecy. But where Government secrecy hinders scientific development and progress on which our national security may well rest, abuse of the secrecy stamp might well turn out to be an enemy's secret weapon.

June 18, 1959

Whose Civil Rights?

Former General Walker and new heavyweight champion Sonny Liston don't have too much in common, but each of them ought to have a little sympathy for the other. Both of them have recently been the victims of some strange encounters with Federal police authorities.

To be sure, the Federal tax authorities had reasonable grounds for suspicion that the Government might not get its due share of the receipts from the Liston-Patterson fight unless it stepped in and grabbed them first. Fight managers and promoters are not noted for their scrupulous accounting or for being pillars of society, and the IRS has had trouble before with the fight's promoters.

Nonetheless, the new champion is not involved in this past dispute. Moreover, the Internal Revenue agents didn't pause long enough to give anybody a chance to make an accounting in good faith. Nor did they content themselves with putting a tab on some reasonable proportion of the fight take. They moved almost as fast as Sonny Liston moved on Patterson, and just as thoroughly. They seized the money first and talked about it afterward.

Possibly also General Walker's speeches contributed to the riots in Mississippi; that is a matter for the courts to decide. But when he was arrested some of the niceties of civil rights got lost in the rush.

He was arraigned without benefit of counsel, and then without even going through the motions of a proper hearing the authorities had him hustled off for "psychiatric examination." His bail was set at the unusually large figure of $100,000, the same figure used for the late Dr. Soblen, a man duly convicted in open court of having spied for the enemies of his country.

We'll leave the lawyers to debate the legal points in these two cases, as they are now doing. Subsequently General Walker's bail was cut in half and he is now out of jail. Doubtless in the end Sonny Liston will receive his proper share of the fight proceeds. But there is something more disturbing here than legal technicalities.

One of these cases puts aside the concept that a man is punished only for crimes committed; here is punishment for tax evasion—certainly seizing all a man's pay is punishment—merely on the policeman's suspicion that taxes might be evaded. The other puts aside the doctrine that a man charged with a crime is entitled to the protection of certain ancient processes of the law, including the right to counsel.

The reply of the policeman in each case is that haste was necessary. If the revenue agents hadn't acted then it might have been too late. The Justice Department had to move swiftly against General Walker to teach a lesson to other people.

Perhaps so; yet it's an argument become all too familiar. A Justice of the Supreme Court makes a ruling, as Justice Black did in the Misssissippi school case, by concluding from conversations what the full court might decide—because everybody was too impatient to wait a few weeks. A corporation angers the Attorney General, as U.S. Steel did by trying to raise prices, and the next day its offices are crawling with Government agents, hustling to find evidence for an indictment not yet drawn.

It may be hard to drum up much sympathy for General Walker or Sonny Liston. But if we are going to set aside all the due processes of law every time the policeman is in a hurry, then no man can be safe from the scowl of the tax collector or the Attorney General.

VERMONT ROYSTER

October 12, 1962

*"I'm chairman of a new committee set up to investigate whatever
sections of American life have so far escaped investigation."*

The Suspicious Policeman

If a large crowd of people standing on the corner all suddenly began walking down the street in one direction, the policeman on the beat would be naïve indeed if he didn't suspect something unusual was going on. It would be his duty to make some inquiry, for while it might be merely the beginning of a parade, it might also be the start of a mob.

Just so the Government has a duty to wonder whether laws are being violated when a number of competitive companies all start going down the street of higher prices simultaneously. Maybe there is some concerted price-fixing going on; then again, maybe not.

The trouble with the Department of Justice, though, is that the trust busters don't always take the trouble to figure out there might be two sides to a suspicion. The missionaries against "big business" have a fixed idea that any price rise all along the line is evidence per se of price-fixing.

The suit against about 30 oil companies and a chemical concern is the most recent example of this fixed idea. In 1956, when Nasser seized the Suez Canal, oil shipments from the Mideast were drastically curtailed and the U.S. Government asked U.S. oil companies to help supply a Europe running dry of oil. The result was that the economic pressure created by the resultant demand here and abroad for crude oil raised prices.

But the Government trust busters decided the oil companies raised their prices not because of competitive demand, but because they saw a chance to make some money; so they conspired to raise crude prices all over. The Government then went before a grand jury and came out with an indictment after presenting its "evidence" of a conspiracy.

And what was the "evidence" on which the Government based its case? The judge who tried it said:

"It is my judgment that the evidence doesn't rise above the level of suspicion."

He added that it was his personal conviction from the presentation of the Government's case that the oil companies were innocent of wrongdoing.

In dismissing the case—the defendants didn't even have to present their side, so weak was the Government's charge—Federal Judge Savage noted that similar language about "suspicion" had been used by two other Federal judges just three months ago in dismissing the

Department of Justice's anti-trust suit against the makers of Salk vaccine. (The vaccine makers also found trouble because the Government asked them to supply a demand.) The makers of Salk vaccine were also indicted on quick suspicion that they were doing wrong.

Like the policeman, the Government has a responsibility to investigate circumstances that arouse suspicion of wrongdoing. But the experienced policeman knows that there may be other reasons for the gathered crowd. And the responsible policeman, unlike the Department of Justice, knows mere suspicion is an unjust excuse for laying about him with his truncheon and rushing people off to jail.

WILLIAM H. FITZPATRICK

February 16, 1960

The Silly Season

Cyrus Eaton, Cleveland, Ohio, industrialist, a frequent critic of policies and practices of his adopted homeland, was awarded this month a Lenin Peace Prize by Moscow. The other day he had a 10-minute conversation at Orly Airport with the Soviet premier just before Mr. Khrushchev departed Paris.

Mr. Eaton, the newspaper reports said, talked to Mr. Khrushchev about George Washington. He told the story of the cherry tree ("I cannot tell a lie, I did it with my little hatchet") and he said that Washington had instructed the country never to base its foreign policy on prejudice or hatred of another nation.

All this was music to Mr. Khrushchev's ears. But it sounded pretty bad on this side of the water.

It sounded so bad to Senator Dodd of Connecticut that in a speech in the Senate he asked that Mr. Eaton be prosecuted under the Logan Act which forbids private citizens to negotiate with foreign powers with intent to influence policy.

Well, doubtless a great many Americans agree that Mr. Eaton acts mighty silly at times. But we don't know very many who think all this foolishness is a danger to us.

So far as prosecution under the Logan Act is concerned, what, for goodness' sake, can Eaton negotiate with Khrushchev aside from an agreement that they both think U.S. policy is wrong? And how in the world can Eaton influence U.S. policy?

Well, it's the middle of spring and the silly season is on. Princeton boys rioted and Barnard girls complained that the Universal Declaration of Human Rights was violated because the dean wouldn't let them wear shorts. But simply because Mr. Eaton seems to observe the season all year round is hardly reason for Senator Dodd to celebrate it, too.

And even less reason for the Department of Justice to accept the Senator's invitation to make us look silly before the whole world.

WILLIAM H. FITZPATRICK

May 23, 1960

"Will you please take your complaints about the state of the nation to your other Senator?"

The Door That Disappeared

The other night, filled with good food and good cheer at the small supper party, we sat for a moment by the fireplace's glow and thought how all was well with us and with so many millions of other Americans enjoying the same security.

And then we caught a drift of conversation across the room. One of the other guests, a man knowledgeable in electronics, was describing some of the latest research to speed the science of communications.

He told us that scientists are working on a device—and they have just about reached their goal—that will read unopened mail, make a picture of it, and speed it on its way in a matter of minutes.

Now this might turn out to be a great help to the Post Office Department, to be sure, in their efforts to speed up delivery of mail from one place to the other, and the knowledgeable man was quick to point that out. But another man, whose interests lie in other fields than speeding letters from here to there, expressed his indignation and he talked about the Bill of Rights and its restraints on Government.

He mentioned particularly the Fifth Amendment and its words about the right of citizens to be secure in their persons, papers, houses and effects against unreasonable searches. He spoke of wire-tapping and the concerted drive to grant such powers to police and Federal agents to listen in on the people's phones. And there was general agreement that, however legal, wire-tapping was nothing but eavesdropping, and reading mail electronically was no different from steaming open private letters.

It may have been only a reflection cast by the street light that accounts for the way the house appeared to look as we left. But though we plainly heard the click of the lock and knew our neighbors were secure for the night, when we turned for a last look it seemed as though beyond the green and silver Christmas wreath there was no door at all.

WILLIAM H. FITZPATRICK

December 31, 1959

The Law's Promise

Predictably, the collapse of the Government's tenuous case against the notorious Apalachin "conspirators" has stirred an outcry against the sort of law that sets free those who scorn the law.

This is a familiar complaint, and a perfectly reasonable one. It is a pity that diligent prosecutors are thus frustrated, and that 20 unsavory characters are thus set at large.

But the prosecution must prove that a crime has been committed, and that a certain person committed it. In the Apalachin case, it could marshal much circumstantial evidence and very strong suspicions, but it did not prove what had to be proved in the judgment of a U.S. Court of Appeals.

Before anyone gets mad at the Federal judges who so ruled, he ought to think of the consequences of bending the law to entrap those whom the police suspect of breaking the law. If the law were flexible, if the police could search and question a suspect arbitrarily, and if courts would admit weak evidence to prove strong suspicions, what would the law's promise of protection mean to any citizen?

RICHARD WHALEN

December 5, 1960

Some Thoughts on American Business

Unlike some of our friends in Washington these days, we are old enough to recall the great depression not as a studied lesson in a history book but as a remembered personal experience. No one needs to tell us that it was a time of troubles.

Yet curiously we find it hard to convince our younger friends that in those days not everyone was sunk in despair or believed the gloomy myth of the day that America was a "mature economy," with all its growth and greatness behind it.

Most of all, our young friends find it hard to believe that such depressed times could also have been times of economic growth. The myth today is that growth and prosperity are one and the same thing, so lack of growth and depression must also be equated. And because the United States does not seem to be growing as rapidly as it has at some other times, the fashion is once again to be gloomy about the future of the mature American economy.

Well, it wasn't quite like that; and we doubt if it's going to be. There's no reason to believe that the pessimists about this country's economic future will be less wrong than they have been in the past. In any event, count us not among them.

This doesn't mean that we are cheerful about all that's being done to the American economy right now, or that we think it can be abused without a price. Rather, it's just that we are convinced by the record that the American economy can take an awful lot of abuse, and that we are skeptical about the durability of high fashion in economic ideas. The delusions of one era pass as surely as those of another.

Take the fashionable ideas about growth. The thirties were, right enough, depression years. They were also years of growth by the yard-sticks it's now the fashion to use. Between 1933 and 1940 the Gross National Product practically doubled and the National Income more than doubled.

This coinciding of growth and depression hardly suggests growth is a bad thing—between 1950 and 1960 there was the same doubling of the figures, and by anybody's standards the fifties were years of prosperity. It's simply a reminder that "growth" and "prosperity" are not synonymous. You can have one without the other, and in our history we frequently have.

Indeed, the history of the United States is strewn with passing economic troubles, recessions, depressions and downright panics, but over the whole span of that history the bright years far outnumber the dark ones and the total record of economic growth and rising material well-being for its citizens is unsurpassed by any country in the world.

One moral from this is to beware of anybody who takes the statistics of a few brief years, gloomily projects them into the future and then says the country is going to hell in a hack if it doesn't forthwith adopt some particular nostrum. There's another moral, too, when you look back at what brought on the times of troubles.

Almost without exception they were preceded by plain foolishness, the belief by people or politicians (or both) that the elementary principles of economic health no longer applied or could be ignored. Land speculation, currency tinkering, wild credit expansion, over-investment, unchecked Government deficits, mounting state debts, attempts to prop prices and a cavalier attitude toward "foreign" balance of payments—all these things have played their roles in the recessions of the past. Each was brought on by the excesses that went before.

The trouble, of course, was that the excesses did not seem like excesses, nor the nostrums like quackery, until it was too late. It would take a bold man, looking at the nostrums now being offered, to say we have outgrown that human frailty.

Yet the real moral is that American business does not succumb easily to abuses. Even in the long and deep depression of 1873–78, as in the depression after 1929, there were many segments of the economy that retained much vigor, and some that even expanded. More to the point, the nation's recuperative powers have been immense.

In the collapse of 1893—brought on by uncertainty over the dollar and a flight of capital to Europe—nearly 500 banks failed and business bankruptcies were numbered in the thousands. Once confidence was restored in the dollar and the gold drain halted, recovery was rapid. Finally, none of the foolishness, or the troubles it caused, stopped the upward march of the American economy.

The reason, we think, lies in the enormous resiliency of private capitalism and a free enterprise society. Repeatedly, as in the 1930s, direct Government efforts failed to recapture prosperity; just as repeatedly, once given a chance the country got itself moving again. Right after World War II, for example, it made liars out of some supposedly learned economists who again wailed that our growth was at an end, as well as our prosperity.

This resiliency is not easy to define in a textbook. For essentially it involves the accumulating effects of thousands of minor decisions of individual businessmen, of their wit or their luck in finding ways under, around or over whatever is the immediate economic problem.

If the problem is depressed business, some people will find a way to sell things even so. If the problem is high taxes, somebody will find a way to accumulate capital and put it to use in spite of the tax collector. If the problem is foreign competition, some businessmen will find a way to meet that competition in spite of high costs. If the problem is inflation brought on by Government tinkering with the money, a great many people will somehow find a way to protect their savings and capital to a marked degree.

Beyond that, the country has always come to recognize bad policies at last and halt them before the damage was irreparable. Nobody argues any more for 16-to-1 silver, any more than they do for prohibition. We still have the farm program, perennial deficit spending, lopsided labor laws, punitive taxes and those who preach inflation as salvation. Yet already all of these things are in doubt if not yet disrepute. Even some politicians are beginning to wonder if you can fool the people forever.

Of course even if you could plot these favorable factors on a piece of graph paper they still would not tell you whether business will be up or down in the next few months. But what this economic discussion is all about, or ought to be, is the reach of America's economic horizon in the years ahead, not just how business will be nursed along between now and the next election.

If that be true, the real pessimists are those who tell us all will be lost if we don't swallow a huge dose of the latest patent medicine brewed by fearful men in Washington. These desperate economic remedies are prescribed only by those who no longer believe in the free economic system.

We still do. Nothing can guarantee this country against some painful consequences from bad economic policies. Yet when you take the enormous resources of this country, add to them the ingenuity and industry of its people, measure these things against its record for recuperation from punishment, and finally project it all against the horizon of opportunity that lies before it—then you cannot really be a pessimist about America's economic future.

VERMONT ROYSTER

March 5, 1963

———◆———

PACKAGE DEAL

In recent years I can't recall
A single carton labeled "Small";
Prior to this subterfuge
I considered "Jumbo" simply huge;
But "Family Size" today is known
To mean for those who live alone.
Still visible to younger eyes
Is one entitled "Giant Size,"
Which makes me heed my toddler's plea
To "Buy the baby one for me."

—LOYD ROSENFIELD

Dismal

In the opinion of some people, the trouble with the Administration's proposed Department of Urban Affairs is not that it's too grandiose but that it's much too modest.

For instance, Senator Clifford Case, writing in the *Saturday Review*, says the plan's "greatest weakness" is its "failure to bring all the Federal programs affecting urban development under one administrative roof." Instead, it would merely elevate the Housing and Home Finance Agency to Cabinet status.

The Senator notes that while the HHFA deals with problems of urban mass transit, these tend to get tangled up with construction of urban roads, an activity under the purview of the Commerce Department. And city transportation, whether by bus or private car, ties into the problem of air pollution, which is the worry of the Department of Health, Education and Welfare (HEW).

Mr. Case indicates it would be a good idea to centralize all these activities in the new department. As a start, he would expand the title to Department of Urban and Suburban Affairs (DUSA).

It's clear the Senator has scarcely scratched the possibilities. The Labor Department is busily retraining workers, a chore that is certainly related to urban development. The Justice Department helps train city police forces, the Agriculture Department provides food for the cities' needy, and where would the cities be without the mail service furnished by the Post Office Department? Why shouldn't these activities, too, be handed over to the new agency?

Indeed, if this approach is pushed far enough, perhaps we can reduce much of the Government to a single agency—something like the Department of Interurban, Suburban, Mechanical and Agricultural Labyrinths.

LINDLEY H. CLARK, JR.

February 15, 1963

Similarity Breeds Content

It has been increasingly noted in late years that the American who prides himself on being a non-conformist in matters of the intellect is a most conforming man.

When he hates a Senator Joe McCarthy, he must hate him with precisely the same intensity and in precisely the same idiom that are exhibited by every other member of the non-conformist lodge. When he decries fin-tailed automobiles, he must sound like every other professional critic of Detroit. When he inveighs against popular culture, or advertising, or the U.S. foreign policy, or businessmen, he must speak as a certified dues payer in the self-proclaimed "liberal" guild.

Since the materials for a study of the conforming non-conformer are all about us, Morris Freedman, a New Yorker who now teaches English in New Mexico, has had a comparatively easy time polishing the creature off in a sprightly book called *Confessions of a Conformist*. Mr. Freedman is, actually, an intellectual who has no desire either to conform or to non-conform; he wants merely to be himself and to like what he likes. But he finds himself pushed into a temporary alliance with the people the non-conformists call conformists.

To ram home his points, Mr. Freedman attacks the shibboleths of the professional non-conformer head-on. For topic head purposes he proclaims that he likes to read advertisements and that he enjoys an interesting billboard along a highway more than he does a stunted or misshapen tree. He prefers a good Hollywood film to a dimly lighted one made in Italy. He doesn't object to some chrome on his car, and he would rather have room to stretch his legs in a Buick or a Chrysler than to coop himself up in a compact importation from Germany.

When one gets past Mr. Freedman's flashy broadstroking of his generic likes and dislikes, however, one comes upon a fairly subtle man. It turns out that Mr. Freedman's real animus is against anybody, whether non-conformer or conformer, who substitutes labeling for thoughtful living. The labeler on both sides, he thinks, provokes the counter-labeler. And as the labelers and the counter-labelers are busy fighting it out (as they happen to be doing at the moment in our school boards as "educationists" and "anti-educationists") the whole question of intelligent weighing of choices tends to get lost. Real clarity disappears.

Take, for one example, the business of trying to deal with American industrial life in terms of labels about conformity and anti-conformity itself. Mr. Freedman says it can't be done in any meaningful way. The truth is that any well-ordered business must be a blend of both the conformist and anti-conformist. In most businesses an individualist in the accountant's office would be totally out of place: balance sheets must balance, and the only way to add a column of figures correctly is to use conventional arithmetic.

Moreover, there are good functional reasons for refraining from dressing like a scarecrow while engaged in door-to-door canvassing. On the other hand, very few businesses choose the narrowly trained conformist for policy-making jobs. The "organization man" is needed, but he generally remains embedded in the ranks. The non-conformist tells him what to do.

Mr. Freedman's basic objection to American intellectual life is that it cuts itself off from intelligence. It runs to unquestioning discipleship, not to independence of judgment. When a Veblen coins a phrase about "conspicuous consumption," a host of Veblenian disciples spring up to practice what Mr. Freedman calls "conspicuous rejection." When a young "rebel" wants to assert his difference by wearing a black turtleneck shirt, black glasses, thong sandals and a rope for a belt, he doesn't do it at home, where it would really be individual, he seeks out the company of a mob of like-minded Bohemians in the North Beach area of San Francisco, where the beatniks react as predictably to stimuli as ever did the Rotarians in Sinclair Lewis' Zenith.

So it goes, as the anti-conformists become the new conformists and the whole world goes Greenwich Village in its reaction to such things as Victorianism and McKinleyism and Babbittry. As for this reviewer, he dropped around to a dinner at his hometown Kiwanis Club the other night. He had an interesting chat with the past president of the club, a tree surgeon who wears a beard and teaches painting in his spare time. He talked with a cheerful individualist who wore a loud vest and who aspires nonetheless to be a high official in a supposedly conformist town. He thought about Mr. Freedman's book as the discussion veered from horses to apples, and back again. And he wondered what was new in the espresso coffee set.

JOHN CHAMBERLAIN

March 14, 1961

THE VIEW FROM 44 BROAD

The Dream and the Reality

When Americans of that generation went off to fight World War I, there were few who doubted that they were fighting to save the world for democracy. It all seemed quite simple to us then.

All we needed was total victory over the enemy. Not merely to halt the Kaiser but to destroy entirely the enemy governments, to break up forever the hateful political institutions of the old world and to create a new world of little democracies after our own image.

When Americans again went off to fight World War II there were few who did not know that its seeds lay in the very totality of that victory 20 years earlier. The achievement of our war aims in Germany left its people in chaos and finally prey to a demagogue preaching vengeance. By destroying the Austro-Hungarian empire we created a new power vacuum in Eastern Europe that plagues us yet. And in the Far East we left a disorder from which the Japanese grew their new empire.

There are few so blind today as not to see from what blunders comes the threat of World War III. Again, we destroyed the enemy entirely only to create a new and greater one. It is not President Kennedy—nor Eisenhower nor Truman—who is to blame for the dangers of the hour. It is our own fatal fascination, which President Roosevelt embodied, with the idea that if we can just win total victory over our enemies, then all will be resolved—that out of the ashes of evil destroyed there will spring the brave new world.

It is a fascination which lingers. For once more there are voices, of which perhaps Senator Goldwater's is the strongest, telling us that our only aim must be "total victory" over the forces of Communism. It is not sufficient that we check Soviet aggressions. Nor that we achieve a balance of power which makes real coexistence a necessity for the Russians. We must destroy Soviet Communism utterly.

Of course those who thus dream of a total victory over Communism do not advocate global war; they would achieve their ends by other means. Yet it is, inexorably, a policy admitting only one instrument for its achievement. No man in the Kremlin will acquiesce in the liquidation of the Russian empire, in the surrender of East Germany or Poland or Czechoslovakia or Hungary. If we are to achieve that kind of victory, the only way is by war—nuclear war.

And if we gained that total victory, what then? Let us suppose that there were a nuclear war between the United States and Russia, suppose even that its end were absolute and complete annihilation of the institutions of Communist Russia. In short, the total victory of which these men speak.

To begin with, we would be confronted with the problem of what to do with the ashes of Russia itself, the vast land mass stretching from the Black Sea to the Pacific. Nor could we expect such a war to come and pass and not leave all Europe as well in destruction. Even in the unlikely event that this country emerged relatively unscathed we should have to take upon our shoulders the staggering burden of occupying, policing, managing and—in time—even rebuilding much of the world.

And what of Red China? Destroying the power of Russia would indeed rid us of one enemy, as we were rid of Hitler and Tojo; but the destruction of one power would again leave an enormous vacuum into which would pour no man knows what forces. Or must we destroy all Asia as well, and take for ourselves hegemony over the whole?

So much of the problem any man can imagine. Yet there is more. For we delude ourselves if we think that by the mere disappearance of Communist Russia we thereby put an end to the ferments of Africa, of South America, of the Middle East, of Southeast Asia.

The truth is, or so it seems to us, that the chaos which would confront the world after such a holocaust defies even those imaginations trained by the failure of our last two efforts to obliterate all the forces of evil in one blow.

This blind faith in the magic of "total victory" is worse than an illusion. It can be fatal because it assumes that evil exists in the world only by sufferance, that all it takes to destroy it is a Godlike power.

A nuclear war we may have, precisely because evil exists in the world. If such a war comes, we must have the courage to face it just as before men have faced wars and death rather than surrender to barbarism. Indeed, if we show that courage to the barbarians we offer the best hope that we will spare the world that tragedy.

But this courage is something else than the delusion that if, somehow, we can just slay the enemy in front of us then we shall put all aright and that the world will live happily ever after in peace. Good men always dream, but wise men never confuse their dream with reality.

VERMONT ROYSTER

October 16, 1961

The Fear of Peace

Not only Soviet propagandists but also many Americans harbor the suspicion that our prosperity is largely defense-based. Senator Humphrey, to mention just one, fears that disarmament could land the economy in a bad fix.

Large-scale disarmament, to be sure, looks remote, but this notion that the economy could not prosper without heavy defense spending deserves to be squashed. And along with it the companion idea that defense contractors are automatically profiteers.

So we think some recent remarks of General Electric Chairman Cordiner are worth consideration, G.E. being the nation's third biggest defense contractor. His company, Mr. Cordiner said, is not attracted to defense work because of the profits—they're too small. Rather plainly, the size and nature of such a firm almost forces it into that activity.

The unprofitability of military work is readily documented. In actual war a contractor's production vastly increases, but here's what happened to U.S. Steel's profits in the last two wars: In 1941 they were $116 million, but thereafter dropped until they finally got down to $58 million in 1945; in 1950, during which the Korean War started, they were $215 million, but by 1952 they were down to $143 million.

As to the impact of disarmament on prosperity, Mr. Cordiner observed that "a lower level of expenditures for defense could permit a corresponding reduction in Federal income taxes. The reduction of taxes, one of the most serious cost factors, would immediately improve the competitive position of United States manufacturers in domestic and overseas markets from the standpoint of both prices and capital formation."

Here again, recent history supports that view. With the end of the fighting in Korea, it was possible to cut military spending. Though this contributed to a mild and temporary slowdown, it also gave the Administration an opportunity to make tax cuts valued at about $7.5 billion, and in the wake of that came a prosperity beyond anything the country had previously known.

Indeed, our whole history refutes the contention that prosperity depends on huge defense outlays. When have we had such outlays, anyway? Only during the war periods themselves and in this partly peacetime decade that began with Korea. Otherwise we have maintained hardly more than a token military establishment and the economy has grown greatly. And so it is likely to be again if we avoid the temptation of the shortsighted to make the Government somehow "take up the slack."

Naturally there are bound to be temporary economic dislocations in even a gradual disarmament; Mr. Cordiner says the temporary idling of workers is the only part of the prospect that does worry him. Also some smaller firms have unwisely sought to make their living almost entirely out of defense contracts, and they could reasonably expect to suffer.

But even the dislocation, as a national problem, can be overemphasized. The convulsions after World War II were considerable, with millions thrown on the labor market and a huge cutback in military spending. Yet the dreaded depression did not ensue; quite the contrary, and quite naturally when these matters are viewed in the light of common sense.

The United States does indeed have something to fear from any sweeping international disarmament agreement—the political traps set by the Soviets. The last thing it has to fear is that the economy will collapse.

For the record is clear: it is peace, not war or war preparation, that has nurtured the prosperity of the world's most prosperous nation.

JOSEPH E. EVANS

December 14, 1959

"What big financial deal? . . . They're figuring out how many
calories they had for lunch."

Cornflakes, Soap and the U.S.A.

It's awfully easy to say, as Vice President Johnson once did, that
a nation capable of popularizing cornflakes should be able to tell the
world about itself.

It is also easy to say that one reason why America may not be wag-
ing the war of ideas around the world more effectively is that President
Kennedy is expected to be a sort of global sales manager for the

United States, in addition to carrying his many other responsibilities.

Advertising executive Charles H. Brower said something of the sort the other day when he renewed a suggestion, which pops up every now and then, that the United States create a new department "dedicated to selling the United States to other nations."

What seems to worry the people to whom the idea of a governmental advertising department appeals is the Soviet Union's generally monolithic image and apparent singleness of purpose. Why, they appear to be saying, can't the United States present a similarly cohesive and determined picture to the world?

Well, for one thing, fortunately for all of us the United States is not run the same way as the Soviet Union is. All the world can hear the daily conflicting opinions of our commentators and politicians. It can watch with unobstructed view the efforts of one Federal department to outmaneuver another. All our crimes and unpleasant domestic problems are recorded plainly in our press. As seen from abroad we may sometimes seem to be disunited, disorganized and uncertain of purpose, a land of dissonant voices, but that is the way things often are in the United States The alternative, rigid and complete unity, is something we do not think anybody really wants, even those who most loudly deplore the confusing picture America presents.

All this is just another way of saying that the United States is not cornflakes or soap. It is a highly complex combination of ingredients, not every one of which appeals to all people, even some who live here. Any attempt to "sell" it faces a number of pitfalls.

We have seen that the present Government propaganda instrument, the United States Information Agency, even with what has been described as a "tin-cup budget," has succeeded in stirring resentment against the United States abroad, an effect just the reverse of what was intended. Any sort of propaganda super-agency runs the real and serious risk of creating disaffection on a much grander scale, and indeed of sounding wholly out of tune with the very thing it is trying to sell.

Just what is it that America has to "sell"? Is it the world's highest standard of living? Is it a picture of a nation with so many automobiles that cities are hard put to find room for them? Is it the labor-saving gadgets in incredible profusion available to American housewives? It is, of course, none of these things, as attractive as they may seem. It is simply the freedom that America offers every man to work out his own destiny.

To disseminate this simple truth requires, it seems to us, no elaborate governmental sales organization. It is a truth that has drawn men to America for more than 350 years and has captured the imaginations of people all over the world. It is a truth so powerful that our chief competitor in the war of ideas goes to great lengths to prevent its citizens from seeing American books and magazines, from listening to American radio transmissions.

Whatever "image" the United States currently may present to people of other nations, we do not believe that the American concept of freedom is losing its appeal. But it could, if we start thinking liberty is something we can sell only if we wrap it in a new package and merchandise it hard enough.

COWL RIDER

November 10, 1961

In Praise of a Junk Dealer

Among our friends is a man who came to this country many years ago and has prospered by buying and selling old automobiles, worn-out refrigerators and other cast-off things.

Now, if we understand him rightly, he has come to days when he is a little saddened by his life, troubled with the feeling that by just being a junk man he has wasted much of it.

Partly, perhaps, this is just an old man's feeling of being distant from his children, who have studied important things at college and speak so much better than he. But part of it is a deep troubling that in a world where so much needs to be done he has done nothing of much consequence.

Of course someone could point out to him that he has passed on two sons and a daughter, raised them to be people of character, educated them, and started them upon their own way. This is no small accomplishment, and he surely must know it. Yet it does not fully comfort him, for he thinks he lives in a world where value is measured by other accomplishments. Buying and selling junk, he has come to feel, is not socially useful.

We suspect that our friend, these days, is not alone in this feeling of despondency of the usefulness of his life. A young girl is taught in college that childbearing and homemaking is a wasted life; she must get out and "do something" for society. A young man is cheered if he turns his talent away from "making money" to some more seemly public service where he will redistribute the money of others.

Buying and selling is a function particularly disdained. Some years ago there was a hit comedy on Broadway that pictured a junk dealer as a sort of parasite, growing rich on a nation's trouble. Another prize-winning play had as its theme the thought that the life of a salesman is a life tragically misspent. In novels, in movies, in television, the man of business may be either hero or villain, but there is never any suggestion that by running a furniture factory the men in the executive suite are performing a social service.

Almost any day our friend can pick up a newspaper, a magazine or a "serious" book and read what a terrible thing it is to be part of an affluent society. To labor, to save, to care for one's own, to prosper —perhaps these things are not to be scorned, but what is there in them that is a contribution to society?

Against such a tide of sentiment, we can offer little to comfort. But we would, if we could, make him see what it is he really does.

He gathers up that which is useless and puts it to use. The debris that would otherwise be waste is collected, sorted, shipped and distributed to return again in the stream of raw materials that feed our factories. The shiny new ambulance which our village has bought, the new factory rising on the outskirts of your town, the highway our Government is building for that backward nation of Asia—all these things would be costlier but for those who buy and sell junk.

And if our friend has prospered it is only because he has learned to do this efficiently. No one rewards him unless he can deliver what the economy needs, at the time it needs it, and at the cheapest cost. No one excuses him if he bungles the job.

In this he no wise differs from all the thousands whose business is buying and selling. Yet the shoes the scornful wear, the bread they eat, the paper upon which they write, the things they use when they go off to uplift the lowly of Africa, these things are there at the place and time because others buy and sell.

Not so glamorous, perhaps, as the Peace Corps. Not so intellectual as writing a book on our ills. Not so much prestige as a desk on the New Frontier. But who can say that in those places men do more for their fellows?

VERMONT ROYSTER

August 8, 1961

Bridge on the River Arno

Seventeen years ago, German troops retreating from the city of Florence blew up the Holy Trinity Bridge spanning the Arno River. Tumbled into the yellow mud were statues representing the four seasons, which had been mounted on the bridge to celebrate a royal wedding in 1608.

In Florence the other day, a painstaking task of rebuilding was completed as workmen cemented in place Primavera, or Spring, the last piece of a treasure that many had feared was lost forever. If he cares to, the modern tourist may once again walk where the Medici wedding party went centuries before.

As 1962 opens, this event appears microscopic in the bulk of the news, most of which relates and foreshadows destruction on a wide scale. Indeed, pessimists argue, not without evidence, that men are contriving to destroy themselves and all the works of civilization. Of what importance, then, is the restoration of a small bridge in an old city outside the mainstream of modern history?

Of no importance, perhaps, except as a passing reminder of continuity, of the tenacity of man, who is not only a destroyer but also a patient and persistent retriever of his follies and failures.

RICHARD WHALEN

January 2, 1962

Nut and Bolt Art

An artist fellow in New York has put together a machine that paints. It grasps some brushes, dips them in paint, and moves them over a canvas, according to an unpredictable pattern suggested by a sort of player-piano punched paper.

This development shouldn't be very surprising. There already are sculptors who create, out of odds and ends, mobile sculptures that blow themselves up, and music of sorts is being composed on electronic machines. Why not machine-made paintings?

Well, one good reason why not is that the machine-made art is indistinguishable from the works—if that is the word—turned out by artists who smear paint on their feet, walk around on a canvas, and then frame the result. So we can't see how a machine that paints represents much progress.

In the invasion of mechanics into the arts, the sculpture that destroys itself is surely head and shoulders above other mediums of expression. For the worst thing about the mechanically induced painting is that, when it's been completed, it just sits there.

August 14, 1961

Fossils Yet Alive

A reader recently challenged a report in this newspaper that horseshoe crabs are inedible. The fact is, the reader said, these creatures are a gastronomic delight.

Because the subject of horseshoe crabs is one that springs up in this office only infrequently, counsel was sought of the scientific community. But even the scientists were none too certain whether this crab is fit for the table ("There is a difference between what is eaten and what is edible," one expert commented).

This exchange of opinion brought to mind some personal experiences with horseshoe crabs and some facts about these peculiar creatures that have rightly been called "living fossils."

Long ago in our youth, during the barefoot days of summer, we stumbled upon our first horseshoe crab. Picking up the crawling thing by its spiny tail, we asked a near-by fisherman if you could eat it. "*You* can, fella," was the reply.

The horseshoe crab (also called the king crab, horsefoot crab, pan crab, and swordtail) resembles a black, overturned wash basin, about a foot in diameter, and featuring a sharply pointed tail also about a foot in length. Underneath the wash basin is a tiny body, composed of a heart, brain, digestive system and spidery legs.

The spidery legs are appropriate, incidentally, because the horseshoe crab is not a crab at all, but a member in good standing of the family that includes the spider and the scorpion.

With such relatives it's not surprising that persons coming upon a horseshoe crab for the first time react much as Emily Dickinson did to snakes (". . . a tighter breathing and Zero at the Bone").

This fairly general attitude toward unpretty animal forms is not without its uses, as young boys have long known. In fact, taking advantage of this fear has been a predilection of the youthful male since an enterprising lad first dropped an earthworm down his sister's back.

Horseshoe crabs are splendidly designed for such sport and we recall an incident that proves their service. This trick involved a dead horseshoe crab and a trap of the kind with a metal bar which, when released, snaps in an arc from one side of a wooden base to the other—a larger version of the conventional mouse trap.

One afternoon, at an hour forever imprinted on fond memory, such a trap was set on the beach, a dead horseshoe crab placed on top of it, and a string tied to the trap's release lever and run under the sand to a point near by where a group of boys sat innocently contemplating the ships at sea. In time a group of strollers came along and their attention was quickly drawn to the strange-looking black object with the swordlike tail. Clearly, they were city folks who had never seen so repulsive a creature, because they dallied at length to examine and discuss the fearsome thing at their feet.

Now there are some activities of men in which timing is all, and it does not strain the bounds of modesty to say that in this instance the timing was magnificent. At the precise moment when the strollers were all bending over to study the crab better, a deft hand pulled the string and the alien monster shot into the air like a Redstone rocket.

Some distant bystanders who were privileged to witness the event said the horseshoe crab reached an altitude of 10 feet. Others held it soared even higher. But all impartial observers agreed that, whatever the mark set by the crab, it was easily bettered by the strollers in immediate attendance.

Our most recent brush with horseshoe crabs came late last spring when, while fishing from a small boat not a hundred yards from the beach, our line tightened severely. Reeling it in we found we had snagged two horseshoe crabs that were coupled together like railroad cars.

A marine biologist in the boat explained that the creatures were not in the process of mating in the usual sense, but that the female had been towing the male to a spot close to shore where she would deposit her eggs. The male would then emit fertilizing fluid around the general area of the eggs and, in time, the few eggs that escaped destruction from storms, birds and fish would hatch and continue the life of a species that has been around for 300 million years.

Unlike almost all other forms of life, horseshoe crabs have not gone through an evolutionary process and today are exactly as they were 100 million years before the first dinosaur appeared on the earth. For this reason they are the subject of unusually intensive study by paleontologists and marine biologists.

No real commercial use has been found for them, although efforts have been made to grind them into fertilizer or poultry feed. If any humans regularly eat them, it is largely a well-kept secret, although some people consider the eggs of the horseshoe crab a great delicacy. *Bon appetit.*

EDWIN A. ROBERTS, JR.

January 16, 1962

Notes on Swordsmanship

NEW YORK—The stage of New York's Metropolitan Opera is hardly the most likely spot to look for an exhibition of expert swordsmanship, but Met audiences, perhaps without knowing it, have been viewing an increasingly skillful brand of onstage fencing during the past three seasons.

The man responsible for the change is a 42-year-old Yugoslav-born fencing maestro named Oscar Frank Richard Gregory Otto Milan Dusan Alexandre Petre Mark Kolombatovich.

"That's to distinguish me from every other Oscar Kolombatovich," he explains. Mr. Kolombatovich, who has already started coaching his "pupils" for the new season, began his association with the Met in 1958. Acting on the advice of a friend, Francis Robinson, who is assistant manager at the Met, he wrote to conductor Erich Leinsdorf, pointing out that he could teach fencing, knew opera, spoke several languages, and could provide sound technical advice on period weapons and armament. Dr. Leinsdorf accepted him, and he became the first and only resident fencing master in American opera.

"Opera people," says Maestro Kolombatovich, "are easier to teach than any other people—because they're such hams.

"But they also have a very good sense of tempo and timing—important in fencing—and they are willing to accept the discipline of fencing, because they have already accepted the discipline of music."

Why are the Met singers interested in learning to fence? According to tenor Barry Morell, he started going to the classes so that he wouldn't look ridiculous on stage with a sword.

"Many people do," he declares.

"My biggest problem," says tenor Albert DaCosta, "is that I am a big man (six-foot-two, 245 pounds). Fencing has been a tremendous help to me in my body movement on stage."

Mr. DaCosta was once a much bigger man—about 100 pounds bigger. The fencing sessions helped him keep his body firm while he was stripping off the excess weight at the rate of four or five pounds a week.

"The best comment I can give," says Mr. DaCosta, "is that serious opera people are eager to attend the sessions because they really get a lot out of it."

If one were to believe singer Ezio Flagello, however, some of the singers get more than fencing out of the sessions. Frequently the women singers report to the sessions wearing skin-tight leotards—not calculated to improve the concentration of the male fencers.

On one occasion, basso Louis Sgarro complained to one curvaceous little miss: "Please—wear some clothes. Those leotards are too distracting. I can't concentrate on the fencing."

He was interrupted by a furious roar from basso Flagello.

"Animale!" shouted the enraged singer. "Shut up! Do you think I come here to fence?"

Maestro Kolombatovich has his own ways of dealing with the ladies. When he discovered that lovely little Lorna Ceniceras of the Metropolitan Opera Studio was standing too stiffly in the *en garde* position, he told her: "A woman and a fencer—you're both now—must be loose to be effective."

The *en garde* of the petite coloratura improved miraculously.

In addition to his fencing classes, Maestro Kolombatovich also helps choreograph the onstage dueling scenes.

"Fencing on stage is like dancing," he tells his pupils. "I lead; you follow. I advance; you retreat. Before the kill, you fence at a distance and make all the flourishes you like. Then on a signal from the winner—you know who he is ahead of time—you move in. The winner makes a feint and thrust and it's done."

The maestro enjoys a second distinction as the only theatrical armorer in America. A few years ago he acquired a large portion of the Met's store of armor and weapons. Just after World War II, he had learned metal casting while working in a foundry. Now he produces period weapons and armor for the stage by casting them from the Met's original models.

The maestro's weapons have an added suitability for the stage. He casts them in a lightweight metal alloy which is easy to handle even for the weakest performers. As a bonus, the metal clangs with a delightfully musical ring when swords clash. For the Met's production of one work, Mr. Kolombatovich manufactured 40 Biblical-style broadswords for use by the Babylonians and the Israelites in the opera.

Of all his various activities at the Met, what does he like most?

"Most of all," he says, "I like to kill tenors."

FREDRIC C. APPEL

October 9, 1961

Rousseau and Modern Tyranny

Jean-Jacques Rousseau may not have intended it, but his political theorizing, which helped extremists take over the French Revolution, makes him one of the more important ancestors of totalitarianism.

When he exalted the concept of the "general will" (meaning that a majority has the right to do what it pleases without reference to the prior rights of individuals), he helped set the stage for all the typical modern tyrannies operating in the name of the "people."

Since he has been one of the great architects of the collapse of the true governmental function (which is to protect citizens in the peaceful exercise of their individual rights), we can hardly have enough information bearing on the genesis of his ideas.

Frances Winwar, author of *Jean-Jacques Rousseau: Conscience of an Era,* does not presume to clarify the nature of her subject's misreading of the history of Roman and Greek republicanism. But her fascinating chronicle of Jean-Jacques' vagabond career in search of self-justification is enough to confirm our worst suspicions.

Long ago Professor Irving Babbitt of Harvard said, in effect, that the trouble with Rousseau was that he never learned to think. Miss Winwar, without making any bibliographical acknowledgment to Babbitt's *Rousseau and Romanticism,* shows how Rousseau managed to evade the first duty of a political or social scientist, which is to learn something about the actual nature of human beings before prescribing what they may or may not do.

If Rousseau had not wreaked such devastation on the human race, his life, as set forth by Miss Winwar, might pass as a comedy of misdirected intellectuality. The young Rousseau was, to put it roughly, a dead beat.

His father, a Geneva watchmaker, apprenticed him to an engraver. No doubt the terms of the apprenticeship were severe, but even if Jean-Jacques had had an angelic being for a master he would still have revolted against completing his vocational education. The boy was just allergic to work.

Well, there is no reason why a young man who wanted to become a writer or a teacher should have been forced to learn a manual trade. But the Rousseau who fled from Geneva was not looking for a real education; he was in search of a soft snap. He found it when he came to Madame de Warens' doorstep in Annecy.

Madame de Warens was a mother to him; she was also his first mistress. To establish himself in Madame de Warens' good graces, the Protestant Jean-Jacques vagabonded his way to Turin in the Italian Piedmont, where he undertook to become a proselyte of the Catholic Church. Miss Winwar does not go so far as to say that he was a religious fraud, but it is obvious that Jean-Jacques, from the day when he first drew breath, never accepted the Catholic doctrine that man is naturally sinful and must wage a personal struggle for redemption. To Rousseau, man was by nature good; it was only his birth into Society, that organized monster, which forced him to become evil.

The ironies mount up as Miss Winwar follows Rousseau's career. As a secretary to the French Ambassador to the Venetian Republic, Rousseau, the professed champion of the idea that all men are equal, insisted on pulling his rank. He found himself a mistress in Paris, a naïve girl from the provinces named Thérèse le Vasseur, and proceeded to have several children by her, all of whom he packed off to foundling homes.

After abandoning his own children, he wrote a book, *Émile,* which endeavored to tell the world how children should be reared. Miss Winwar says with a straight face that *Émile* was the product of Rousseau's "conscience." She does not, however, indicate that the author was ever bothered in his conscience by the fact that he had had no personal experience whatsoever in the raising of children.

Rousseau's *Nouvelle Héloïse* was acclaimed throughout Europe as a love story. But Rousseau himself was incapable of losing himself in love. His *Social Contract* was seized upon by the revolutionary generation of 1789 as a justification for creating a republican State.

But Rousseau, the small-town Genevan, had not envisaged the possibility that the "general will" could be made the excuse for sending members of recalcitrant minorities to the guillotine. The man who had exalted the individual conscience had failed to make provision in his political thought for the idea that majorities might be just as monstrous as kings.

In short, Rousseau, who never thought of the individual as a person with responsibilities to self, family or the rights of one's neighbors, was a mountebank when he undertook to speak for the common man.

JOHN CHAMBERLAIN

November 6, 1962

A Tale for Our Times

It's an entertaining tale, this not so recent novel of William Golding's that has become the latest campus rage and is making a belated bid for the bestseller list. But *Lord of the Flies* is something more than a well-spun yarn, and we hope its point will not be lost.

The story is a simple one. A group of schoolboys are shipwrecked on an island. There they must not only struggle for survival but start from scratch to build some sort of society. One of them, a nice young lad named Ralph, wants the island to be run fairly, with peace and order. Jack is the strong man of the young toughs, whose idea is that everything belongs to the strong and the ruthless.

As it often does in fairy tales, fate intervenes; rescuers arrive to save young Ralph just as, broken and friendless, he is being hunted down by the savage Jack. Mr. Golding himself is not very hopeful about how otherwise the struggle between good and evil would have ended.

"My sympathies are all with Ralph," he remarked in a recent interview with *The National Observer*, "but I don't think he will necessarily win out because he is likable . . . The 'nice guy' frequently loses."

It is often hard for Americans to believe it. The standard fare of our fairly tales—they come to us these days on television—is that no matter how dark the peril the defenders somehow save the innocent, and when the gunsmoke has cleared the good sheriff protecting peace and order stands tall and victorious over the vanquished villain.

The fable colors much of our outlook on the world. Did we not, as weak colonists, slay the dragon of St. George and gain our independence because we were right? True, we have since then had many a perilous hour, but from Bull Run to Pearl Harbor the good cause has always emerged triumphant. If anyone doubts the invincibility of righteousness, let him ask Hitler or Mussolini or Tojo.

So it is that a great many Americans today have a simple faith that our ultimate victory over predatory Communism is somehow foreordained because our cause is just.

There are those who think that if we will be patient when pushed around, then the Communists will be impressed by our moral virtues and in time come to share them. There are others who say we must not meet force with force lest we lose our friends. Still others that because we know war to be a moral evil we can do nothing to risk it even to defend ourselves against a moral evil.

Finally, there are those who, while not sharing these views, nonetheless believe that we need not go in haste to face the foe. We can postpone that day until tomorrow, confident that when patience is exhausted, and we have been pushed back into the final corner, then we can arouse ourselves and as before emerge triumphant. To nearly everyone the picture of the United States defeated, of America overrun, of Communism victorious, is almost inconceivable.

Yet the allegory of a schoolboy's island is not without its precedent in history. No doubt the citizens of Rome felt the same disbelief even as they saw the peril. But their civilization, their laws, their culture, their advancement in knowledge, the numbers of their legions did not keep them from being vanquished by barbarians, tough, determined and ruthless. Rome died bit by bit, sliced up like a piece of salami.

What we may be in danger of forgetting is that America does not stand tall in the world merely because it stands for peace and justice but because, at least until this hour, it has been willing to meet roughness with toughness in the name of its good causes.

It's just as well to have a teller of tales remind us that nice guys don't always win. For however it may seem on television, on the real frontier the ruffians lost only because peaceful citizens learned to use a forty-five.

VERMONT ROYSTER

October 5, 1962

The Foe of Man

Both the Soviet Communist Party's wordy "draft program" and Khrushchev's speech this week contain a restatement of a familiar theme: Capitalism is in crisis and decay and therefore the triumph of Communism is certain everywhere in the world.

Unfortunately a good many people fear that such may turn out to be the case; some, indeed, are ready to throw away their manhood and rush to the servitude of the new masters.

So it is perhaps useful to take another look at what might be called

the spiritual values of Communism—for it does presume to spirituality
—and our own.

In one sense, Communism is just another form of the tyranny of the
State that has dogged man throughout his difficult history. But it is also
something far more than that; it is a peculiarly aberrant system of
belief—a pretentious secularized religion, as Dr. Niebuhr has called it.

The key to this pseudo-religion is falsity. Practically every other word
in the new party program is a demonstrable and preposterous lie; for
example, Soviet society alone "insures the real liberty of the individual."

In considerable part, the falsity goes right back to Marx and his
philosophical progenitors. Just about everything Marx predicted about
the world's economic and political evolution turned out to be dead
wrong. The man probably was sincere enough; his trouble was a woe-
fully deficient understanding of history and of human nature.

For this reason, Marx has been a terrible headache for the Russian
Communists from the moment they seized power. They have had to
revise him constantly, and the new party program contains some further
revisions. More importantly, in practice they have had to distort or
deny much of his fundamental thinking; otherwise they couldn't make
anything go at all. Thus, only a few years after the revolution, Lenin
had to introduce a sort of free-enterprise "new economic policy" for a
while.

The result is that today the Soviet economy is a weird patchwork of
socialist and capitalist practice. The impossibility of running a Marxist
economy turned Stalin to terror, but that was self-defeating, and ever
since the Red rulers have been making some concessions to human
nature. To that extent, human nature has won out over Marx. Yet this
ridiculous shambles of an ideology, this tissue of lies and perversions,
goes on; and it is this which is offered to the world.

So it is a question whether the world can reasonably be expected,
short of force by arms, to buy such an absurdity. There are, to be sure,
many gullible people in the world, but there have always been; despite
them, other men have made considerable progress in constructing a
coherent set of spiritual values, a tenable philosophy of freedom, and
nowhere so well as in the West.

Whether expressed in religious or secular terms, this philosophy does
not attempt to deny man's instincts but proceeds from truths about
them ascertained and verified in the long struggle up from the cave.
It is a truth, not a figment of someone's imagination, that the individual has an intense concern about his individuality, which is displayed
in his obstinate determination to be free. And because man also has the
capacity to reason, he has been able to build whole intellectual systems
of value, especially in the West, based on this fundamental instinct.

These values obviously inspire all the art, science and philosophy that we lump together as Western culture. They are the genesis of the free-market economy and its political twin, the complex and sophisticated mode of government we loosely call democratic. In sum, there is an inherent logic in our values, flowing straight from truths about man to the establishment of free institutions.

Despite that, Communism could conceivably win the world, though the nature of man suggests it could not hold it long. Meantime, as we gird for the long struggle, it should strengthen us to reflect that we face a foe whose power rests on a basic weakness: an anti-intellectual, irrational non-philosophy which is the foe not of us alone but of man himself.

JOSEPH E. EVANS

August 9, 1961

Some Shop Talk About a Strike

In what follows we will talk about some problems of shrinking markets, competition, rising costs, make-work rules, strikes, and other things not without public interest. Yet it is only fair to warn the reader that mostly we will be talking about family matters, the affairs of a business we love and in which we have spent a lifetime.

No one ever foresees precisely the consequences of cataclysmic events; you know only that afterward everything will be different. For our business we suspect the New York newspaper strike will prove such an event. Perhaps things will be better when it is over, perhaps worse. But never the same.

One reason for this is that the strike itself is merely the culmination of long events. The simple truth of the matter is that the shape of metropolitan journalism has already changed in almost every other big city in America; in New York it has struggled to remain what it was a generation ago in terms of the number and kind of newspapers that dwell there.

These shaping forces involve much more than union problems. Television fills better than newspapers one function which once belonged to the newspaper page. The arrival of the daily paper in the home is no longer, as it was in the days of our childhood, a big family event, entertaining the children with the comics, Mother with a description of the First Lady's new gown and Father with a picture of the Yankee ball game.

The newspaper, moreover, is no longer the only source of news about the outside world. TV reporting has its limitations. But some things it does superbly; it can and does bring you quickly a simple recital of the big events of the day, often letting you participate in a way no newspaper can.

Meanwhile, the growing and thriving "suburban" newspapers are filling another void. In a sprawling city like New York or Chicago or Los Angeles the average dweller couldn't care less about the affairs of a neighborhood across town. For what happens in their own neighborhood, readers today are better served by their local newspaper than by the big-city paper.

True, all this provides a pallid diet for a good many people; they want something more than they can get from either TV or their community paper. On the other hand it is sufficient for a great many other

people, and these sources fulfill the function of the kind of mass newspaper of the past that never offered much more than that anyway.
We suspect New York's strike has brought this home to New Yorkers;
sad to say, many of them are going to buy fewer newspapers hereafter.

All of this is, in a way, quite obvious, just as it is obvious that television has cut a big hole in one of the big sources of a newspaper's
revenue, its advertising. But apparently its meanings have not yet sunk
into sociologists, newspaper managers and labor union officials.

The sociologists will mourn the passing of any big-city newspaper on
philosophic grounds (as we do on personal grounds) without realizing
that those which pass do not always leave a vacuum in society's needs;
often they pass because there is no longer any need for them. Sociologists can be comforted (as we can) by the fact that the newspaper
business as a whole is actually growing; its dynamic character is shown
by the very changes it is undergoing.

But the changes strike deep. One of the most important of these is
that the newspaper business can no longer support the kind of uneco-
nomic practices which it may have been able to do in the days when
the big-city newspaper was the lord of the news domain.

A simple example is the fact that the standard-size New York City
newspapers are now all going to sell at a ten-cent price. The nickel
newspaper has been bad economics for years; retaining it was largely
an effort to keep circulation figures up to compete with TV or other
media, which is ridiculous. We happen to think a good newspaper is
a thing of value, not a giveaway; certainly its value can be greater and
the public better served when its balance sheet is healthier.

But the most important example of change unadjusted-to lies in the
area of labor costs and union practices.

For while it is true that metropolitan newspapers have been hurt by
inevitable competition, it is also true that they are less able to meet that
competition and to survive it when they are saddled with senseless labor
costs growing out of union demands enforced by a monopoly position
of the unions.

It would be unfair to blame the printers' union for all this, although
it precipitated the New York strike. Relatively speaking anyway, the
printers have been more realistic than many other unions in accepting
new equipment and methods. But the point, really, is not to assign
blame to specific unions.

The fault lies, in the first place, with a type of union thinking which
holds that labor is served merely by gouging pay for non-work or by
"protecting" the worker from more efficient tools, all with a total
disregard for what this is doing to the enterprise which must provide
the workers' wages. How are their interests served by helping to put
newspapers out of business?

The fault is aggravated by the very number of unions the New York newspapers must deal with—a total of ten. Time after time this strike has seemed near settlement, only to come unstuck as this or that union membership balked. It happened again just Wednesday night with the last union still on strike, a bitter blow for the men who had their papers ready to roll. How can anyone be expected to run a business on that basis?

The fault is then compounded by a public attitude, expressed in public laws, which permits a union leader—in this case, any one of the ten separate unions—to enforce his demands by the power to close down what enterprises he will. The printer or the reporter who wanted to work in New York all these months could not and cannot do so. The laws and ways of society stopped him.

Naturally this is especially saddening because it touches our own business, and we happen to believe that the public suffers by any diminution of its ways to understand what is happening in the world. A free press that can't print is not only not free; it is useless.

But the public also suffers when, on another day, there is a diminution of steel or of shoes. For us the newspaper strike is a personally poignant reminder that something is wrong when society can find no other way to meet change except to stop men from producing useful things.

VERMONT ROYSTER

March 29, 1963

"How can you get out of politics—what else are you fit for?"

The Paradox of Profits

Just about everybody in this country understands profits for the simple reason that he has to. So it is a curious thing that the whole idea of profits continually encounters so much apparent misunderstanding and vehement opposition.

This week, as it happens, several voices were trying to clear up the confusion, or whatever it is.

Former President Eisenhower put profits in down-to-earth terms when he wrote in the *Saturday Evening Post:* "The proprietor of the cleaning-and-pressing establishment, the corner delicatessen, the filling station and millions of other small-business operators—and their employees—depend just as much on a fair return on the money they have invested as do America's giants of industry."

What profits mean to employees was explained by the National Association of Manufacturers' Charles Sligh, Jr., answering a union demand for explanation. "It is business activity undertaken in the expectation of profit which creates jobs. If the profits are realized, the jobs continue and perhaps grow in number. If the profits are not realized, the jobs and the companies which offer them eventually disappear."

And the inescapable relation of profits to economic growth was touched on by U.S. Steel President Leslie Worthington. If corporate profits had grown as did other parts of the economy, he observed, they would have reached more than $40 billion last year instead of about $23 billion.

If profits had thus kept pace, Mr. Worthington said, "then an additional $17 billion could have helped to modernize and replace more of the nation's estimated $100 billion worth of obsolete plant and equipment. . . . But, unfortunately, profits of $23 billion cannot be stretched to perform a $40 billion job."

Why aren't all these facts better understood? Even more important, why does the Government, which is so concerned about unemployment and inadequate economic growth, exhibit so little concern about this engine of economic activity?

Any genuine misunderstanding is in part, we suppose, a relic of the image of the old-time tycoon grinding down the workers out of his own insatiable greed. Whatever it may have been, the image is false today.

For one thing, the whole structure of corporate management has radically changed. Corporations are rarely one-man operations; they are operated by managers and owned by some 17 million stockholders.

More than that. Profitable business not only means jobs and economic expansion and paying the 17 million owners. It also means, as President Eisenhower notes, such agreeable additional benefits for employees and their families as company pension plans, insurance plans, medical-care plans and all the rest.

For anyone deliberately to perpetrate a false image of business and its profits is mischievous indeed, for it is playing fast and loose with this nation's economic potential. Unfortunately just that is being done. There are too many people in this country today, notably in unions, in universities and in Government, who simply do not like the American economy, whether it is called capitalism, a profit-and-loss system or the free market.

In some cases such people are prisoners of prejudices based on personal resentment or on academic theories which fail to realize that no economy, not even a Communist one, can run without profits. In other cases there are people who quite plainly want to substitute a different kind of profit economy. Not necessarily nationalization, but a more sophisticated kind of Government control of practically everything business and individuals do. For with control goes profit and power.

So the paradox that profits are at once obvious and seemingly abstruse is not so mysterious after all. What is certain is that a nation which persists in shortchanging the profit system is an extremely shortsighted nation.

JOSEPH E. EVANS

August 10, 1962

A Sense of Purpose

It was not so long ago, or so it seems to us, that the young men of Oxford were vowing not to fight for king or country and the campuses of America were dotted with pacifist clubs. Those were the days when Hitler looked down from Berchtesgaden and Tojo talked of walking into Washington.

Today, of course, Hitler and Tojo are no more. And as they passed on they must have found it passing strange that all this happened because thousands of these very same young men were willing to fight and many of them lie in the deeps of the English Channel or in the sands of Tarawa.

Yet, curiously, once more a good many people seem to have been taken by the idea that the Americans and the British have grown too soft, too bemused by the hope of peace and too dismayed by the fear of war, to stand up to the Russians.

Certainly the Russians seem to have had this idea. Mr. Khrushchev acts as if he put some stock in the ancient idea of frightening one's enemies with a fierce visage. He talks as if he thinks the West is too afraid of war to risk it, and that put to the hard test in Berlin or elsewhere, the West will give in.

And if he has such an idea, he may well have gotten it from ourselves. Englishmen have been filling Trafalgar Square, beneath the statue of their greatest warrior, with huge crowds demanding some sort of accommodation with the Russians and decrying more armaments for nuclear war. It was British pacifism, as much as anything else, that forced the Summit conference in the first place.

Nor is the same mood unnoticed here. We are always talking among ourselves about how in the next war there will be no victors, only a holocaust for civilization. In the columns of letters to the editor (including those of this newspaper) some people even write about how we should consider surrender rather than an "unthinkable" nuclear war.

There are, once more, pacifist clubs on campuses, though they go now by other names. And in the press and on platforms, supposedly wise men ask whether we have become so demoralized we will no longer risk dying to defend freedom. A national magazine, disturbed, is running a whole series of articles posing the question, have we lost our sense of national purpose?

Perhaps. But we would like to suggest a look at what has happened, not only in this country but throughout the Free World, since the events of last week.

Here the Summit conference, that great hope of peace, not only failed but ended with insults and threats. And so what has been the people's reaction? Timidity? Irresolution? Disaffection among our fearful allies? Pleas to appease the Russians when the Russians say all they want is an "apology"?

Quite the contrary. Among the people the threats of the Russians transcended any recriminations about possible blunders on our part. The British and the French came resolutely to our side. And anyone who will spend five minutes talking to people will see that the Americans reacted by getting their dander up. A week ago a politician could talk of "accommodation"; to do so today would be to commit political suicide.

This doesn't mean that we Americans have turned warlike, or that we fear an atomic war any less than before. None of us has any illusions about the terrible price the world would pay for a war, whoever won.

It does mean that despite the way we talk, in moments of tranquillity, about how cynically we are going to weigh the values of survival against the loss of freedom, in troubled times we reassert our faith that survival, without freedom, is valueless.

So it was a generation ago, and a generation before that. And though it may seem passing strange to some, so will our national sense of purpose lead us again to the same choice, if ever we must choose.

VERMONT ROYSTER

May 23, 1960

"I used to think he was a crackpot!"

The Prospects of Man

A European living in the middle of the 14th century had every reason to suppose the world was coming to an end. Many did think so, and in consequence were swept into all sorts of psychological frenzies, with whole groups of people publicly repenting the sins they believed were bringing doomsday.

For the Black Death was more than decimating the continent. In some places it killed three-fourths of the population. In Europe as a whole, it is estimated the plague took 25 million lives, or no less than one-fourth of all the people.

In many other times past—almost any era you can think of—
calamities so enormous have occurred as to put mankind's future, or at
least a particular civilization's, in grave doubt. Numerous civilizations
have in fact gone under, and our own Western civilization went into
eclipse for some 500 years after the barbarians sacked its center.

Who in any of the distant reaches of past catastrophes could reasonably have hoped his descendants could see civilization magnificently
flowering anew?

Today in our civilization's nuclear crisis we all tend to telescope these
things in our minds. We forget the annihilating force of a medieval
plague, forget what the future must have looked like to that European
with death on every side. No other age but ours, we say, ever faced
such a threat of the extinction of mankind or at least of civilization,
because no other age ever had to face the destructive potentiality of
nuclear energy.

Our proclivity to consider ourselves uniquely beset is perfectly
understandable. But it is not very useful when it leads people to say,
as many Americans are saying, that even if survival is possible for some,
they do not want to live in such a world nor do they want their
children to. As an attitude for rational beings, this has a profound
defect: it not only forgets the past but presumes to know the future.

So we have people declaring flatly that it is ridiculous for families
to build any kind of home shelter. In our great urbanized nation, they
argue, father would be caught downtown and the children in school;
even if the family were together, they couldn't survive when they came
out. Now how does anyone know such things for a certainty?

Others concede Americans might survive in some parts of the country
but contend there is absolutely no hope for anyone in a 15-mile radius
of the center of, say, New York City. How do they know for sure that
if Khrushchev drops a bomb on New York it will be a 50-megaton,
a 5-megaton or a 5-kiloton one—or even that Khrushchev would
positively bomb New York in a nuclear war?

Then there are those who, assuming some survival, insist that life
would not be worth living; society would break down and everyone
would be shooting each other in a ferocious outburst of greed and
rivalry. But it was not so inside Britain and inside Germany after the
horror bombings of World War II; it was not so in the catastrophes
that have befallen this nation. The reaction is more often one of helping others and trying to get a community going again.

For many people the most gruesome prospect of all is that of serious
mutations in the survivors' children and succeeding generations. This
is in truth a frightful prospect, and there is scant comfort in the reflection that the human species has always been in a process of mutation,
some of it quite radical. Still, even in this ominous area, we cannot

predict with certainty; no one has the omniscience to state categorically today whether human beings will be better or worse 50 or 500 years from now.

The truth is that the future is all conjecture. It is a wildly irrational conjecture when uninformed citizens predict total devastation for America and assert that survival is either impossible or intolerable. This is defeatism—essentially the same defeatism which leads so many in the world to demand that we surrender now to the slavery of Communism rather than run even the risk of nuclear war.

But there are degrees of validity in conjecture. It is a conjecture backed by scientific knowledge and historical understanding when a nuclear physicist says a 90 per cent survival rate and resumption of national life is possible for Americans if they take precautions— possible, be it noted, not certain.

Since common sense tells us anything is possible, a nuclear war is not inevitable in any case. If it does come no one can prophesy its effects. It could introduce another dark age lasting centuries or millennia; equally, it could be an event from which we could recover and from which we should try to recover in our individual and national interest. Man is not foredoomed to any certain fate, good or ill.

What is absolutely certain is that this remarkably resilient creature has in fact survived—some experts now think for nearly two million years—through all manner of devastations of his own and nature's contriving. Against that incredible span even centuries and millennia count for little. And always the survival instinct has won; men have rebuilt, women have borne children, and the community has sought to organize even amid the death and desolation of pestilence, flood and war.

None of us can prejudge man's prospects. But only if we see man in perspective can we hope to act like mature men.

JOSEPH E. EVANS

October 31, 1961

ACKNOWLEDGMENT

THIS BOOK could not have been put together without the cooperation of a number of people on the staff of *The Wall Street Journal,* to whom I am gratefully indebted.

And special thanks to Bernard Kilgore, president of Dow Jones Company, publishers of *The Wall Street Journal.*

—C. P.

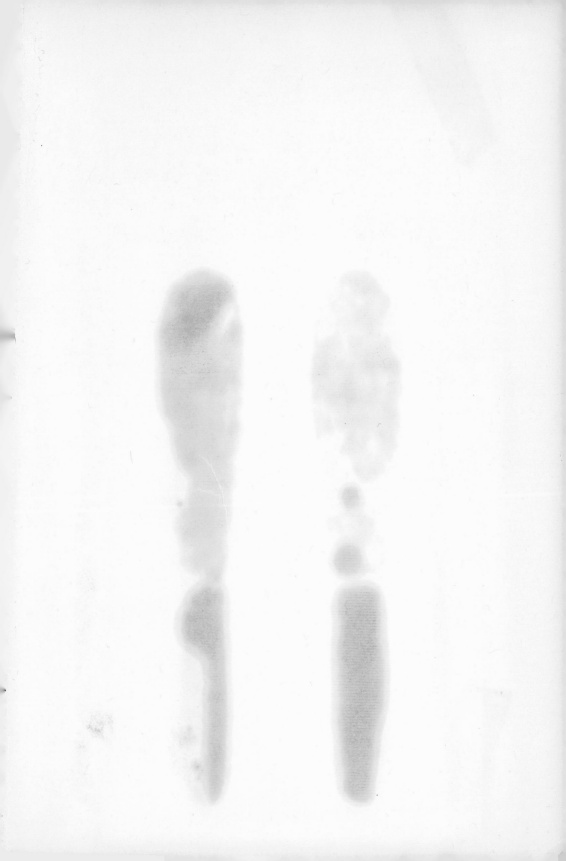

12-15-63

THE WALL STREET JOURNAL
THE NEW WORLD OF THE
WALL STREET JOURNAL.

DATE DUE

GAYLORD   PRINTED IN U.S.A.